The Ground of Holy Life

The Ground of Holy Life

A Reformed Response to the Holiness Movement in America with Progressive and Definitive Sanctification

David D. Cho

RESOURCE *Publications* • Eugene, Oregon

THE GROUND OF HOLY LIFE
A Reformed Response to the Holiness Movement in America
with Progressive and Definitive Sanctification

Copyright © 2021 David D. Cho. All rights reserved. Except for brief quotations in critical publications or reviews, no part of this book may be reproduced in any manner without prior written permission from the publisher. Write: Permissions, Wipf and Stock Publishers, 199 W. 8th Ave., Suite 3, Eugene, OR 97401.

Resource Publications
An Imprint of Wipf and Stock Publishers
199 W. 8th Ave., Suite 3
Eugene, OR 97401

www.wipfandstock.com

PAPERBACK ISBN: 978-1-6667-0271-2
HARDCOVER ISBN: 978-1-6667-0272-9
EBOOK ISBN: 978-1-6667-0273-6

08/09/21

All Scripture quotations, unless otherwise indicated, are taken from the Holy Bible, New International Version®, NIV®. Copyright ©1973, 1978, 1984, 2011 by Biblica, Inc.™ Used by permission of Zondervan. All rights reserved worldwide. www.zondervan.com The "NIV" and "New International Version" are trademarks registered in the United States Patent and Trademark Office by Biblica, Inc.™

Contents

Preface | vii

Chapter 1 : The Hole in Protestant Theology | 1

Chapter 2 : Historical and Theological Background of the Holiness Movement in America | 7

Chapter 3 : Benjamin Warfield's Response to American Perfectionism | 42

Chapter 4 : Other Reformed Theologians' Response to Perfectionism | 72

Chapter 5 : Keswick's View of the Victorious Christian Life | 101

Chapter 6 : John Murray's Response to Keswick's Sanctification | 147

Chapter 7 : Comparison of Keswick's Sanctification and John Murray's Definitive Sanctification | 182

Chapter 8 : Definitive Sanctification in Salvation of Man | 198

Chapter 9 : The *Duplex Gratia* in the Protestant Church | 238

Bibliography | 259

Preface

"Justification by faith alone" was the central doctrine in the Reformation. It is understandable that the historical situation compelled the reformers to emphasize the forensic nature of salvation as opposed to Roman Catholic Church's infused grace. However, the overemphasis on the forensic doctrine of justification at the expense of sanctification in the Reformation created a gap, or an abrupt change, between justification and sanctification. Justification has been taught as an immediate and once-for-all grace of God whereas sanctification was understood primarily as a process involving man's works guided by the Spirit. This created a disjointed relationship between justification and sanctification, and the imbalance between the *duplex gratia* in the salvation of man. Also, this has produced many nominal Christians who profess to be saved, or justified, but shows no sign of the new life in their lives.

Many Christian leaders and theologians have wrestled with this problem, and some have attempted to rectify the problem by emphasizing man's works in salvation or introducing the concept of final justification at the end of life. Most of spiritual movements and theologies focusing on the holy life of a Christian fall into this camp. The issue at the core is to present sanctification by faith also just like justification, and to stress man's works in sanctification without falling into Arminian or Pelagian theology. So the holy life of a Christian is stressed with monergistic nature of salvation taught in Scripture. Doctrine of definitive sanctification formulated by John Murray satisfies this condition and is the best corrective measure to fill the gap between justification and sanctification, thereby balancing the *duplex gratia* in a biblical way.

Holiness is a serious matter for all Christians. It is what makes them different from all others in the world. There will not be believers in Christ and the Christian church without holiness. With holiness Christians have the right and power to lead and change the world, and without it they become followers and servants of the world. Holiness in Christians is the visible sign that God dwells in them.

Chapter 1

The Hole in Protestant Theology

FOR MANY YEARS SANCTIFICATION has been treated as a secondary doctrine behind justification since the Reformation. But recently many scholars have begun to stress the importance of sanctification in the Christian life. Richard F. Lovelace argues for the importance of sanctification for the renewal of the church in the world today.[1] Also, the theologians from different theological traditions are engaged in a robust discussion on sanctification with their distinctive views.[2] These theologians collectively bring out sanctification as one of the very important elements in salvation. J. I. Packer, for example, also focuses on the concept of sanctification in relation to the Christian's holy life.[3] All of these writings and many other scholars' studies on this subject published recently show the emergence of the importance of the doctrine of sanctification in Christian theology, especially in relation to holiness of the Christian life.[4]

Sanctification and the Holiness Movement

A consideration of sanctification in our time is not possible without a careful examination of the holiness movement in the nineteenth century from which many present-day concepts of sanctification sprang forth. Whereas some groups, whose teaching on sanctification owe their genesis to the perfectionism as taught by the holiness movement, view this movement positively, others regard it without much value in American Christianity. Some theologians such as Melvin E. Dieter of the Wesleyan group, Stanley M.

---

1. Lovelace, *Renewal*, 102.
2. Alexander, "Riddle of Sanctification," 7–11.
3. Packer, *Keep In Step*, 127.
4. Peterson, *Possessed by God*, 15; Piper, "Miracle," 29; Ferguson, *Devoted to God*, 31; Park, *Driven by God*, 13; Payne, *Already Sanctified*, 13.

1

Horton of the Pentecostal group, and J. Robertson McQuilkin of the Keswick group place a high value on the holiness movement in the nineteenth century in America.[5] However, the Reformed theologian, Anthony A Hoekema, does not highly regard the holiness movement in relation to sanctification in American Christianity.[6] Whether one views the holiness movement positively or negatively, one cannot deny that many present-day teachings on the holy life of a Christian trace their roots to the holiness movement in the nineteenth century. Therefore, it is important to examine the holiness movement and reactions to it in the nineteenth and early twentieth centuries, in order to better understand divergent teachings on sanctification today and to assess them in the broad context of Protestant theology.

The Holiness Movement and Warfield

American perfectionism owes its genesis to Wesleyan perfectionism. In the nineteenth century, Wesleyan Methodism was the catalyst of the holiness movement in America. Sydney E. Ahlstrom describes this movement:

> In the great surge of interest in Christian perfection and complete sanctification, on the other hand, the Wesleyan legacy was primary. During the Gilded Age the Methodist churches, North and South, were swept by a great Holiness Revival, and the preaching and the practice of this doctrine led to religious manifestations which most Methodist leaders tended to discountenance as disruptive and unseemly.[7]

Soon this movement spread to Presbyterian churches aided by the powerful preaching of Charles Finney. As Finney's teaching of perfectionism, based on Pelagian theology, flowed into the Presbyterian churches, the clash with the Princeton theologians, then the vanguard of conservative Presbyterianism and Reformed theology, was inevitable. Herein lies the interest of our study. The response of Reformed theologians led by B. B. Warfield was severely critical of Finney's perfectionism. However, today, about a hundred years later, the reassessment of perfectionism and the assessment of Warfield's response itself are necessary in order to analyze this action-reaction movement in a broad historical and theological context, and to understand

---

5. Dieter, "Wesleyan," 37; S. Horton, "Pentecostal," 106; J. R. McQuilkin, "Keswick Perspective," 153.

6. Hoekema, "Reformed," 83.

7. Ahlstrom, *Religious History*, 817.

the development of the Reformed doctrine of sanctification in the dynamics of this historical and theological context.

Keswick, often called the Victorious Life Movement, in the twentieth century is an important offshoot of the holiness movement in the nineteenth century. Keswick toned down the Pelagian theology of perfectionism and emphasized the instantaneous nature of crisis sanctification. In the mid-twentieth century Barabas presented Keswick's teaching in an orderly manner in *So Great Salvation*. Not only was it the definitive presentation of Keswick's teaching, but it also was an indirect response to Warfield's criticism on the holiness movement. In this book Barabas criticized Warfield's teaching of a gradual eradication of the old nature.[8] Thus, the theological debate between Reformed theologians and advocates for perfectionism continued. Keswick elicited a particular concern from Reformed theologians because its apparently mild Calvinism attracted many lay people as well as leaders from Reformed and Presbyterian churches. Although Keswick abandoned the radical form of perfectionism of the nineteenth century, it followed the tradition of the holiness movement by emphasizing the immediate and instantaneous nature of sanctification.

John Murray's Response

After the publication of Barabas's *So Great Salvation*, John Murray, then a professor of systematic theology at Westminster Theological Seminary, responded to Keswick's teaching. Although Murray criticized the Arminian and Pelagian elements in Keswick's teaching, his response to Keswick was somewhat different from Warfield's response to perfectionism in the nineteenth century. In responding to Keswick, Murray formulated the doctrine that deals with the definitive aspect of sanctification, which he saw was lacking in Warfield's response to perfectionism. So, the holiness movement and the Reformed response, especially Murray's response with definitive sanctification, should be viewed and evaluated in this historical and theological context as to a contribution, whether positive or negative, each movement or response made to the development of the doctrine of sanctification in American Christianity.

---

8. Barabas, *So Great Salvation*, 73.

Sanctification Dialogue in Protestant Theology

Also, the American holiness movement and the Reformed response to it should be viewed within a broader context of Protestant theology since the Reformation. Protestant or Reformation theology stressed the forensic nature of justification in order to counteract Roman Catholicism's doctrine of infused grace. The upshot of this overemphasis on the forensic nature of justification in the Protestant theology was the creation of a gap or an abrupt transition between justification and sanctification. Keen theologians such as G. C. Berkouwer, B. B. Warfield, and Herman Ridderbos detected this imbalance in the soteriology of Protestant theology. In dealing with the doctrine of sanctification Berkouwer argues:

> If we would keep this center, as well as the softer and harder lines flowing from it, in true perspective, we must be thoroughly aware that in shifting from justification to sanctification we are not withdrawing from the sphere of faith. We are not here concerned with a transition from theory to practice. It is not as if we should proceed from a faith in justification to the realities of sanctification; for we might as truly speak of the reality of justification and our faith in sanctification. Indeed, nearly all the problems of sanctification are bound up with the question of this "transition" from justification to sanctification. One of the complaints which assail us constantly is that sanctification is being cut loose, or abstracted, from justification.[9]

Berkouwer places the *Sola fide* at the heart of both justification and sanctification.

The imbalance of soteriology in Protestant theology has also been observed by Warfield. He discerns concerning this matter, "The strong emphasis laid by the Reformers upon the objective side of salvation, in the enthusiasm of their rediscovery of the fundamental doctrine of justification, left its subjective side, which was not in dispute between them and their nearest opponents, in danger of falling temporarily somewhat out of sight."[10] In a similar vein, Ridderbos expresses the same concern, "Reformation theology, broadly speaking, found this main entrance in Paul's preaching of justification by faith. In the great struggle with Roman Catholic legalism and mysticism the forensic pronouncements in Paul's epistles to the Romans and the Galatians were of fundamental significance."[11] Ridderbos, in another

---

9. Berkouwer, *Sanctification*, 20.
10. Warfield, *Theological Studies*, 373.
11. Ridderbos, *Time*, 44.

place, also writes, "The concept of 'Christ-for-us' has developed a far greater force in the whole conscious mind of Reformation faith than the Pauline 'we-in-Christ.'"[12] Thus is seen the overemphasis on justification compared to sanctification in the Reformation. This has created the imbalance of the *duplex gratia* in the soteriology of Protestant theology.[13]

If the holiness movement in America and the Reformed response to it are viewed in this historical and theological backdrop of the Reformation, then the holiness movement, perfectionism in particular, may be seen as a logical consequence of the Reformation which created a gap, or hole, between justification and sanctification. The holiness movement attempted to fill this gap with perfectionism emphasizing the experiential nature of sanctification. But perfectionism could not fill this gap with Pelagian theology which destroyed the monergistic nature of salvation. Murray's definitive sanctification, on the other hand, should not only be understood as a response to Keswick but also as a theological attempt to bridge the gap between justification and sanctification from the Reformed perspective.

Purpose of the Study

Therefore, the purpose of this study is fourfold. First, it is to show that the response of Reformed theologians led by Warfield to the holiness movement was primarily from the progressive aspect of sanctification. John Wesley's perfectionism, which left an indelible mark on the American holiness movement, is included as a background study for perfectionism in America. Following Wesleyan perfectionism, perfectionism taught by Charles Finney and other Christian leaders is presented with an analysis of their ideas and theology. In response to perfectionists' teaching Warfield's evaluation of Oberlin perfectionism is presented in detail as a major response by a Reformed theologian.

The second purpose of this study is to show that Murray's doctrine of definitive sanctification was a response to a modified form of perfectionism, i.e., Keswick, with a definitive aspect of sanctification, thereby complementing Warfield's response to perfectionism. To this end Keswick's teaching and Murray's response to it along with his own teaching on the once-for-all aspect of sanctification, definitive sanctification, are presented.

Third, it is to demonstrate the importance of the doctrine of definitive sanctification in the soteriology of Protestant theology. Building on Murray's

---

12. Ridderbos, *Time*, 45.

13. John Calvin speaks of justification and sanctification as a double grace (*duplex gratia*) in salvation. *Inst.* 3.11.1

ideas of definitive sanctification, my own formulation of this doctrine is documented. The aim is to fill the gap—or fix the "transition," to use Berkouwer's word—between justification and sanctification, which was created by the overemphasis on the forensic doctrine in the Reformation, with a biblical doctrine that maintains monergistic nature of salvation.

Fourth, it is to show that many spiritual movements and theologies sprung up after the Reformation are religious or theological efforts to fill the gap between justification and sanctification. Even though this is not the primary purpose of this study and thus the analysis is not exhaustive, six spiritual movements and theologies included in this study show that there have been earnest attempts by Christian leaders and theologians to rectify the problem of the imbalance of the *duplex gratia* in Protestant theology. However, it has been proven that it is impossible to maintain monergistic nature of salvation without definitive sanctification in the *ordo salutis*.

Chapter 2

Historical and Theological Background of the Holiness Movement in America

THE DOCTRINE OF SANCTIFICATION, especially in America, is closely related to the holiness movement in America in the late nineteenth and early twentieth centuries. Since the doctrine of sanctification deals with the holy life of believers, there is invariably an interdependence and mutual influence between the practical life and the formulation of the doctrine. We all agree that a doctrine has to be founded on Scripture and also has to be theologically sound. But the formulation of a doctrine is often influenced by spiritual milieu of the time, and the doctrine is likely shaped by the theological tradition in which it is developed.

Therefore, it is critical to examine the historical and theological background of the holiness movement and reactions to it without predisposed ideas, in order to understand the development of the doctrine of sanctification in America, especially the definitive aspect of sanctification. A study of the doctrine of sanctification, including definitive sanctification, in America from a purely exegetical point of view without examining the historical background of holiness movement is tantamount to presenting the doctrine of justification without the backdrop of the Reformation. This historical and theological background provides us a proper perspective to understand the formulation of the doctrine of sanctification which has a distinctive emphasis depending on the tradition of theology.

John Wesley's Influence on the Holiness Movement in America

The root of the holiness movement in America goes back to John Wesley of England. He founded Methodist church, and he was the towering figure of the evangelical revival in the eighteenth century. Wesley's life and teaching were deeply influenced by Moravian church which taught the primacy of holy life of believers.

As the Methodist churches were planted and multiplied in many parts of America in the eighteenth and nineteenth centuries, Wesley's unique brand of teaching on the holiness of Christian life spread into lives of many believers in America. His emphasis on sanctification of believers left an indelible mark on the doctrine of sanctification in American Christianity.

Life of John Wesley

John Wesley was born in a village called Epworth in England, in 1703. He was brought up in strict Christian discipline by parents who had strong Puritan roots. While he was growing up, his devotional reading included such books as Lorenzo Scupoli's *Spiritual Combat*, Thomas à Kempis's *Imitation of Christ* and the Scottish mystic Henry Scougal's *The Life of God in the Soul of Man*.[1]

Wesley entered Christ Church, Oxford, in 1720.[2] At Oxford he developed a respectable scholarship, but he was still yearning for a personal experience that would satisfy his spiritual need. This spiritual need led him to join the Holy Club. The members of the Holy Club studied the Bible together and followed a strict religious discipline to seek personal holiness. He describes the experience of a member of the Holy Club, "Upon this encouragement we still continued to meet together as usual; and to conform one another, as well as we could, in our relations, to communicate as often as we had opportunity, (which is here once a week); and do what service we could do to our acquaintance, the prisoners, and two or three poor families in the town."[3] In 1725, Wesley was ordained a deacon by John Potter, the Bishop of Oxford, yet he was still not sure of his spiritual life.

During the years between 1735 and 1737 Wesley labored as a missionary in Georgia in the New World, America. In spite of his hard labor and toil Wesley, with a disappointed and defeated heart, returned to England after a fruitless ministry in America. While on the ship coming back home he met a group of Moravians whose bold confidence in the midst of a terrible storm left him questioning his own spiritual life. Wesley was even more disillusioned when he could not give a satisfactory answer to the question

---

1. Tuttle, *Wesley*, 48.
2. Ayling, *Wesley*, 28.
3. Wesley, *Journal*, 95–96.

asked by the Moravians whether he knew Jesus Christ. He describes his own spiritual condition during this time:

> I went to America, to convert the Indians; but oh, who shall convert me? Who, what is he that will deliver me from this evil heart of unbelief? I have fair summer religion. I can talk well; nay, and between myself, while no danger is near. But let death look me in the face, and my spirit is troubled. Nor can I say, "To die is gain"![4]

After returning to England Wesley went through now the famous Aldersgate conversion experience while listening to Luther's preface to the *Epistle to the Romans*. It was a decisive event for him. He now felt sure that he did trust in Christ alone for salvation and that his sins were taken away. Wesley writes this experience:

> In the evening I went very unwillingly to a society in Aldersgate Street, where one was reading Luther's preface to the *Epistle to the Romans*. About a quarter before nine, while he was describing the change which God works in the heart through faith in Christ, I felt my heart strongly warmed. I felt I did trust in Christ, Christ alone for salvation; and an assurance was given me that He had taken away my sins, even mine, and saved me from the law of sin and death.[5]

Wesley now had Jesus as his master in his heart and mouth. He drew his strength from the master rather than fighting with all his might under the law as in his former state. He had now peace with God. Yet, we find Wesley confessing that his soul was in heaviness because of manifold temptations even though his soul continued in peace.[6]

From this point on, the quest in Wesley's life was to reach absolute holiness, or Christian perfection, in his life. He had an ongoing interaction with Moravian Quietism and sought to incorporate it into his teachings on perfectionism. Wesley's chief writing on the subject of perfectionism was his book, *A Plain Account of Christian Perfection*, which we will examine in detail in the next section.

It is said that John Wesley is often misquoted and misrepresented by many. This is understandable because Wesley was not a systematizer of theology, which even people in the Wesleyan camp admit in writing.[7] Wesleyan

---

4. Wesley, *Journal*, 418.
5. Wesley, *Journal*, 475–76.
6. Wesley, *Journal*, 478.
7. Keefer, "Wesley's Arminianism," 91.

theologians often apologetically refer to John Wesley as the "unsystematic theologian," or practical theologian.[8] A study on his writings labels him as a "mystic ascetic."[9] But Thomas C. Oden, a Wesleyan theologian, strongly objects to this view.[10] While it is unfair to call Wesley an ascetic, a strong influence on mysticism in his theology and life cannot be denied. Other scholarly works on Wesley show a strong influence of mysticism in his theology and life.[11] While it is still debatable how much Wesley was influenced by mysticism, what we are mainly concerned with in this work, however, is Wesley's Arminianism in his theology, particularly in his perfectionism.

John Wesley's Doctrine of Perfectionism

Although John Wesley's writings may not be considered as systematic theology with an overarching theme, his doctrine of perfectionism constitutes one of the main principles in his theology. This doctrine of perfectionism has exerted an enormous influence on the holiness movement in America in the nineteenth century. Therefore, it is appropriate for us to study Wesley's doctrine of perfectionism in examining the holiness movement in America.

Definition of the Doctrine

The definition Wesley gives to Christian perfection is a psychological definition, not a theological one, even though Wesley himself deems it biblical. He defines Christian perfection thus, "It is 'perfect love.' 1 John 4:18. This is the essence of it: its properties, or inseparable fruits, are, rejoicing evermore, praying without ceasing, and in everything giving thanks."[12]

Wesley further defines it, "By perfection I mean the humble, gentle, patient love of God and our neighbor, ruling our tempers, words, and actions."[13] But this definition is only a description of an outward disposition of Christian perfection, and still is not a theological definition.

Wesley equates Christian perfection with "perfect love," "entire sanctification," or "holiness." Thus, he defines Christian perfection positively as perfect love, while he sees it as deliverance from all sins in the negative

8. Tyson, "Sin," 77.
9. Kim, "Tension," 58.
10. Thomas C. Oden, letter written to D. Clair Davis on March 12, 1992.
11. Tuttle, "Influence," 241; R. H. Wilson, "Sanctification," 4.
12. Wesley, *Perfection*, 60.
13. Wesley, *Perfection*, 112.

sense. In his sermon, "On Perfection," Wesley defines Christian perfection in more detail as following:

> It is the complying with that kind of command, "My son, give me thy heart." It is the "loving the LORD his God with all his heart, and with all his soul, and with all his mind." . . . Another view of this is given us in those words of the great Apostle: "Let this mind be in you which was also in Christ Jesus." . . . It is one undivided fruit of the Spirit, which he describes thus: "The fruit of the Spirit is love, joy, peace, longsuffering, gentleness, goodness, fidelity, meekness, temperance." . . . The moral image of God consists "in righteousness and true holiness." By sin this is totally destroyed. And we never can recover it, till we are "created anew in Christ Jesus." And this is perfection . . . perfection is another name for universal holiness . . . "a living sacrifice unto God;" to whom ye were consecrated many years ago in baptism. When what was then devoted is actually presented to God, then is the man of God perfect. . . . And this salvation from sin, from all sin, is another description of perfection.[14]

In studying Wesley's definition, or description, of Christian perfection, I agree with Lindstrom that there is a close affinity between Wesley and practical mysticism.[15] Once we see a strand of mysticism in Wesley's theology, it is easy to understand Wesley's tendency to define Christian perfection in psychological terms, rather than theological terms. In summary, we could say that Wesley's idea of Christian perfection is indwelling pure love, deliverance from all sins, and humble and total dependence on God. We may say, in short, that Wesley's Christian perfection is empoweredness with love in the heart of the believer to imitate the life of Christ.

Place in the Order of Salvation

Wesley places Christian perfection between justification and glorification. According to Wesley, the believer goes on unto perfection after he is justified. He writes, "It is not so early as justification; for justified persons are to go on unto perfection. It is not so late as death; for St. Paul speaks of living men that were perfect."[16] Wesley thus sees the new birth and entire sanctification, or Christian perfection, as two isolated phenomena in the order of salvation.

14. Wesley, *Works*, 6:413–15.
15. Lindstrom, *Sanctification*, 413–15.
16. Wesley, *Perfection*, 106.

Wesley sees justification and the new birth as the beginning stage of salvation. Justification and the new birth are given to man at the same instant. He defines the new birth as the change of an earthy mind into the mind of Jesus Christ and justification as the forgiveness of sins. He sees the new birth as "what God does in us, in renewing our fallen nature, and justification as what God does for us, in forgiving our sins."[17] While Wesley sees the close connection between justification and sanctification, he clearly distinguishes them. He describes the difference between the two:

> What is justification? This is the second thing which I proposed to show, and it is evident, from what has been already observed, that it is not the being made actually just and righteous. This is sanctification; which is, indeed, in some degree, the immediate fruit of justification, but, nevertheless, is a distinct gift of God, and of a totally different nature. The one implies what God does for us through his Son; the other, what he works in us by his Spirit.[18]

Thus, Wesley places sanctification after justification in the order of salvation.

After justification comes assurance. Assurance means that one is assured of forgiveness of his sins by God, so that he has peace with God without fear. This is based on testimony by the Holy Spirit. Assurance of justification brings to the believer an awareness of God's love and reconciliation through the blood of Jesus Christ. Wesley exhorts believers to have full assurance. Those who have full assurance firmly believe that they are forgiven and that they have a clear perception that Christ abides in them.[19]

Wesley sees sanctification beginning at the moment of justification. Sanctification is defined by him as "an instantaneous deliverance from all sin; an instantaneous power then given, always to cleave to God."[20] Whereas Wesley sees justification as a one time act of God's forgiving our sins, he sees the beginning of sanctification as the onset of God's work of renewing our mind. Thus, it marks the beginning of the eradication of all our sins. Wesley writes:

> When does inward sanctification begin? In the moment we are justified. The seed of every virtue is then sown in the soul. From that time the believer gradually dies to sin, and grows in grace.

---

17. Wesley, *Works*, 6:65.
18. Wesley, *Works*, 4:56.
19. Wesley, *Works*, 8:393.
20. Wesley, *Works*, 12:207.

> Yet sin remains in him; yea, the seed of all sin, till he is sanctified throughout in spirit, soul, and body.[21]

Wesley affirms both gradual and instantaneous sanctification. But he teaches the followers to seek the instantaneous sanctification which is far better. He writes, "But it is infinitely desirable were it the will of God, that it should be done instantaneously; that the LORD should destroy sin by the breach of his mouth, in a moment, in the twinkling of an eye."[22] Wesley admits that Christian perfection, or entire sanctification, is impossible in this life if it includes a deliverance from evil thoughts and speeches. However, defining Christian perfection as pure love, he asserts that it is consistent with the teaching in the Bible and that it can be attained by faith in this life.

The final stage of salvation is glorification. With the glorification of the believer the eternal plan of salvation of man by God is accomplished. Wesley writes, "This is the order wherein, according to the counsel of his will, the plan he has laid down from eternity, he saves those whom he foreknew; the true believers in every place and generation."[23] For Wesley, glorification is in a sense final justification. In the life of a believer sanctification is a condition of this final justification. The believer is qualified for the final justification, or glorification, only through sanctification of life. Thus, we see Wesley's principal idea of sanctification in his teaching of the salvation of man.

Attainability

Wesley teaches that Christian perfection is an attainable experience by believers in this life. He gives an example of those in the Bible who attained this perfection. Citing the passage in 1 John 4:17, Wesley gives Saint John and those mentioned in this passage as the believers who attained Christian perfection in this life.[24] While not claiming he ever attained this perfection, Wesley testifies that he knew and personally met some believers who attained this perfection in this life.

In *A Plain Account of Christian Perfection*, Wesley lays down the means to achieve this experience of perfection. According to him, one ought to zealously obey the commandments, deny himself daily by taking up the cross, pray earnestly, and fast in order to attain the experience of perfection.

---

21. Wesley, *Works*, 8:285.
22. Wesley, *Works*, 6:53.
23. Wesley, *Works*, 6:228.
24. Wesley, *Perfection*, 14.

Wesley especially stresses prayer for the means of diligently seeking perfection. He exhorts believers thus:

> Prayer especially is wanting. Who continues instant therein? Who wrestles with God for this very thing? So "ye have not because ye ask not," or because "ye ask amiss," namely: "that you may be renewed before you die." Before you die! Will that content you? Nay, but ask that it may be done now, today, while it is called today! Do not call this "setting God a time." Certainly today is his time, as well as tomorrow. Make haste, man—make haste![25]

Although Christian perfection can be attained by zealously employing the means suggested by Wesley, it can also be lost. Thus Christian perfection, once attained, is not always permanent in the believer's life. Wesley writes, "It is amissible; capable of being lost of which we have had instances."[26] It seems that Wesley in the beginning thought this perfection experience was permanent in the life of a believer. In the later years of his life Wesley taught that perfection can be lost by the believer who does not abide in pure love by zealously walking with God everyday.

Agent of Christian Perfection

As in justification, faith is the indispensable instrument in sanctification also. For Wesley faith is the only condition of sanctification. Just as justification is impossible without faith, so is sanctification without faith. He furthermore says that faith alone is the sufficient condition for sanctification in the life of the believer. Wesley writes:

> Exactly as we are justified by faith, so are we sanctified by faith. Faith is the condition, and the only condition, of sanctification, exactly as it is of justification. It is the condition: None is sanctified but he that believes; without faith no man is sanctified. And it is the only condition: This alone is sufficient for sanctification. Every one that believes is sanctified, whatever else he has or has not. In other words, no man is sanctified till he believes: Every man when he believes is sanctified.[27]

He also affirms that faith is a gift of God. Faith itself is freely bestowed upon man as a gift of God.

25. Wesley, *Perfection*, 25.
26. Wesley, *Perfection*, 61.
27. Wesley, *Works*, 6:49.

As faith is the condition for sanctification, the Holy Spirit is the operator of sanctification. As the operator of sanctification, the Holy Spirit supplies power and the will to pursue holiness and perfection in the life of a believer. Wesley writes, "And as the increase of perfection, so the original of faith, is from the Spirit of God, by an internal illumination of the soul."[28] In the process of sanctification the Holy Spirit renews man in all the parts and faculties of his soul. The inclination to obey the will of God is wrought in a man by the Holy Spirit.

According to Wesley, the Holy Spirit also leads, directs, and governs man's actions and conversation. Those who are led by the Holy Spirit are those who are walking in the Spirit. Those who walk in the Spirit produce the fruit of the Spirit which is pure love, which Wesley equates to Christian perfection. For Wesley, the Holy Spirit is the divine agent who fills the believer's heart with pure love, thus bringing perfection in him.

Limitations of the Doctrine

Wesley teaches that there are limitations in his doctrine of Christian perfection. Christian perfection is not absolute perfection, which belongs to God alone. Nor does it make a man infallible. A believer who attained perfection is still fallible while he remains in the body.

Christian perfection does not mean perfect knowledge, says Wesley. Since man does not have perfect knowledge, Christian perfection does not mean to be free from ignorance. Since man is not omniscient and has limited knowledge, he would be ignorant even after attaining Christian perfection. Nor does Christian perfection mean that man is free from mistakes. Wesley sees mistakes as an unavoidable consequence of having a limited knowledge. However, he differentiates the two kinds of mistakes in the life of the believer. He states, "It is true, the children of God do not mistake as to the things essential to salvation. . . . But in the things unessential to salvation they do err, and that frequently."[29]

Christian perfection also does not mean to be free from infirmities. For Wesley infirmities are "all those inward or outward imperfections which are not of a moral nature."[30] Christian perfection does not include the renewing of man's defects in conversation or behavior. According to Wesley, the believer cannot be perfectly freed from these defects until he dies and goes to heaven.

28. Wesley, *Works*, 8:100.
29. Wesley, *Works*, 6:3.
30. Wesley, *Works*, 6:4.

Furthermore, temptations are excluded from Christian perfection. Man cannot be wholly free from temptation in this life. Wesley explains, "Neither can we expect till then to be freed from temptations; for the servant is not above his Master. But neither in this sense is there any absolute perfection on earth."[31] He admits that man can temporarily reach a state where he feels no temptation. But it is temporary and cannot be permanent. Wesley explains, "But this state will not last always; as we may learn from that single consideration, —that the Son of God himself, in the days of his flesh, was tempted even to the end of his life. Therefore, so let his servant expect to be; for 'it is enough that he be as his Master.'"[32]

Theology of John Wesley

In order to get to the root of the Christian perfection taught by John Wesley, it is necessary for us to examine his theology. His theology is undoubtedly Arminian. Wesley's unique brand of theology, which became the chief instrument in the revival in eighteenth-century England, is sometimes called evangelical Arminianism.[33] A close examination of Wesley's doctrines pertinent to Christian perfection reveals extensive Arminianism in his theology. The doctrines examined in this section are election, prevenient grace, sin, free will, and assurance.

Election

Wesley's fundamental conception of God is a loving God rather than a sovereign God as in Calvinism. In his sermon on free grace Wesley strongly rejects the Calvinistic doctrine of election, especially double predestination. The absolute and unconditional election of man by God for the purpose which could only be found in the depth of his infinite wisdom is untenable for Wesley. He clearly states his rejection:

> Call it therefore by whatever name you please, election, preterition, predestination, or reprobation, it comes in the end to the same thing. The sense of all is plainly this, —by virtue of an eternal, unchangeable, irresistible decree of God, one part of

---

31. Wesley, *Perfection*, 4.
32. Wesley, *Works*, 6:5.
33. Pask, "Influence of Arminius," 259. Evangelical Arminianism is the Wesleyan brand of Arminianism in which the doctrine of general atonement is emphasized in the practical application of the Gospel in a crusade for the salvation of a world parish.

mankind are[sic] infallibly saved, and the rest infallibly damned; it being impossible that any of the former should be damned, or that any of the latter should be saved. But if this be so, then is all preaching vain. It is needless to them that are elected; for they, whether with preaching or without, will infallibly be saved. . . . This, then is a proof that the doctrine of predestination is not a doctrine of God, because it makes void the ordinance of God.[34]

After rejecting the Calvinistic doctrine of election, Wesley sets forth his own doctrine of election. He divides the election into two different kinds of appointments by God. First, Wesley sees a divine appointment of some particular men to be "absolute and unconditional." But this divine appointment is not necessarily connected to salvation of man by God. He explains:

> Thus Cyrus was elected to rebuild the temple, and St. Paul, with twelve, to preach the gospel. But I do not find this to have any necessary connexion with eternal happiness. Nay, it is plain it has not; for one who is elected in this sense may yet be lost eternally. "Have I chosen" (elected) "you twelve?" saith our LORD; "yet one of you hath a devil." Judas, you see, was elected as well as the rest; yet is his lot with the devil and his angels.[35]

Second, for Wesley election means a divine appointment of men to eternal salvation. He sees this election to be conditional. According to Wesley, the election concerning salvation depends upon the response of a man. Man is not elected from eternity past for salvation. Rather, man becomes elected of God when he actually believes the LORD for salvation. He toils to explain this concept, "In like manner, God calleth true believers, 'elect from the foundation of the world'; although they were not actually elect, or believers, till many ages after, in their several generations. Then only it was that they were actually elected, when they were made the 'sons of God by faith.'"[36] Wesley's doctrine of election naturally stems from his fundamental conception of a loving God in his theology. Without detecting the depth of the doctrine of election, he bends and distorts the doctrine in order to preserve his principal concept of a loving God. Wainwright points out, "What Wesley might have learnt from Calvin was both the sheer difficulty of perseverance and perfection and also the need for an active determination on God's part to see us through to the goal of permanent and complete holiness. Perhaps the whole thing is both higher

---

34. Wesley, *Works*, 7:375–76.
35. Wesley, *Works*, 10:210.
36. Wesley, *Works*, 10:210.

and deeper than Wesley perceived."³⁷ Wesley's theology is a theology of love. Wesley's God is a loving God, rather than a sovereign God. As such, his God is a God bounded by love, not a sovereign free God. Wesley's Arminian theology yields a God who must act in all cases according to the principle of love overriding all other divine characteristics such as justice, in order to bring eternal happiness to man. Thus, God becomes the means for a man to achieve his end. As Cornelius Van Til aptly pointed out, the Arminian theology eventually leads to human autonomy.³⁸

Prevenient Grace

The doctrine of prevenient grace is one of the doctrines that are unique to Wesley's theology. In Wesley's theology the fall of man deprived him of the moral character, so that he is totally unwilling and unable to save himself from sin. To this man is given prevenient grace by God in order that he may more or less see the light, moral absoluteness and goodness. Wesley explains prevenient grace:

> No man living is entirely destitute of what is vulgarly called natural conscience. But this is not natural: It is more properly termed, "preventing grace." Every man has a greater or less measure of this, which waiteth not for the call of man. Every one has, sooner or later, good desires; although the generality of men stifle them before they can strike deep root, or produce any considerable fruit.³⁹

Thus, for Wesley conscience is a manifestation of prevenient grace.

Not only is prevenient grace a natural conscience in man, but also it is the beginning of salvation in man. Wesley writes, "Salvation begins with what is usually termed (and very properly) preventing grace; including the first wish to please God, the first dawn of light concerning his will, and the first slight transient conviction of having sinned against him."⁴⁰ All these imply some degree of salvation. It is the "beginning of a deliverance from a blind, unfeeling heart." Prevenient grace carries a man to repentance where he is further exposed to a larger measure of self-knowledge and is delivered from the heart of stone.

---

37. Wainwright, "Perfect Salvation," 904.
38. Van Til, *Defense*, 139.
39. Wesley, *Works*, 6:512.
40. Wesley, *Works*, 6:509.

What Wesley does not make clear is whether the prevenient grace given to a man in regeneration is an extension of the prevenient grace given to all men, or it is a separate gift from God. His doctrine of prevenient grace is a natural byproduct of his Arminian doctrine of election. It is incorrect to state that Wesley's "particular development of prevenient grace allowed him to walk a narrow ledge between Calvinism and Pelagianism."[41] Rather, Wesley's Arminian doctrine of conditional election forced him to devise such a doctrine as prevenient grace. What Wesley wishes to do here is to make election conditional so as to show that God is morally tolerable in his redemptive plan and to make salvation not dependent, or unconditioned, upon human merit so as to show that man is totally responsible for his own damnation. In this attempt a synergistic characteristic of Wesley's theology is clearly detected.

Wesley's synergistic tendency in his theology is a natural consequence of his endeavor to readjust the doctrines fundamentally based on Arminianism, which he sees as too Pelagianistic, to orthodox doctrines of Reformation and Calvinism. This tendency is also detected in his doctrine of Christian perfection where the meat of the Arminian doctrine of sanctification is flavored with the Calvinistic doctrine of sanctification.

Sin

The doctrine of sin is an absolutely fundamental and indispensable doctrine in Christian theology. As such, the definition of sin needs to be stated as precisely as it can be because Christian theology revolves around the solution of this sin-problem. Wesley's definition of sin does not fully satisfy this requirement. He sees sin as voluntary transgressions of a known law. Wesley explains the concept of sin to one of his followers:

> Nothing is sin, strictly speaking, but a voluntary transgression of a known law of God. Therefore, every voluntary breach of the law of love is sin; and nothing else, if we speak properly. To strain the matter farther is only to make way for Calvinism. There may be ten thousand wandering thoughts, and forgetful intervals, without any breach of love, though not without transgressing the Adamic law.[42]

Wesley does not speak about unconscious sins. He stresses the volitional nature of sin of man. In dealing with the nature of sin Wesley often speaks about

---

41. Keefer, "Wesley's Arminianism," 90.
42. Wesley, *Works*, 12:394.

defects, imperfections, and mistakes of man, but he does not call them sins. These are human infirmities that are necessarily connected to the imperfect body, which always remains an imperfect organ in this life.

In his "Sermon on the Mount" Wesley calls sins diseases, "Indeed we are already bound hand and foot by the chains of our own sins. . . . They are diseases that drink up our blood and spirits, that bring us down to the chambers of the grave."[43] Salvation is seen as a healing, and man is healed from a disease. Whereas sin is seen as guilt in justification, it is seen as a disease in sanctification. Thus, Wesley views sin materially and medically in regard to sanctification. Although some Wesleyan theologians attempt to vindicate Wesley from his definition of sin as a disease in materialistic and medical sense, their arguments for Wesley's diverse definitions of sin are not convincing.[44] Other theologians correctly interpret his concept of sin and thus catches the importance of his treatment of sin as a disease.[45] Lindstrom writes, "The basic corruption of natural man is again portrayed as a disease, salvation as a restoration to health."[46] In Wesley's theology such a view of sin is derived from his doctrine of sanctification. The doctrine of sanctification is the driving force in Wesley's theology of salvation. The goal of sanctification is Christian perfection; sanctification is God's method of healing a disease in man.

Thus, Wesley's concept of sin is determined by his idea of sanctification, and the concept of sin is vitally and organically connected to the idea of sanctification. In making the idea of sin dependent upon the idea of sanctification, Wesley attempts to present the solution to the problem before he identifies what the problem is. In so doing his subjective view of sin reveals a practical and mystical nature of his theology. Lindstrom comments, "An orthodox outlook, or rather an orthodoxy modified by Moravianism, is thus crossed by a line of thought reminiscent of Pietism and William Law and practical mysticism, and the latter gains the ascendancy."[47]

Free Will

Wesley believes that man after the fall of Adam does not have free will except in things of an indifferent nature. The idea expressed in "things of an

---

43. Wesley, *Works*, 5:339.
44. Cox, *Concept of Perfection*, 54. Hynson, "Original Sin," 69.
45. Sangster, *Perfection*, 113. Lindstrom, *Sanctification*, 42.
46. Lindstrom, *Sanctification*, 42.
47. Lindstrom, *Sanctification*, 44.

indifferent nature" is meant as that which is not related to the salvation of man. He states his position on the matter of the free will of man:

> I believe that Adam, before his fall, had such freedom of will, that he might choose either good or evil; but that, since the fall, no child of man has a natural power to choose anything that is truly good. Yet I know (and who does not?) that man has still freedom of will in things of an indifferent nature.[48]

While denying the natural free will of man, he still affirms that man does have a free will restored to him by prevenient grace. He rejects the Calvinistic presupposition that a natural man is totally dead spiritually. Wesley writes, "No man living is without some preventing grace; and every measure of grace is a degree of life."[49] And he continues, "Every man has a measure of free-will restored to him by grace."[50] Therefore, for Wesley a natural man has free will to choose and do good works as commanded by law. But natural man by exercising his free will cannot obtain eternal salvation.

In essence Wesley's doctrine of free will shows that man has free will to respond to the gospel of loving God but does not have free will to save himself. Such a doctrine of free will is a natural and necessary consequence of the doctrines of election and prevenient grace in his Arminian theology.

Assurance

The doctrine of assurance shows much defect in Wesley's theology. Flew says that Wesley is confused in his dealing with assurance.[51] Sangster calls the doctrine of assurance "the hardest and least defensible part of Wesley's doctrine."[52] First, Wesley teaches there is an assurance of justification. Man is not only to be saved but also he knows he is saved. He explains it:

> I believe that conversion, meaning thereby justification, is an instantaneous work; and that the moment a man has living faith in Christ, he is converted or justified. . . . I believe the moment a man is justified he has peace with God: Which he cannot have without knowing that he has it.[53]

---

48. Wesley, *Works*, 10:350.
49. Wesley, *Works*, 12:453.
50. Wesley, *Works*, 10:392.
51. Flew, *Idea of Perfection*, 338.
52. Sangster, *Perfection*, 160.
53. Wesley, *Works*, 8:370.

God puts a glad confidence in the believer's heart that all sins are forgiven, says Wesley. The Holy Spirit bears witness and gives the assurance in the heart of a believer. For Wesley this testimony in the case of justification is not a perceptible testimony. He writes, "They no more speak of Scripture, than of miracles. They manifestly speak of what passes in the heart, the spirit, the inmost soul of a believer, and that only."[54]

Second, there is an assurance of sanctification. Wesley confirms that one can be assured of sanctification as well. He answers to the question how one can know he is sanctified:

> I can know it no otherwise than I know that I am justified. Hereby know we that we are of God, in either sense, by the Spirit that he hath given us. We know it by the witness and by the fruit of the Spirit. And, First, by the witness. As when we were justified, the Spirit bore witness with our spirit, that our sins were forgiven; so, when we were sanctified he bore witness, that they were taken away.[55]

As in justification the Holy Spirit bears the internal testimony. But unlike justification, in the case of sanctification there is the outward testimony, the fruit of the Spirit, by which the genuineness of the assurance of sanctification is tested. Wesley gives the answer to a question:

> By what fruit of the Spirit may we know that we are of God, even in the highest sense? By love, joy, peace, always abiding; by invariable long-suffering, patience, resignation; by gentleness triumphing over all provocation; by goodness, mildness, sweetness, tenderness of the spirit; by fidelity, simplicity, godly sincerity; by meekness, calmness, evenness of spirit; by temperance, not only in food and sleep, but in all things natural and spiritual.[56]

Thus, an assurance of sanctification could be tested by outward signs whereas an assurance of justification could not be tested. There are inconsistencies and much confusion between the assurance of justification and the assurance of sanctification in Wesley's doctrine. Sangster aptly points out the nature of these problems:

> He carried over, without any apparent sense of crossing a gulf, the conviction that we could be assured that our sins were forgiven, and affirmed that we could be assured of sanctification as well. It is impossible to believe that a man of Wesley's mental

---

54. Wesley, *Works*, 12:94.
55. Wesley, *Works*, 11:420.
56. Wesley, *Works*, 11:422.

acuteness was unaware of the different character of these assurances, or counted it as unimportant that one could be submitted to tests which were impossible for the other.[57]

In Wesley's assurance one may have any assurance that he could be free of all sins, but he is not assured that it has taken place in his life. As in other doctrines in Wesley's theology, his unsuccessful attempt to incorporate the Calvinistic concepts into his fundamentally Arminian theology is also seen in his doctrine of assurance.

American Holiness Movement in the Nineteenth Century

The American holiness movement in the nineteenth century was a product of American revivalism and Wesleyan perfectionism during that era.[58] America in the early nineteenth century inherited the doctrine of natural ability which was a product of the Great Awakening and revivals in the previous century. The revival meetings in the nineteenth century stressed the immediate duty of a sinner. They taught that a man had the natural ability to respond to the gospel; so he should respond to the gospel affirmatively right now. Thus, the emphasis on man's ability and voluntarism were prevalent in nineteenth-century America.

Along with the revivalism came the pietistic impulse driven by Wesleyan perfectionism. In 1837, Phoebe Palmer, who was a Methodist laywoman, claimed that she experienced "entire sanctification." Mrs. Palmer emphasized that she had had three aspects of experience: entire consecration, faith, and confession. After this experience of entire sanctification, she started to hold meetings called the "Tuesday Meeting" to disseminate her teaching on perfectionism to Christians. She held these meetings for over thirty years during which time many Christians including well-known ministers came to hear and to learn from her personally her teaching on the life of holiness. Through Palmer's active ministry to promote the holiness in the believer's life, the teaching of entire sanctification, or perfectionism, spread to many churches in America. Her ministry was not limited to America. She and her husband, Walter Palmer, traveled to England to hold meetings on the teaching of entire sanctification.

Another key figure who played an important role in the holiness movement in the nineteenth century was Asa Mahan. Unlike Phoebe Palmer, Asa Mahan was a well-educated minister and scholar. He served as the president

---

57. Sangster, *Perfection*, 161.
58. Dieter, *Revival*, 18.

of Oberlin College where he formulated and taught Oberlin perfectionism. Using his philosophical mind, Mahan endeavored to defend scripturally his understanding of perfectionism for the spread of the holiness movement.

But it was Charles Finney who, more than any other person, exerted the greatest force in the holiness movement in nineteenth-century America. Ordained as a Presbyterian minister in the beginning of his ministry, he served as an evangelist, Congregationalist minister, professor and president of Oberlin College during his life. Although a Presbyterian minister initially, Finney rejected Calvinistic theology and preached New Haven theology and Wesleyan perfectionism. He was a great evangelist. Many people were converted to Christianity under his ministry, and his teaching of perfectionism was spread to many parts of the country through his powerful preaching. Finney's powerful preaching and teaching cut across the denominational boundaries and touched many hearts in various churches in America in the nineteenth century. In the following sections we will examine teachings of these key figures in the holiness movement in America: Phoebe Palmer, Asa Mahan, and Charles Finney.

Phoebe Palmer

Phoebe Palmer, virtually unknown today, was a dominant figure in the holiness movement in nineteenth-century America. As a devout Methodist, she zealously followed John's Wesley's teaching on sanctification and dedicated her life in teaching her modified form of sanctification to promote the holiness of Christians in the nineteenth century.

Life of Phoebe Palmer

Phoebe Palmer was born in New York in 1807. Her parents were both devout Methodists. She was brought up in a religious environment filled with Bible reading and prayer. Her childhood education is not known, but one could infer that she either attended a public school or received education at home.[59]

In 1827, Phoebe Palmer married Walter Palmer, a physician and a member of the Methodist Episcopal Church. During the early years of the marriage Phoebe and Walter Palmer experienced a deep grief because of the loss of their three children in early ages. Taking the loss of their children as God's sign for them to entirely devote their lives to God's service, she committed

---

59. Raser, *Palmer*, 21.

her life as a living sacrifice to God. She realized that she then experienced the entire sanctification as taught in Wesleyan Methodism. Thus, in 1837, Phoebe Palmer experienced what she thought was "entire sanctification," or Christian perfection, and it became the turning point of her life.

She began to hold meetings to share her experience and to teach her own perfectionism. Devoting her entire energy and whole being into this work, she published books and magazines and traveled to England several times to preach what she thought was the secret of powerful life, perfectionism. While teaching this perfectionism, she involved herself in other ministries such as defending women's ministries, aiding the poor, and establishing the settlement houses. She worked tirelessly preaching the gospel and her brand of perfectionism throughout her life until her death in 1874.

Phoebe Palmer's Teaching on Perfectionism

Although Phoebe Palmer cannot be thought of as a theologian and nor did she want to be called such, but what she taught in her doctrine of entire sanctification carried theological implications. What she taught in perfectionism was essentially the Wesleyan doctrine of Christian perfection. Her main contribution was to popularize Wesley's doctrine of entire sanctification and to make it applicable to every believer in the church. In the process of popularizing the doctrine, Mrs. Palmer made three important modifications of the original Wesleyan doctrine of perfection.

First, Mrs. Palmer makes Christian perfection immediately applicable to every believer by introducing the "altar theology." She exhorts believers to commit their entire life as a living sacrifice to God. The entire devotion and commitment of the believer as a living sacrifice to God is necessary in order to attain entire sanctification. And Christ is the altar on which to offer this living sacrifice to God. Mrs. Palmer writes:

> "What is the evidence of entire sanctification?" is another inquiry. How might an offerer at the Jewish altar arrive at an evidence that his offering was sanctified? In the first place, God had explicitly made known just the sacrifice required, and the manner in which it should be presented. If the offerer had complied with these requirements, he, of course, knew that he had done so, or in other words, had the testimony of his own spirit to assure him of this fact. In immediate connection with this, the witness of the Holy Spirit is given as a consequence of relying upon the faithfulness of God. The moment his offering was laid

> upon the altar, he had evidence of God's word that his offering was sanctified.[60]

She also emphasizes the instantaneous experience of entire sanctification. She exhorts her followers to give their entire devotion to God to experience entire sanctification "immediately." She teaches:

> Now is God's time! Will you choose any further period? If so, you take your own time. And is not this exceedingly perilous? Do you say, "It is but meet that I should count the cost?"
>
> Well, dear sister, begin just now to make the calculation, and let it be with the decision fixed irrevocably, that you will abide by the reckoning. I entreat you, in the name of the LORD Jesus, to pause, and now bring this matter to an issue.[61]

Thus, Mrs. Palmer takes out the gradual aspect of sanctification from the believer's life and makes sanctification all instantaneous. The tension between gradual and instantaneous sanctification is eliminated in Mrs. Palmer's teaching on Christian perfection.

Second, Mrs. Palmer places entire sanctification at the beginning, instead of the end, of the conversion experience. For her, entire sanctification is no more the goal of Christian life as it was for John Wesley. Mrs. Palmer teaches that Christian life begins with entire sanctification rather than ending with it. For Mrs. Palmer sanctification is either past or present, not future. She insists that a believer must be holy not only to go to heaven, but also to live a powerful life on earth. Mrs. Palmer writes:

> Now do you still ask, How soon may I expect to arrive at this state of perfection? Just so soon as you come believingly, and make the required sacrifice, it will be done unto you according to your faith. Christ came to take away our sin, to destroy the works of the devil, and to purge us from all iniquity. The purpose of man's redemption is not accomplished until he is presented perfect in Christ Jesus. When the Saviour said, "It is finished!" then this full salvation was wrought out for you. All that remains is for you to come complying with the conditions, and claim it.[62]

Thus, as Dieter aptly points out, Mrs. Palmer makes perfection the beginning of Christian life "instead of a point somewhere at the culmination of struggle and growth."[63]

60. Palmer, *Faith*, 242.
61. Palmer, *Faith*, 95.
62. Palmer, *Faith*, 53.
63. Dieter, "Development," 64.

Third, Mrs. Palmer devises a specific way to seek and achieve entire sanctification. She presents a simple three step process of achieving entire sanctification: entire consecration, faith, and confession.[64] Mrs. Palmer insists that entire consecration, which is man's work aided by the Holy Spirit, must precede entire sanctification. Then comes faith in the Word of God. Entire sanctification is completed by confession which sets man completely emancipated from sin. Mrs. Palmer explains this process:

> In relation to the attainment, or retainment, of entire sanctification, the inquiries first in importance with you should be, do I comply with the conditions upon which God promises this blessing? Do I come out from the world, and am I resolved to manifest my detachment from its spirit and customs? Have I set myself apart, fully purposed to devote all my redeemed powers to God alone, with the intention that all my earthly interests and affections shall be subservient, in every minute, to the service of my Redeemer? Do I now present myself a living sacrifice to God, through Christ. . . . If I come to this point, it matters not what my feeling may be. . . . The condition upon which the blessing of entire sanctification is promised, has in your case, been met.[65]

Unlike John Wesley who did not elaborate a specific way to attain perfection, Phoebe Palmer, by showing a specific way to attain perfection, made sanctification a pragmatic doctrine in part of the American holiness movement in the nineteenth century.

Asa Mahan

Asa Mahan, a Presbyterian minister in the beginning of his career, was an Arminian theologian and educator at Oberlin College. With his philosophical mind Mahan played an important role in the holiness movement by supplying a theological framework for perfectionism in nineteenth-century America.

Life of Asa Mahan

Asa Mahan was born in Vernon, New York in 1799. During his childhood he was influenced by the strong faith of his mother. He was concerned about his peace with God. But he did not know the way of salvation.

---

64. White, "Holiness," 26.
65. Wheatley, *Palmer*, 536–37.

Mahan confesses that his understanding of salvation was dominated by the "straitest sect" of Calvinism. He was confused and bewildered by the answers he received from Christians about the way of salvation. Mahan recounts his experience, "Having been absolutely taught that I could do nothing whatever effective in the matter. . . . Thus inquiring, and thus waiting, the agony of suspense which I endured deepened at length into the rayless midnight of blank despair."[66]

Helped by New England Calvinism, Mahan experienced conversion in 1816. From 1821 he spent four years at Hamilton College and three years at Andover Theological Seminary for college and seminary training, respectively. Four years at Hamilton College were uneventful years for Mahan. At Andover he was taught New Haven theology, and he embraced it. After graduating from the seminary and ordination, he was called to minister a church in a Cincinnati Presbytery. There he became acquainted with Charles Finney and enthusiastically supported his revival meetings and teaching.

At the age of thirty-five, Mahan became the president of Oberlin College in Ohio. At Oberlin, he along with Finney, formulated the doctrine of sanctification known as Oberlin perfectionism and threw himself into teaching and defending the doctrine. Mahan with his philosophical mindset endeavored to delineate and defend the doctrine theologically. He and Finney formulated and documented the doctrine of perfectionism which became a theological foundation of the American holiness movement in the nineteenth century.

In his later years Mahan became a British citizen and lived there. He taught and preached perfectionism at every opportunity provided to him. He led a quiet life in old age in England and died in 1889.

Asa Mahan's Teaching on Perfectionism

Asa Mahan starts his doctrine of perfectionism from philosophical ground. Mahan gives a philosophical definition of perfection:

> Every being . . . was created for a certain sphere of existence and action, and is endowed accordingly with . . . internal capabilities which perfectly adapt it, when these capabilities are fully developed, to that sphere. When such a being . . . is subject to such influences, that all these internal capabilities receive the most full and harmonious development possible, then such a creature . . . is in a state of perfection.[67]

---

66. Mahan, *Out of Darkness*, 10.
67. Mahan, *Philosophy*, 338–39. Cited by Hamilton, "Philosophy," 57.

Mahan teaches that any created being can be perfect so far as its action meets the requirements of its sphere to its maximum capabilities. For Mahan any creature can be perfect at any given moment. This also applies to man as a moral being. So, for Mahan, man is morally perfect when his moral activities satisfy the moral law to his maximum capabilities.

Mahan's concept of perfection is based on his idea of man's free will. Rejecting what he thinks is Calvinistic determinism, Mahan asserts man's free will. He makes a connection between the freedom of the will and entire sanctification, or Christian perfection.

In his major work on Christian perfection, *The Scripture Doctrine of Christian Perfection*, Mahan generally follows the typical Wesleyan Methodist holiness theology. He teaches that sanctification is by faith and it is produced in the believer by Christ. In an article on sanctification, Mahan explains his doctrine:

> When the believer looked to Christ for sanctification, he found that the evil tendencies and habitudes of his mind were broken up, and he was confirmed and strengthened in his obedience. This is sanctification by faith, a form of sanctification which Christ Himself produces in us, in connection with present obedience, and after such obedience has been rendered. This form of sanctification does not result from faith itself, as effect from cause, but wholly and exclusively from the grace of Christ received by faith.[68]

In his doctrine of sanctification Mahan describes the difference between sanctification as an act and sanctification as a state. In sanctification as an act man's voluntary acts are in full harmony with the known will of God. But in sanctification as a state man's will is confirmed in its habits of obedience.

In his later work, *Baptism of the Holy Ghost*, Mahan shows some progress in his doctrine of sanctification. In this work he uses the term "baptism of the Holy Ghost" rather than "Christian perfection." Mahan explains the nature of this baptism of the Spirit:

> We learn, 1. That the gift of the Spirit was not expected in, but after conversion: "Have ye received the Holy Ghost since ye believed?" The same fact is referred to and affirmed, Eph. 1. 13: "In whom ye also trusted, after that ye heard the word of truth, the gospel of our salvation; in whom also, after that ye believed ye were sealed with that Holy Spirit of promise." 2. We are here taught also, that, in the judgment of inspired men, believers are

---

68. Mahan, "Sanctification," 35.

not fully qualified for their sphere of Christian activity until this baptism is received.[69]

Emphasizing the work of the Holy Spirit in this manner, Mahan makes a shift from the Christ-centered doctrine of sanctification to the work of the Holy Spirit. He also makes the baptism of the Holy Spirit as the proper qualification for Christian activity.

Several important theological points may be observed in Mahan's doctrine of sanctification and holiness theology. First, there is Arminianizing of American theology in his holiness theology.[70] Mahan endeavored to fuse between New Haven theology and Wesleyan perfectionism with the fundamental idea of Arminian theology. Second, Mahan made the shift from Wesleyan Christ-centered perfectionism to Holy Spirit-centered perfectionism. Third, the emphasis was shifted to the special experience and event, which are vitally related to the power and work of the Holy Spirit, from the Wesleyan emphasis of the fruit of the life of Christian perfection.

Charles Finney

Charles Finney, a famed revivalist and an innovator of revival meetings, had a profound impact on the history of American Christianity. Ordained as a Presbyterian minister but rejected Calvinism, he moved away from Presbyterianism and espoused perfectionism of the Methodist church. Finney absorbed Wesleyan perfectionism and developed it into his own brand of perfectionism utilizing the theology bordering Pelagianism.

Life of Charles Finney

Charles Finney is the key figure when it comes to the study of the American holiness movement in the nineteenth century. There is little doubt that the influence of Finney on American society in the nineteenth century was monumental, whether positively or negatively. He is sometimes called "*the crucial figure of American evangelicalism since Jonathan Edwards*," and he is considered to be ranked on the same level with "Andrew Jackson, Abraham Lincoln, and Andrew Carnegie among the most important public figures in nineteenth century America."[71] To others, he is the catalyst in the

---

69. Mahan, *Baptism*, 38.
70. Hamilton, "Academic Orthodoxy," 57.
71. Noll, "Finney," 22.

dissolution of American Calvinism and the one who brought in the demise of evangelical theology in the nineteenth century.

Charles Finney was born in Litchfield County, Connecticut, in 1792. When he was two years old, his family moved to central New York and he spent his childhood there. Neither of Finney's parents was Christian. Finney confesses that he "seldom heard a Gospel sermon from any person" when he was growing up.[72] Following his preceptor's advice Finney finished his college education at home and entered a law office as a student. After finishing a legal apprenticeship Finney practiced law and became a successful lawyer.

Finney started to read the Bible after finding that the authors of his law textbook frequently quoted Scripture. While reading the Bible one day, he went through the conversion experience. Finney recounts this experience, "But after this distinct revelation had stood for some little time before my mind, the question seemed to be put, 'Will you accept it now, today?' I replied, 'Yes; I will accept it today, or I will die in the attempt.'"[73] After being converted, he pursued theological training for ministry by being personally tutored by his pastor, George Gale. Gale was trained in the Old School Presbyterian tradition, and Finney challenged and rejected Gale's Calvinistic doctrines.

Finney, ordained as a Presbyterian minister, began his ministry by teaching and preaching at revival meetings. He developed his own method of preaching the gospel and introduced many innovative methods such as the "anxious bench" in his revival meetings. He was so successful in his revival meetings that he became well-known throughout the country. Many parts of the country were affected for the cause of Christianity as a result of his ministry. But after sensing that his New Haven theology and innovative methods of preaching were not well-received by some of the fellow Presbyterian ministers, Finney left the Presbyterian church and joined the Methodist camp of the Christian church.

In 1835, Finney came to Oberlin College and began his teaching ministry at the college. At Oberlin, Finney along with Asa Mahan formulated the so-called Oberlin perfectionism and spent much time and effort in defending the doctrine. Finney pastored the First Congregational Church in Oberlin from 1837 to 1872 while teaching at the Oberlin College, first as a professor and then as the president of the college. In his later years much of his effort was spent on writing memoirs and theological books about his life and his own doctrinal views. Such books as *Revival Lectures* and *Lectures on Systematic*

---

72. Finney, *Memoirs*, 5.
73. Finney, *Memoirs*, 18.

Theology are Finney's well-known books to many Christian churches. After finishing a long and fruitful life Finney died peacefully in 1875.

Charles Finney's Doctrine of Perfectionism

Perfectionism or entire sanctification is the primary doctrine in Finney's theology. In his work, *Christ Our Sanctification*, he describes Christ's offices and relations to the believer in sixty-one different ways. The key to entire sanctification is to accept all the offices and relations of Christ. Finney writes, "The personal and individual acceptance of Christ in all His offices and relations as the *sine qua non* of entire sanctification seems to me to be seldom either understood or insisted on by ministers of the present day, and of course little thought of by the Church."[74] Thus the entirely sanctified person has Christ as the absolute ruler in his soul. He explains:

> There is no degree of sanctification that is not to be thus ascribed to Christ; and that entire sanctification is nothing else than the reign of Jesus in the soul; nothing more nor less than Christ, the Resurrection and Life, raising the soul from spiritual death, and reigning in it through righteousness unto eternal life.[75]

After describing entire sanctification, Finney defines the term, "I shall use the term entire sanctification to designate a state of confirmed, and entire consecration of body, soul, and spirit, or of the whole being to God."[76] He means that an entirely sanctified person does not and will not sin. But he does not mean that there will be no struggle or warfare with temptation in the rest of Christian life.

After defining entire sanctification Finney asserts that entire sanctification is attainable in this life. He bases his argument on the concept of the natural ability of man. Finney writes:

> It is self-evident, that entire obedience of God's law is possible on the ground of natural ability. To deny this, is to deny that a man is able to do as well as he can. The very language of the law is such as to level its claims to the capacity of the subject, however great or small that capacity may be. "Thou shalt love the LORD thy God with all thy heart, with all thy soul, with all thy mind, and with all thy strength." Here then it is plain, that all the law demands, is the exercise of whatever strength we

---

74. Finney, *Christ Our Sanctification*, 31.
75. Finney, *Sanctification*, 46.
76. Finney, *Finney's Lectures*, 405–6.

have, in the service of God. Now, entire sanctification consists in perfect obedience to the law of God, and as the law requires nothing more than the right use of whatever strength we have, it is, of course, forever settled, that a state of entire sanctification is attainable in this life, on the ground of natural ability.[77]

Finney thus not only argues that a believer can attain entire sanctification by his natural ability, but also insists that entire sanctification is in fact a promise of God. Quoting such Scripture passages as Deuteronomy 30:6, Jeremiah 31:31–34, and Hebrews 8:8–12, Finney insists that entire sanctification is implied in this promise and that this promise was made to the Christian church. He in fact makes perfection a duty of a Christian. Finney states, "I argue that Christian Perfection is a duty, because God has no right to require anything less."[78] Thus Finney teaches that a believer not only can attain entire sanctification but also must attain it.

In the discussion of the conditions for attaining entire sanctification, Finney warns the believers not to imitate the experience of others. He states:

> A state of entire sanctification cannot be attained by attempting to copy the experience of others. It is very common for convicted sinners, or for Christians inquiring after entire sanctification, in their blindness, to ask others to relate their experience, to mark minutely the detail of all their exercises, and then set themselves to pray for, and make direct efforts to attain the same class of exercises, not seeming to understand, that they can no more exercise feelings in detail like others, than they can look like others.[79]

Repudiating the Arminian concept of converting grace and the Calvinistic approach of using the means of grace, Finney sets his own conditions for attaining entire sanctification. He teaches that there are two kinds of works: works of law and works of faith. Both justification and sanctification are by faith, without works of law. Works of law achieve nothing. For Finney, entire sanctification is attained by faith alone. Finney explains the importance of faith, "This state [entire sanctification] is to be attained by faith alone. Let it be forever remembered, that without faith it is impossible to please God, and whatsoever is not of faith, is sin. Both justification and sanctification are by faith alone."[80] For Finney sanctification by faith is tantamount to sanctification by the Holy Spirit. Thus, for him faith is rather

77. Finney, *Finney's Lectures*, 407.
78. Finney, *Professing Christians*, 342.
79. Finney, *Sanctification*, 15.
80. Finney, *Sanctification*, 18.

the "instrument or condition," than the efficient agent that induces a state of entire sanctification. Faith simply receives Christ as reigning king in the soul. According to Finney, "it is Christ, in the exercise of His different offices, and appropriated in His different relations to the wants of the soul, by faith, who secures our sanctification."[81]

As we shall see in the examination of his theology in the next section, Finney fell into semi-Pelagianism in making a man autonomous by endowing him with natural ability. As such, an individual *earns* entire sanctification, or perfection, in Finney's concept of perfectionism. Even though he paints his theology with the term "grace," no such concept exists in Finney's theology.

Theology of Charles Finney

The theology of Charles Finney is unique in that he claimed to follow neither Arminian nor Calvinistic theology. However, he did not show originality in his theology as his theology is widely known as Taylorism. Foster dismisses Finney's theology with one word "Taylorism."[82] Nathaniel Taylor was primarily responsible for developing New Haven theology in the nineteenth century. Finney's theology owes much to Taylor's theological system. In this section Finney's doctrines such as man's ability, sin, the depravity of man, and the atonement, which are pertinent to his doctrine of perfection, are examined.

Man's Ability

Finney begins his discussion on man's ability with the recognition that "the question of ability is one of great importance." He expresses his primary reason for asserting this doctrine, "To deny the ability of man to obey the commandments of God, is to represent God as a hard master, as requiring a natural impossibility of his creatures on pain of eternal damnation."[83] Rejecting the Edwardsean notion of natural ability, Finney argues that ability is a "first-truth of consciousness, a truth necessarily known to all moral agents." Man, according to Finney, as a moral agent has the natural ability to obey God. He writes, "In all our judgements respecting our own moral character and that of others, we always and necessarily assume the liberty

---

81. Finney, *Sanctification*, 19.
82. Foster, *History*, 453.
83. Finney, *Finney's Lectures*, 350.

of the human will, or natural ability to obey God."[84] Thus, for Finney a person does not believe in Christ not because he cannot, but because he does not want to believe. There is no inability in Christian life but only unwillingness. Finney writes:

> Nothing was more foreign from the apostle's purpose, it seems to me, than to affirm a person's inability of will to yield to the claims of God. Indeed, he affirms and assumes the freedom of will. "To will," he says, "is present with me;" that is, to resolve. But resolution is an act of will. It is a purpose, design. He purposed, designed to amend.[85]

Moving on to the discussion of gracious ability, Finney dismisses it as an absurdity. He shows the reason for rejecting it, "To admit the assumption, that men had really lost their ability to obey in Adam, and call this bestowment of ability for which they contend, grace, is an abuse of language, an absurdity, and denial of the true grace of the gospel not to be tolerated."[86] Finney defines grace thus, "I maintain that the gospel, with all its influences, including the gift of the Holy Spirit, to convict, convert, and sanctify the soul, is a system of grace throughout." But for the salvation of man the grace of God alone is not sufficient in Finney's system. He presents man's part in the salvation of man, "But to maintain this, I must also maintain, that God might justly have required obedience of men without making these provisions for them. And to maintain the justice of God in requiring obedience, I must admit and maintain that obedience was possible to man."[87] In Finney's system both God and man become partners and make contributions to the salvation of man. In endeavoring to defend God's justice with his rationality Finney moves away from orthodox theology and falls into semi-Pelagianism. As Vulgamore notes in his article, in Charles Finney the dissolution of American Calvinism has begun.[88]

Sin

In dealing with the doctrine of sin, Finney shows that his concept of sin is closely tied to his fundamental concept of moral law and man as a moral

---

84. Finney, *Finney's Lectures*, 326.
85. Finney, *Finney's Lectures*, 361.
86. Finney, *Finney's Lectures*, 352.
87. Finney, *Finney's Lectures*, 352.
88. Vulgamore, "Finney," 33.

agent in his theological system. Sin is a transgression of moral law and it is voluntary, says Finney. He states the definition of sin:

> What is sin? Sin is a transgression of the law. The law requires benevolence, good willing. Sin is not a mere negation, or a not willing, but consists in willing self-gratification. It is willing contrary to the commandment of God. Sin, as well as holiness, consists in choosing, willing, intending. Sin must be voluntary; that is, it must be intelligent and voluntary. It consists in willing, and it is nonsense to deny that sin is voluntary. The fact is, there is either no sin, or there is voluntary sin. Benevolence is willing the good of being in general, as an end, and, of course, implies the rejection of self-gratification, as an end. So sin is the choice of self-gratification, as an end, and necessarily implies the rejection of the good of being in general, as an end.[89]

For Finney sin is a voluntary choosing of one of two possible choices, self-gratification or good of being, as one's ultimate end in life. Sin and holiness are eternal opposites and antagonists, and both sin and holiness consist in choice.

Finney teaches that there are only two alternatives in life: selfishness and benevolence. The intention for this ultimate selfishness is sin. Thus, in Finney's concept sin is quantified, a unit. Sin is a voluntary choice of selfishness.

Depravity of Man

As was expected from his concept of sin, Finney's understanding of the depravity of man deviates from orthodox theology. He begins the discussion on this subject by making a distinction between physical and moral depravity and giving a definition for each one. "Physical depravity is the depravity of constitution, or substance, as distinguished from depravity of free moral action."[90] Finney again writes, "Moral depravity is the depravity of free-will, not of the faculty itself, but of its free action. It consists in a violation of moral law."[91]

After affirming man's physical and moral depravity, Finney begins to move away from orthodox theology to Pelagianism. He sees moral depravity in "yielding the will to the impulses of the sensibility, instead of abiding

---

89. Finney, *Finney's Lectures*, 122.
90. Finney, *Finney's Lectures*, 228.
91. Finney, *Finney's Lectures*, 229.

by the law of God, as revealed in the intelligence." Finney describes how moral depravity is formed from birth:

> The sensibility acts as a powerful impulse to the will, from the moment of birth, and secures the consent and activity of the will to procure its gratification before the reason is at all developed. The will is thus committed to the gratification of feeling and appetite, when first the idea of moral obligation is developed. This committed state of the will is not moral depravity, and has no moral character, until the idea of moral obligation is developed. The moment this idea is developed, this committal of the will to self indulgence must be abandoned, or it becomes selfishness, or moral depravity.[92]

Thus, Finney sees the reason for man's moral depravity is physical: slow development of reason compared to that of sensibility in infant or childhood years of life. In stating this view Finney outrightly rejects the teaching of the original sin of man as understood in orthodox theology. According to Finney, there is no connection or relation existing between Adam and his posterity as far as original sin is concerned. Man is morally depraved because "will is committed to the gratification of feeling and appetite" due to the slow speed of the development of reason compared with that of sensibility in early childhood. It is interesting to note that Finney, as eager as he is to defend the justice of God, does not notice the apparent injustice of God in his system of having man subject to moral depravity by giving man slow development of reason in early childhood.

Although Finney rejects the idea of original sin and the sinful nature of man, he insists that sin is natural to man. This is not because man's nature is sinful, but it is because the "appetites and passions tend so strongly to self-indulgence." Once the will is given to sin, argues Finney, it is very natural to sin. Once the will is committed to self-indulgence as its end, selfish actions become spontaneous. But when all the powers of man are developed, man as a moral being does not tend to sin, but "strongly in an opposite direction." He argues, "When reason is thoroughly developed by the Holy Spirit, it is more than a match for the sensibility, and turns the heart to God."[93] But the problem is that the "sensibility gets the start of reason, and engages the attention in devising means of self-gratification, and thus retards, and in great measure prevents, the development of the ideas of the reason which were designed to control the will."[94]

92. Finney, *Finney's Lectures*, 253–54.
93. Finney, *Finney's Lectures*, 257.
94. Finney, *Finney's Lectures*, 257.

In Finney's concept of depravity man is made totally autonomous. He is not a sinner, but morally depraved due to the nature of the development of man. He seeks to preserve the justice of God by making a man an independent and wholly responsible sinner. In the process he has to introduce the source of sin in man. To satisfy this purpose Finney's own concept of moral depravity is introduced in his system.

Atonement

Charles Finney's theology of the atonement is designed to sustain God's moral law and to show the integrity and love of God. His idea of the atonement is closely tied to his fundamental concept of God's moral government in his theological system. He shows how these are related:

> The governmental bearings of this scheme are perfectly apparent. The whole transaction tends powerfully to sustain God's law, and to reveal His love and even mercy to sinners. It shows that He is personally ready to forgive, and needs only to have such an arrangement made that He can do it safely as to His government.[95]

For Finney, the atonement is not so much to satisfy God's honor, as Anselm said, and not so much to satisfy retributive justice, as the Reformers taught. God as the moral governor rules the universe according to his moral law. Man sinned against God by breaking a moral law of God. Finney argues that the atonement is a "governmental expedient to sustain law without the execution of its penalty on the sinner." God has accomplished this purpose most perfectly by having Jesus Christ die on the cross.

Finney denies the concept of a commercial transaction and retributive justice in the atonement. He argues, "It is naturally impossible, as it would require that satisfaction should be made to retributive justice. Strictly speaking, retributive justice can never be satisfied, in the sense that the guilty can be punished as much and as long as he deserves; for this would imply that he was punished until he ceased to be guilty, or became innocent."[96] In other words, according to Finney it is impossible to satisfy retributive justice, even by offering the perfect God-man, Jesus Christ, for this purpose! He could not accept the idea that Christ could suffer the eternal punishment that was due to the elect.

---

95. Finney, *Gospel Themes*, 211.
96. Finney, *Finney's Lectures*, 271.

But for Finney the atonement of Christ is to satisfy public justice. In order to satisfy public justice, there are two ways God could choose: "either by the full execution of the penalty or by some substitute." In either case God's view of the value of the law must be shown with equal force. God chose to satisfy public justice by having the substitute in the God-man Jesus Christ. Finney writes:

> The thing to be done, then, required that Jesus Christ should honor the law and fully obey it; this He did. Standing for the sinner, he must, in an important sense, bear the curse of the law—not the literal penalty, but a vast amount of suffering, sufficient, in view of His relations to God and the universe, to make the needed demonstration of God's displeasure against sin, and yet of His love for both the sinner and all His moral subjects. On the one hand, Jesus represented the race; on the other, He represented God. This is most divine philosophy.[97]

In Finney's theory of the atonement man's sin is forgiven or forgotten in the arbitrary will of God. This is the place where his semi-Pelagian theology would end up in the theory of atonement. Since he did not have a clear biblical concept of sin, he did not have a clear solution to the sin problem, the atonement.

On the subject of the extent of the atonement Finney argues for universal atonement. He states, "All holy beings are, and must be, benefited by it, from its very nature, as it gives them a higher knowledge of God than ever they had before, or ever could have gained in any other way."[98] His concept of universal atonement is a natural consequence of his concept of a benevolent God who confers blessings upon mankind.

Charles Finney's theology is semi-Pelagian aiming at pragmatic and revivalistic Christianity. His aim is to convert the sinner and keep him perfect the rest of his life. The doctrines in his theological system are centered around this theme. And many, if not all, of his doctrines are diluted and stripped of orthodox Christian and biblical truth. Reeves correctly observes that there is no sense of tragedy in Finney's doctrine of sin, consequently there is no sense of triumph in his doctrine of atonement.[99] In Charles Finney the Christian theology of America was deprived of Calvinism and even of Arminianism and turned into semi-Pelagianism which was in essence only a synthesis of Enlightenment humanism and Christian piety.

---

97. Finney, *Gospel Themes*, 209–10.
98. Finney, *Finney's Lectures*, 275.
99. Reeves, "Holiness and the Holy Spirit," 314.

Conclusion

The root of American perfectionism in the holiness movement goes back to John Wesley of England in the eighteenth century. Wesley defined perfectionism as pure love, deliverance from sin, and humble and total dependence on God. The purpose of perfectionism is to introduce the empowered life of the Christian. Though Wesley himself never claimed Christian perfection or perfectionism personally, he preached and disseminated this teaching diligently. However, the idea of perfectionism was founded on Arminian theology. Wesley's fundamental concept of God was a loving God rather than a sovereign God as in Calvinism. His doctrines of election, prevenient grace, sin, free will, and assurance showed that his fundamental theology was Arminianism. Thus, American perfectionism had its beginning in John Wesley's perfectionism, founded on unsound Arminian theology.

Wesley's perfectionism filtered into the American churches through Methodist teachings. A Methodist laywoman who was greatly affected and changed by Wesleyan perfectionism was Phoebe Palmer. Though not a theologian, she taught the Wesleyan doctrine of perfection with her entire devotion. She popularized the doctrine of Wesleyan perfectionism and made it applicable to every believer in the church. Her three-step process of achieving Christian perfection introduced a specified technique to follow in order to attain perfectionism. Mrs. Palmer's technique was a forerunner of many prescribed techniques taught by various holiness groups such as Keswick, in order for a man to achieve the epitome of holiness in the Christian life.

Unlike Phoebe Palmer, Asa Mahan was a trained theologian who was also greatly influenced by perfectionism. As the president of Oberlin College, he formulated and taught perfectionism. He endeavored to give a legitimate philosophical and theological foundation to perfectionism. He rejected Calvinism and followed Arminianism in his teaching of perfectionism. In his later works Mahan introduced the term "baptism of the Holy Ghost" instead of using "Christian perfection." In his teaching of perfectionism is seen a mixture of New Haven theology and Arminian theology. Also, his emphasis on the baptism of the Holy Spirit shows a shift from Wesleyan Christ-centered perfectionism to Holy Spirit-centered perfectionism.

Charles Finney more than Mrs. Palmer and Asa Mahan was undoubtedly the most dominant figure in the holiness movement in America in the nineteenth century. He was known as a preacher and a theologian, though a very poor one from a Calvinistic perspective, for perfectionism. He defined perfectionism as the entire consecration of body, soul, and spirit and taught that it was attainable in this life. The examination of Finney's theology reveals that his theology is semi-Pelagian and is even called Pelagian by some theologians. Finney rejected Calvinism and even moved away from Arminianism and embraced Taylorism which was basically Pelagianism. The study of Finney's doctrines of man's ability, sin, depravity of man, and atonement exposes the semi-Pelagian and Pelagian nature of his theology.

The movement of perfectionism from John Wesley in England to Charles Finney in America crossed several theological boundaries. Perfectionism based on Arminianism became perfectionism based on Pelagianism through the inroads of New Haven theology. Though founded on unsound theology, perfectionism gained a large following and influenced many churches including Presbyterian churches in the nineteenth century. Reformed theologians and Presbyterian ministers responded to perfectionism from a Calvinistic perspective of sanctification. The foremost and ablest Reformed theologian responding to perfectionism in the late nineteenth century was B. B. Warfield. In the next chapter we will examine Warfield's analysis of the theology of perfectionism and his exposition of the true nature of this doctrine.

Chapter 3

Benjamin Warfield's Response to American Perfectionism

As THE HOLINESS MOVEMENT with its doctrine of perfectionism made inroads and spread into American Christianity, the reaction to the holiness movement came from various people in American evangelicalism. But more than anyone else, the most comprehensive response to perfectionism came from the pen of Benjamin B. Warfield. Warfield, professor of theology at Princeton Theological Seminary from the late nineteenth to the early twentieth centuries, responded to perfectionism with sharp criticism from the position of Reformed theology. His detailed work on perfectionism, *Studies in Perfectionism*, is said to be the most thoroughgoing treatment on the subject of perfectionism as far as the critical evaluation of the subject is concerned.

Evaluation Of Asa Mahan's Teaching

In the first part of *Studies in Perfectionism*, Warfield deals with the teachings of Asa Mahan as he is considered the key figure in the beginning of the development of Oberlin perfectionism. In this section he examines in detail Asa Mahan's teachings such as sanctification, the relationship between justification and sanctification, the transformation in sanctification, the baptism of the spirit as well as Mahan's use of Scripture in formulating these doctrines.

Sanctification

Warfield begins his critical evaluation of Asa Mahan's doctrine of sanctification by showing the supernaturalness of salvation in Mahan's doctrine.

Warfield writes, "It is as an assertion of the supernaturalness of the whole of salvation, that he understands the declaration that our sanctification as well as our justification is by faith, by faith alone."[1] Although sanctification by faith is a biblical concept, he exposes a false theological logic behind Mahan's statement. Warfield shows Mahan's reasoning:

> The committal of our sanctification to Christ in faith is a confession that we cannot sanctify ourselves; and the prescription of this method of sanctification by the Scriptures is their testimony that we cannot sanctify ourselves. The main facts in the case accordingly are that we are incapable of sanctifying ourselves, and that it is precisely because we are incapable of sanctifying ourselves that sanctification is by faith, that is to say, by Christ in response to the commitment of it to Him.[2]

Warfield criticizes the utter passiveness of man in the work of sanctification in Mahan's teaching. He sees the eventual consequence of Mahan's reasoning—the immediate, instantaneous, and complete sanctification of man. But in this reasoning Warfield notes the supernaturalness in Mahan's perfectionism. Warfield writes:

> Here we have the foundation of Mahan's reasoning. Some of the corollaries which he draws from it are, that because this sanctification is wrought by Christ alone, it may be and is immediate, instantaneous and complete. His perfectionism is thus distinctively a supernatural perfectionism. Christ's people may be perfect, precisely because it is Christ the LORD who makes them perfect, and not they themselves.[3]

Reacting to Mahan's statement that Christians should expect to obtain justification and sanctification at the same time and to the same extent by faith in Christ, Warfield shows that Mahan is teaching that sanctification must be as instantaneous and complete as justification. He rejects Mahan's teaching of the instantaneous nature of sanctification and simultaneous occurrence of sanctification with justification. Warfield comments on Mahan's view:

> He[Mahan] is not insisting that justification must be as progressive as sanctification; but, just the contrary, that sanctification must be as instantaneously complete as justification. He means to say that it is absurd to suppose that we are completely justified all at once—as we certainly are—and not to suppose that we are

1. Warfield, *Perfectionism*, 95.
2. Warfield, *Perfectionism*, 95.
3. Warfield, *Perfectionism*, 95–96.

> completely sanctified at the same time: and it is as wicked as it is absurd, since then we should be asserting that we are saved *in* and not *from* our sins. This, however, is all the more strongly to assert the absolute coetaneousness of justification and sanctification in its completeness; and compels us not only to give its full validity to the phrase "at the same time," but to throw a strong emphasis upon it. Justification and sanctification in its completeness are thus affirmed in the most uncompromising way to take place together.[4]

Warfield sees that Mahan's teaching of the instantaneous and simultaneous occurrence of justification and sanctification as incredible.

Commenting on Mahan's concept of the legal and the evangelical spirits, Warfield says that sanctification by effort and sanctification by faith are not in mutually exclusive opposition to one another. The Christian's efforts to be holy, says Warfield, are themselves part of the sanctifying effects of the faith by which they are united with Christ. So, in sanctification the efforts and faith are mutually indispensable. Warfield explains his view, "Effort and faith cannot in themselves be set in crass opposition to one another, as if where the one in the other cannot be. They rather go together in a matter like sanctification which consists in large part of action."[5]

After presenting his own view on the relationship between effort and faith in sanctification, Warfield criticizes Mahan who sets himself in opposition to sanctification from personal efforts. Warfield refutes Mahan's view:

> The matter for us is to note now is that by setting himself in opposition to those who "expect sanctification from personal efforts," and by the very inconsiderateness of this opposition, it is made the clearer that Mahan thinks of himself as teaching that sanctification is obtained not at all by "personal effort," but by faith alone, and is the work of Christ exclusively, into which no other work of man enters except faith alone.[6]

For Warfield sanctification always involves efforts which themselves are the sanctifying effects of the faith. Thus, he sees sanctification as a progressive and gradual process in the Christian life. As such, Mahan's concept of instantaneous sanctification without any effort at all cannot be accepted by Warfield.

---

4. Warfield, *Perfectionism*, 97.
5. Warfield, *Perfectionism*, 105.
6. Warfield, *Perfectionism*, 105.

Relationship between Justification and Sanctification

After stating the Reformed view that it is by one and the same act of faith that we receive Christ both as our justification and as our sanctification, Warfield shows the difference between this view and the Mahan's view which says that "by this single act of faith we not only obtain both justification and sanctification, but obtain them both at once in their utmost completeness."[7] By this statement Mahan seems to teach that if the individual is not perfectly sanctified at the moment of his justification, he is in a sense saved *in* his sin. Warfield observes this false teaching and spews a caustic criticism on this inept reasoning:

> What is really declared then is that every believer is perfect, in the sense that he is freed from all sin from the moment of his believing. That carries with it the consequence that no one is a believer—that no one is justified—that no one is saved in any sense, to whom there clings a single, even the tiniest sin. Christ's salvation is *from* sin and never *in* sin. Now Mahan does not in the least believe that. He is only for the moment caught in the meshes of his own chop-logic, and is reasoning on a submerged premise, assumed not only without but against proof—that sanctification takes place all at once and occupies no time.[8]

Sensing the discrepancy in his reasoning, Mahan endeavors to correct it by saying that "we must have a special faith for every particular benefit received of Christ."[9] Thus, Mahan introduces the concept of justifying faith and sanctifying faith. For Mahan different kinds of faith are needed for justification and sanctification. Warfield finds Mahan's differentiation of faith totally unacceptable. He writes:

> It is equally absurd to speak of a special "sanctifying faith" adjoined to "justifying faith"; "justifying faith" itself necessarily brings sanctification, because justification necessarily issues in sanctification—as the chains are necessarily knocked off of the limbs of the acquitted man. The Scriptures require of us not faiths but faith.[10]

Warfield sees Mahan's separation of faith in relation to justification and sanctification totally unacceptable and unscriptural. For Warfield, Mahan

---

7. Warfield, *Perfectionism*, 97.
8. Warfield, *Perfectionism*, 97–98.
9. Warfield, *Perfectionism*, 100.
10. Warfield, *Perfectionism*, 100.

introduces the separation of justification and sanctification which are considered as the particular benefits from Christ which may be received by different kinds of faith. Warfield contends that this is the result of false reasoning and is totally foreign to the scriptural teaching. Warfield gives his final analysis on this matter:

> However Mahan may have endeavored to conciliate for himself such conflicting lines of thought, he emerges into the open with the clear and firm conviction that justification and sanctification are two distinct and separable benefits to be sought and obtained by two distinct and separable acts of faith.[11]

In spite of his original intention of making justification and sanctification the instantaneous and simultaneous events, Mahan creates a gap between justification and sanctification by making them two distinct and separable benefits attainable by different kinds of faith in Christ.

Transformation in Sanctification

Warfield begins the evaluation of Mahan's view of transformation with Mahan's citation of Ezekiel 36:25–27. He reproduces Mahan's statements. Mahan writes:

> Three great blessings, in all fullness, are here specifically promised; namely, full and perfect, cleansing from all sinful dispositions, tendencies, and habits; an equally full and perfect renewal, "the gift of a new spirit," and "a heart of flesh," in the place of the heart of stone which "had been taken out of the flesh"; and the "gift of the Holy Ghost," by whose indwelling the believer is "endued with power" for every good word and work, and perfected in his obedience to God's statues and judgments.[12]

In these statements Warfield sees a complete explication of what Mahan's sanctification is. Warfield writes, "Negatively, everything sinful is eradicated from the believer—including every sinful disability he may be supposed to have. Positively, holiness is infused into him, carrying with it power to do every good word and work."[13] Affirming the Scripture's teaching of "growth in grace," Warfield points out the difference between this "growth in grace" and Mahan's concept of the "process of becoming holy." He notes

---

11. Warfield, *Perfectionism*, 101–2.
12. Warfield, *Perfectionism*, 108.
13. Warfield, *Perfectionism*, 108.

that Scripture speaks of the expansion and development of the already holy person whereas Mahan's concept is of a "supernatural, instantaneous, entire transformation—a transformation which is total not only in the extensive sense but in the intensive sense."

What Warfield finds incredible in Mahan's sanctification is his understanding of the transformation in sanctification as a transformation of nature and not merely of activities. Warfield calls this sanctification the "physical" salvation, or physical sanctification. He states his critical evaluation of Mahan's concept:

> For one of the most notable features of it is the emphasis with which it is declared that the transformation is a transformation of nature and not merely of activities. "The body of sin is destroyed"; and that is defined as meaning that "evil dispositions and tendencies are 'taken out of our flesh'": a "full and perfect cleansing" is made "from all sinful dispositions, tendencies, and habits." A new heart is placed within us: and we are made "partakers of a Divine nature." A work like this cannot well be called other than "physical."[14]

Warfield points out that Mahan is teaching a two-stage salvation. For Mahan, the "physical" salvation, or sanctification which is reserved for the second stage salvation, is a result of an alleged second conversion. Warfield describes Mahan's awkward teaching of two conversion salvation:

> The convert in his own strength can avoid open and gross immoralities; but, nothing having happened to him within, he is unable to resist the impulses which arise from his unaffected "old man." It is a curious condition this, and one cannot see that there can be attributed to it anything that can justly be thought of as a state of salvation. We are told that the believer has escaped the penalties due to his sins—is a pardoned man: but he remains in precisely the same inward condition in which he was before. He is still in the condition of the natural man seeking to reform himself.[15]

Warfield accuses Mahan for discounting or eliminating the importance and necessity of justification by making sanctification the physical salvation.

---

14. Warfield, *Perfectionism*, 109.
15. Warfield, *Perfectionism*, 110.

Baptism of the Spirit

Mahan's doctrine of the baptism of the Spirit presents the concept of the mode of the Spirit's sanctifying work. He describes the work of the Spirit in sanctification, "He[Spirit] enlightens the intellect, and carries on the work of sanctification in the heart, by presentation of truth to the mind and . . . the Spirit sanctifies by presenting Christ to the mind in such a manner, that we are transformed into his image."[16] Reacting to these statements, Warfield raises a question as to how the Spirit makes Christ vivid and impressive to a believer in Mahan's concept of sanctification. He writes:

> We are left . . . in darkness as to how the indwelling Spirit is thought to enlighten the mind, or as that is here explained, to present truth or to present Christ to the mind. It does not seem to be meant that the Spirit reveals new truth to the mind, or reveals to it the old truths afresh. His action does not appear to be conceived as, in the strict sense revelatory, but rather as in its nature clarifying and enforcing: he gives clearness and force and effectiveness to the things of Christ. He makes Christ, in all that Christ is as our sanctification, vivid and impressive to us. What puzzles us is how He does it.[17]

Warfield further notes that Mahan's statement that the Spirit illuminates the soul by giving it knowledge in the form of absolute knowledge, still does not give an adequate answer. He continues, "It seems to involve the assumption of an effect wrought by the Spirit on the man himself, that is on his heart, which cannot be called anything but 'physical,' and that seems to demand such a 'physis' for man as is susceptible to such an operation."[18] Observing Mahan's statement that he was made absolutely conscious of God's pardoning of him by an action of the Spirit though he could not tell how, Warfield calls him a mystical perfectionist. He explains:

> It seems to be represented as merely an ungrounded conviction; the ground of it is assumed to be the Spirit; and the guarantee of this assumption appears to be merely the absoluteness of the conviction. So explained, it falls within the category of revelations, and we observe Mahan, on a later page, laying claim to special supernatural experiences which fall in nothing short of particular revelations.[19]

---

16. Warfield, *Perfectionism*, 115.
17. Warfield, *Perfectionism*, 116.
18. Warfield, *Perfectionism*, 117.
19. Warfield, *Perfectionism*, 117.

Warfield equates Mahan with the New York Perfectionists of whom such mystical experiences are characteristic in their religious life.

Scriptural Proof

Mahan used several Scripture passages to support his concept of sanctification. One of the passages used by Mahan to support his view was Acts 19:2–7. Commenting on Mahan's use of this passage, Warfield writes:

> This is so much the main passage on which he relies in proof of his cardinal contention that the baptism of the Spirit is a subsequent benefit, sought and received by a special act of faith, "after we believe," that he weaves it into the statement of his doctrine with an iteration that becomes irksome.[20]

Mahan claims from this passage that the promise of the Spirit awaits the believer after conversion. In other words, the Spirit is not expected *in* but *after* conversion, according to Mahan. To this statement Warfield responds that Mahan's wrong doctrine is based on an incorrect reading of the text. He continues that the aorist should be fully rendered and should be read "Did you receive the Holy Ghost when ye became believers?"

Another Scripture passage Mahan uses to support his view of sanctification is Ephesians 1:13 which says, "having also believed, you were sealed in Him with the Holy Spirit of promise." Mahan claims that the sealing in him and giving of the Spirit do not go together because we may give our seal to God long before he vouchsafes his to us. Warfield says this is an utterly wrong interpretation of the passage. He states the correct interpretation, "What the Apostle really says is of course, that we were sealed 'on believing'—intimating that the sealing occurred at once on our believing, and that it occurs, therefore to all that believe."[21] It is clear that Warfield does not highly regard Mahan's exegetical skill of Scripture. Warfield evidences that Mahan's wrong concept of sanctification is based on incorrect interpretations of the passages. He writes:

> The sealing of the Spirit belongs according to their very nature as such, to all Christians, It is not a special privilege granted after a while to some; but at once to all. Alford would have set Mahan right here, too. He renders the passage: "in whom on

---

20. Warfield, *Perfectionism*, 123.
21. Warfield, *Perfectionism*, 124.

your believing, ye were sealed," and remarks that "this use of the aorist makes the time when the act of belief first took place."[22]

Evaluation of Oberlin Perfectionism

Warfield describes the development of the Oberlin teaching in his *Perfectionism*. He shows that Oberlin perfectionism was not developed by one man but that several people contributed their theological insights to the development of the doctrine. Warfield particularly points out three people who played a key role in the development of Oberlin perfectionism. These people are Asa Mahan, William Cochran, and Charles Finney. Mahan especially played an important role in the beginning of the development of the doctrine whereas contributions from William Cochran and Charles Finney came as the development of the doctrine progressed.

Influence of Asa Mahan

Asa Mahan undoubtedly was the one of the dominant figures in the development of Oberlin perfectionism. Especially in the early stage of the development of the doctrine the dominant influence came from him. Warfield notes that Mahan's doctrine of sin and man's ability played the crucial role in the shaping of Oberlin perfectionism in the early stage of the development.

Mahan denies original sin in man and says that "sin is exclusively a personal matter, a state of the inner man, a form of voluntary moral activity."[23] "The soul becomes sinful, not from necessity, but choice," according to Mahan. He gives his own view of sin:

> We derive no sin from our ancestry, near or remote; and we have no form or degree of merit or demerit which does not attach to us personally and to no one else but us. "Personal criminality" and nothing else is sin to us. But however, we have become sinful, we are all entirely sinful. All sin consists in alienation and estrangement from God, His character, His will, and the law of duty; and this alienation and estrangement from all the claims of God and of His moral law, affects all our moral movements.[24]

---

22. Warfield, *Perfectionism*, 124
23. Mahan, *Out of Darkness*, 13–15. Cited by Warfield in *Perfectionism*, 126.
24. Mahan, *Out of Darkness*, 104–5. Cited by Warfield in *Perfectionism*, 126.

Thus, for Mahan there is always a "total failure to do that which is good." Warfield calls it "inability to good" even though Mahan himself does not use this term. Regarding Mahan's concept, Warfield writes, "He avoids the word 'inability,' but he is compelled to recognize some sort of a 'human impotence' to good; a 'self-impotence', a 'total self-impotence.'"[25] Warfield shows that Mahan thinks that his teaching is better than the New England doctrine of natural ability which, wholly neutralized by moral inability, leaves no ability at all. However, Mahan went "too far and left no disability at all," writes Warfield.[26]

Mahan insists on man's inability and that man is dependent on God's grace for right choices. Man's inability is overcome by light and grace. Mahan says that man has power to accept or reject God's grace offered to him as he will. However, he does not have a power to perform without grace what can be performed only with grace. Thus, for Mahan grace is the instrument for working certain effects; man must use it if he wishes those effects. Responding to these statements, Warfield points out that Mahan is not actually teaching the doctrine of inability to good but a doctrine of absolute ability with a complementary doctrine of right instrumentation. He comments that according to Mahan we are perfectly able to do what is right—to love God, to serve him, to be perfect; but of course, we are not able to do any of these things except we use the proper instruments for their performance.[27] Mahan thinks that he is teaching the ability dependent for its exercise on grace. But he is not. He is teaching grace dependent for its operation on ability. Warfield dissects Mahan's concept and reveals a faulty logic in his teaching. He explains:

> The whole truth is that Mahan has raised the problem of ability and inability, and then—has dodged it. He has left us with man on our hands "impotent" to good: and as he has not made it quite plain to us why he is impotent to good, so he has not given us any ground whatsoever to believe.... Clearly these problems can find no solution except in the frank postulation on the one hand of the sinfulness of human nature disabling it for good, and on the other of recreative grace recovering it to good.[28]

In dealing with the doctrine of salvation from sin Mahan says that there occurs a "fundamental change and a renewal of our propensities" in salvation. He writes, "We have 'a new heart', and 'a new spirit', 'a divine

25. Warfield, *Perfectionism*, 126.
26. Warfield, *Perfectionism*, 127.
27. Warfield, *Perfectionism*, 127.
28. Warfield, *Perfectionism*, 128.

nature', which impels us to love and obedience, just as our old nature impelled us to sin."[29] Thus, Mahan argues for the saving Spirit's work in salvation as a physical effect. Warfield observes the inescapable woe Mahan is trapped in, "He is no longer able to escape ascribing to unregenerate man a sinful 'nature' which determines his actions; or to the saving Spirit a 'physical' effect on this nature by which it is made good and the proximate source of our renewed activities."[30]

Mahan teaches that the words 'the divine nature' imply not only the holiness and blessedness of the divine mind, but also that divine *disposition* or nature in God which induces his holiness and blessedness.[31] According to Mahan, as a believer the individual not only obeys the divine will but also receives from Christ a new or 'divine nature', which "prompts him to purity and obedience." In this statement, says Warfield, Mahan is teaching impartation of the new nature by the Holy Spirit to the believer. Warfield writes, "A tendency appears here to think of the new nature imparted to us as if it were a separate entity implanted within us: and this is identified with the Holy Spirit whose coming into our hearts brings the 'disposition' of Christ with Him."[32] He also points out that Mahan's employment of the phrases "God sends the Spirit of His Son into our hearts" shows Mahan's mystical tendency in his concept.

Mahan summarizes his view, "It is as much the nature of the 'new man', or the promptings of his new divine tendencies, to be pure in heart and life, as it was that of the 'old man' to obey the law of sin."[33] Warfield calls it a physical change as Mahan's concept is physical corruption and physical holiness. Such concept is the foundation of Mahan's doctrine of sanctification, which Warfield calls "sanctification of the sensibility."

Influence of William Cochran

William Cochran, whom Warfield calls "a brilliant young man," was a student at Oberlin College and later served a few years as a professor at the college. Warfield credits Cochran for developing what was known as "the simplicity of moral action" and thus making a permanent mark on Oberlin perfectionism. The essence of this doctrine is stated in Warfield's *Perfectionism*:

29. Warfield, *Perfectionism*, 128–29.
30. Warfield, *Perfectionism*, 128.
31. Warfield, *Perfectionism*, 130.
32. Warfield, *Perfectionism*, 130.
33. Warfield, *Perfectionism*, 131.

> The doctrine maintains the impossibility of a divided heart in moral action. The sinner, in his sin, is utterly destitute of righteousness, and the good man, in his obedience, is completely, entirely obedient: sin on the one side and obedience, on the other belonging only to voluntary states. The division of the will between the two contradictory moral attitudes of sin and holiness is a metaphysical impossibility.[34]

According to this doctrine, a man is either good or bad as volitions are either good or bad. There is no spectrum of good and bad. Either the man is completely good or completely bad. There is no moral grey area in the volition of man. The implication of this concept to the doctrine of sanctification is far-reaching—it eliminates the whole concept of progressive sanctification. Warfield notes, "There can therefore be no such thing as a partially sanctified believer; and the whole conception of progressive sanctification is excluded."[35] He continues to explain the implication of this doctrine:

> Over against the general doctrine of the churches which denies the existence of perfect holiness, this doctrine sets the denial of the possibility of imperfect holiness. You are either perfectly holy, or you have no holiness at all. Holiness is a thing that does not admit of abscission and division. The idea is generalized into the proposition that "holiness must be supreme in degree to have the character of holiness at all"—a proposition which might appear to mean that a little sin neutralizes any amount of holiness, but no amount of holiness can affect the quality of existing sin at all, except that the very conception of progressive holiness is excluded.[36]

Thus, the church at any moment is made up of perfectly holy and perfectly wicked people in the same group. Therefore, this doctrine eliminates the concept of two classes of Christians and of a second conversion. "To be a Christian at all is to be perfect: and the concern of the Christian is not to grow more perfect, but to maintain the perfection which belongs to him as a Christian and in which, not into which, he grows."[37] In Christian life what the believer seeks is not more perfection but "establishment."

The doctrine of the simplicity of moral action supposes that man is oscillating between perfect goodness and perfect badness. This doctrine thus has been called "the pendulum theory of moral action." The goal of the believer is

---

34. Warfield, *Perfectionism*, 138.
35. Warfield, *Perfectionism*, 139.
36. Warfield, *Perfectionism*, 139.
37. Warfield, *Perfectionism*, 140.

to stop the oscillation between perfect goodness and perfect badness and to abide permanently in perfect goodness. When this state is attained, he is not only entirely sanctified but also permanently sanctified.

The influence of the doctrine of the simplicity of moral action is profound and permanent in Oberlin teaching. Warfield remarks, "The interpolation of this doctrine, as a controlling factor, into Oberlin thinking had the effect of antiquating the doctrine of perfection as previously taught at Oberlin."[38] Both Mahan and Finney make the readjustment of their view of sanctification, in order to incorporate this doctrine into their system. Warfield observes that in developing the simplicity of moral action the Oberlin men made the doctrine of sanctification the supreme doctrine in salvation. He writes:

> The doctrine of salvation becomes almost nothing indeed but a doctrine of sanctification. One of the results of this is that when the formal treatment of sanctification is reached, despite the copiousness with which it is dealt with, little is left to be said of it. In this exigency the term is retained and its meaning altered. "Entire sanctification" no longer stands as the end of the saving process as the final goal towards which the Christian's heart yearns.[39]

In the evaluation of William Cochran's simplicity of moral action Warfield does not seem to have the fuming criticism toward him as he has toward Mahan and Finney. However, Warfield remarks that the effect of this doctrine on Oberlin teaching from 1841 on is permanent, "And the characteristic feature of this new Oberlin perfectionism is that it is the product of the conception known as 'the simplicity of moral action.'"[40]

Influence of Charles Finney

It is no doubt that the most dominant figure for developing and disseminating Oberlin perfectionism is Charles Finney. Warfield reserves the most acrimonious evaluation of Oberlin teaching for Charles Finney. Warfield gives the most space for the evaluation of the perfectionist teaching to the teaching of Finney. While the comprehensive evaluation by Warfield of the theology of Finney is presented in the next section, Finney's peculiar

---

38. Warfield, *Perfectionism*, 140.
39. Warfield, *Perfectionism*, 141–42.
40. Warfield, *Perfectionism*, 143.

concept of justification and sanctification, which is so vital to his teaching of perfectionism, needs to be examined at this time.

Out of many theological concepts proposed by Finney, Warfield presents Finney's concept of justification and sanctification as that which left a lasting mark on Oberlin perfectionism. Warfield begins by showing Finney's differentiation between condition and ground of justification. According to Finney, the only ground for justification is "the disinterested and infinite love of God," whereas the conditions of justification are the atonement of Christ, repentance, faith in the atonement, and sanctification.[41] He distinguishes between present and future justification, making the former conditional upon *present* repentance, faith, and sanctification and the latter conditional upon *future* repentance, faith, and sanctification. Finney continues, "It is only an error of some theologians to make justification a condition of sanctification, instead of making sanctification a condition of justification."[42] Warfield observes that the relation of sanctification to justification in this case is of causal condition, which means that one can have sanctification without justification, but not justification without sanctification. In other words, man's acceptance with God is always conditional upon his complete obedience to law—one has to be holy before being accepted by God.

Finney also asserts that justification occurs only in sequence to the four conditions: atonement, repentance, faith, and sanctification. There is a sequential relationship in which justification always follows these four conditions. Warfield observes a fallacy in this logic and shows that Finney is teaching the justification by man's own righteousness. He remarks:

> There is a relation here of precedence and sequence; of cause and consequence. Justification depends on these things, its occurrence is suspended on them; as they do not depend on it, their occurrence is not suspended on it. And that carries with it that justification depends on, is suspended on, "man's own obedience or righteousness."[43]

Warfield perceives that Finney is working from the rectoral theory of atonement, in which the work in Christ is reduced to induce man to repent and believe. Although Finney works very hard to make God both benevolent to forgive sin and sovereignly free, Warfield points out that Finney's God is not free but is tied up with governmental obligations. Warfield states, "The love of God cannot fulfill itself in the actual justification of sinners, therefore,

41. Warfield, *Perfectionism*, 152.
42. Finney, *Finney's Lectures*, 555. Cited by Warfield in *Perfectionism*, 152.
43. Warfield, *Perfectionism*, 153.

consistently with His governmental obligations, except in the case of those who have been brought by the Atonement (serving the purposes here of punishment) to repentance and faith, with the consequent amendment of life which is sanctification."[44] Thus, says Warfield, Finney is teaching that the "reformation of life" is the actual justification of man by God. Warfield accuses Finney of teaching a work-salvation which is purely Pelagianism. He shows Finney's wayward deviation from the orthodox position:

> When Finney strenuously argues that God can accept as righteous no one who is not intrinsically righteous, it cannot be denied that he teaches a work-salvation, and has put man's own righteousness in the place occupied in the Reformation doctrine of justification by the righteousness of Christ.[45]

Warfield thus sends forth the most broadly appealing accusation against Finney in which he is shown to be endeavoring to turn back the clock and undo singlehandedly the Reformation to which the Protestant church owes her birth and existence.

Finney boldly rejects the doctrine of justification in a forensic sense. He asserts, "Now this is certainly another gospel from the one I am inculcating. It is not a difference merely upon some speculation or theoretic point. It is a point fundamental to the gospel and to salvation, if any one can be."[46] Warfield explains the reason for Finney's rejection of the forensic doctrine of justification:

> And the precise point on which his opposition turns is that the Reformation doctrine, by interposing an imputation of the righteousness of Christ as the ground on which the sinner is accepted as righteous, does not require perfect intrinsic righteousness as the condition precedent of justification.[47]

Finney calls the forensic doctrine a "doctrine of justification in sin." He cries out, "It certainly cannot be true that God accepts and justifies the sinner in his sins. I may safely challenge the world for either reason or Scripture to support the doctrine of justification in sin, in any degree of present rebellion against God."[48] It is unthinkable for Finney to have God justifying an im-

---

44. Warfield, *Perfectionism*, 154.
45. Warfield, *Perfectionism*, 154.
46. Warfield, *Perfectionism*, 155.
47. Warfield, *Perfectionism*, 155.
48. Warfield, *Perfectionism*, 155.

pure, unsanctified sinner. Warfield remarks, "The attainment of sinlessness with Finney is the first, not the last step, of the religious life."[49]

In responding to Finney's challenge to adduce any Scripture to support the forensic doctrine of justification, Warfield points to Romans 3:21–26 and says that "Paul might seem to have written a great part of his epistles expressly to provide materials for meeting the challenge."[50] Then he seems to give a lesson to Finney on the exposition of the Scriptures. He writes:

> Precisely what Paul says in the cardinal verses (23, 24) is that "all—a very emphatic "all," declaring what is true of all believers without exception—that "all" have sinned"—the view-point being taken from their present state as believers—"all have sinned and know themselves to be without the approbation of God"— the present tense, middle voice, declaring a lack of which they were conscious—"and are therefore justified freely, by His grace, by means of the reasoning which is in Christ Jesus. . . . It is distinctly asserted here that those justified are sinners, and are conscious of standing as such under the condemnation of God at the moment when they are justified; that their justification is not in any sense in accordance with their deserving, but is very distinctly gratuitous, and proceeds from the grace of God alone; ant that God can act in this gracious fashion toward them only because He has laid a foundation for it in the ransoming which He has wrought out in Christ.[51]

Thus, Warfield shows that Scripture teaches otherwise even though Finney contends that man must be totally free from sin before being justified by God.

Finney also makes perseverance, along with sanctification, a condition of justification. He says, "Perseverance in faith and obedience, or in consecration to God is also an unalterable condition of justification, or of pardon and acceptance with God."[52] Warfield notes that Finney makes the continuance of justification dependent upon perseverance instead of perseverance dependent upon justification. He also remarks that Finney's teaching is totally humanistic, making God subject to human will. Warfield states, "In the Biblical view it is God, in Finney's it is man, who determines the issue: the whole standpoint assumed by Finney is that of a God responsive to human actions, rather than that of a man operated upon by

---

49. Warfield, *Perfectionism*, 156.
50. Warfield, *Perfectionism*, 156.
51. Warfield, *Perfectionism*, 156–57.
52. Warfield, *Perfectionism*, 158.

divine grace."[53] Warfield is amazed at Finney's statement such as that "the Christian is justified no further than he obeys, and must be condemned when he disobeys." Finney teaches that once the believer commits a sin, he ceases to be a believer and must do his first works all over again. Thus, the believer might have to go through many times the lapse and reworking for salvation during his life until the time of final justification. Warfield finds this doctrine totally false, and not based on Scripture.

As Warfield moves to the closing paragraph of Finney's lecture on justification, he finds Finney rejecting also the Augustinian doctrine of sin and soteriology. Finney writes, "Constitutional depravity or sinfulness being once assumed, physical regeneration, physical sanctification, physical divine influence, imputed righteousness, and justification, while personally in the commission of sin, follow of course."[54] Confirming the necessity of the Augustinian doctrine of sin and soteriology, Warfield points out that Finney's doctrines form a "concatenated system, rooted in his denial of innate depravity." He further says that Finney's soteriology revolves around his Pelagian doctrine of sin. Warfield writes, "there is no need of righteousness of Christ to supply his lack; and none is provided and none imputed—the sinner's acceptance with God hangs solely on his own self-wrought righteousness," thus echoing Finney's Pelagian theology.[55]

Evaluation of the Theology of Charles Finney

In his *Perfectionism*, Warfield devotes an entire chapter to the evaluation of the theology of Finney. Such a treatment underscores the importance and influence of Finney's theology on American perfectionism. Warfield sees Finney as the key figure in the American holiness movement in the nineteenth century. He gives a thorough treatment of the theology of Finney. In particular, Warfield deals with such doctrines as election, ability of man, sin, depravity of man, and sanctification, which are pertinent to the study of perfectionism.

Election

According to Finney, election proceeds on the foresight of salvability. He teaches that God gives each man whatever grace it seems to him wise in

---

53. Warfield, *Perfectionism*, 158.
54. Warfield, *Perfectionism*, 160.
55. Warfield, *Perfectionism*, 160–61.

order to accomplish his end. Thus, God secures the salvation of those who are salvable under the wise government and leaves those who are not salvable in their sins. Finney's doctrine of election shows that men are elected on the ground of their salvability. In the evaluation of Finney's doctrine of election, Warfield points out that there is no sovereignty of God in his doctrine of election. He writes:

> There is no sovereignty exhibited in their election itself, except in the sense that God might have left them also in their sin; if He were to save any, these were the only ones He could save—under the wise government established by Him. The only place in the transaction in which any real sovereignty is shown, lies in God's having established the particular government which He has established, and which determines who are salvable and who not[sic].[56]

Warfield shows that in Finney's doctrine of election, election is on the foresight of salvability and only ultimately can it be called sovereign.

Finney's doctrine of election teaches the salvation of "just these and none others" rather than the salvation of some rather than others. Finney writes, "The best system of means for securing the great end of benevolence, included the election of just those who were elected, and no others."[57] He continues, "The fact, that the wisest and best system of government would secure the salvation of those who are elected, must have been a condition of their being elected." To these statements Warfield raises the question, "Why are just those who are elected, elected?" After raising this thought-provoking question, Warfield answers his own question by saying that in Finney's system "the real reason of the election of the elect is their salvability, that is under the system of government established by God as the wisest."[58] He shows that Finney's teaching leads to a conclusion that there is an intrinsic difference between the elect and the non-elect. Warfield remarks about this:

> God elects those whom He *can* save, and leaves unelected those whom He *cannot* save, consistently with the system of government which He has determined to establish as the wisest and best. And this seems strongly to suggest that there is an intrinsic difference between the objects of election and others, determining their different treatment.[59]

---

56. Warfield, *Perfectionism*, 169.
57. Warfield, *Perfectionism*, 169–70.
58. Warfield, *Perfectionism*, 170.
59. Warfield, *Perfectionism*, 170.

It is clear in his writing that Finney wants to exclude any concept of an arbitrary criterion in election in his system. He explains his own position:

> I supposed that God bestows on men unequal measures of gracious influence, but that in this there is nothing arbitrary; that, on the contrary, he sees the wisest and best reasons for this; that being in justice under obligation to none, he exercises his own benevolent discretion, in bestowing on all as much gracious influence as he sees to be upon the whole wise and good, and enough to throw the entire responsibility of their damnation upon them if they are lost. But upon some he foresaw that he could wisely bestow a sufficient measure of gracious influence to secure their voluntary yielding, and upon others he could not bestow enough in fact to secure this result.[60]

In these statements Warfield detects that Finney wishes to have God who elects all that it is wise for him to elect. He also sees here that "Finney wishes to make it appear that election is in some sense the cause of salvation." Warfield points out the awkward position Finney puts himself in. Finney wants to deny that election is arbitrary and to represent salvation depended on the voluntary action of men. Warfield writes, "In order to protect this voluntariness of salvation he wishes to confine all of God's saving operations within the category of persuasion. And above all and governing all he wishes to make benevolence the one spring of the divine action."[61] He further shows Finney's God who has to allow some men to perish for the happiness of others. Warfield states, "The ultimate result is that, representing God as ordering the universe for the one end of the production of the greatest happiness of the greatest number, he finds himself teaching that men are left to perish solely for the enhancement of the happiness of others."[62]

Ability of Man

Regarding the ability of man Finney teaches that man's obligation is limited by his ability. In other words, man is able to do all that he is under obligation to do and nothing which he cannot do lies within the range of his duty. Finney presents this concept as the fundamental principle of his teaching. It is indubitable that he has a high view of man in saying that "it is possible for man to be all that he is under an obligation to be" and that "by willing he

---

60. Warfield, *Perfectionism*, 170–71
61. Warfield, *Perfectionism*, 171.
62. Warfield, *Perfectionism*, 172.

can directly and or indirectly do all that God requires him to do." In a statement like this, Warfield observes that Finney is teaching more than what the New England divines taught regarding the so-called "natural ability." What Warfield sees in Finney's teaching is that man has the inherent power or ability to obey God perfectly. Warfield writes:

> The ability which he thus ascribes to man as his inalienable possession is not merely that so-called "natural ability" which the New England divines were accustomed to accord to him, and which only recognized his possession of the natural powers by which obedience could be rendered were it not inhibited by man's moral condition. He means, on the contrary, that man has by his natural constitution as a free agent the inalienable power to obey God perfectly.[63]

For Finney, this ability is a natural ability of man. Because of this ability man does not need much help from God except some persuasion from him. Warfield remarks, "In possession of this inalienable ability man's salvation requires and admits of no other divine operation than persuasion."[64]

Along with the teaching of man's ability Finney also asserts man's unwillingness to obey God. Finney writes, "I admit and maintain that regeneration is always induced and effected by the personal agency of the Holy Spirit. It is agreed that all who are converted, sanctified and saved, are converted, sanctified and saved by God's own agency; that is, God saves them by securing, by his own agency, their personal and individual holiness."[65] Warfield notes that the mode of the divine agency in this operation is purely persuasive. Finney says, "All God's influence in converting men is moral influence. He persuades them by His word and His Spirit. If men will not yield to persuasion, they must be lost." He again asserts that the actual turning of the sinner is his own act and he can change his mind. In Finney's teaching like this, Warfield sees nothing but the repetition of the teachings of the New Divinity and Taylorism. After clearing the foliage of much verbiage and fallacious logic from Finney's theology, Warfield declares it to be nothing original, but just simple Pelagian theology.

In relation to man's ability, Warfield tackles Finney's concept of "power to the contrary." Finney asserts the "equal possibility of a contrary effect" in the will of man. Even though Finney claims that the action of the Spirit is persuasive, Warfield points out that the "action of the Spirit on the elect has the appearance of having a character more causal in nature than is expressed

---

63. Warfield, *Perfectionism*, 174.
64. Warfield, *Perfectionism*, 174
65. Warfield, *Perfectionism*, 175.

by the term persuasion." Warfield describes the strange phenomenon ascribed to man by the concept of the "power to the contrary." He writes:

> It is at least an arresting phenomenon that the human will, inalienably endowed with an equal power to either part, should exhibit in its historical manifestation two such instances of absolute certainty of action to one part—in one instance affecting the whole mass of mankind without exception, and in other the whole body of those set upon by the Spirit with a view to their salvation.[66]

Warfield finds Finney's concept incredible and totally humanistic. He remarks that Finney makes man a totally autonomous being who is quite able to save himself by his own power. Warfield closes this part of the discussion by posing the question, "How can man be affirmed to be fully able and altogether competent to an act never performed by any man whatever, except under an action of the Spirit under which he invariably performs it?"[67]

Sin

For Finney, all sin is sinning and sinning is purely personal. Finney allows that man may receive "a certain amount of moral injury through the physical deterioration that has come to them by evil inheritance." Warfield rejects the relationship between the moral injury and the physical deterioration of man. He is especially disturbed by Finney's suggestion that the physical deterioration could be corrected through a wise dietetic system so that "the sin into which they have fallen partly through its influence might in a generation or two disappear too." Warfield dismisses Finney's equation of physical deterioration with moral depravity. He says, "Nevertheless physical deterioration and moral depravity are different things, different in kind, and must not be confused with one another. The one we may receive from our progenitors, the other can be produced only by our own moral action."[68]

According to Finney there is no imputation—no transmitted corruption of heart. It becomes natural for Finney to deny the Augustinian doctrine of original sin. He writes, "All sin is actual, and . . . no other than actual transgression can justly be called sin."[69] He rejects any notion of a sinful nature. He continues, "We deny that the human constitution is

---

66. Warfield, *Perfectionism*, 177.
67. Warfield, *Perfectionism*, 178.
68. Warfield, *Perfectionism*, 179.
69. Warfield, *Perfectionism*, 188.

morally depraved . . . because it is impossible that sin should be a quality of the substance of soul or body. It is, and must be, a quality of choice or intention, and not of substance."[70] For Finney, sin is either choice or intention, and nothing else.

Warfield has harsh words for Finney's notion of sin and rejection of original sin. He shows that Finney's notion of sin is a Pelagian doctrine of sin. Warfield writes:

> The affiliations of Finney's notion here are obviously with that Pelagianizing doctrine of concupiscence which infested the Middles Ages and was transmitted by them to the Roman Church. It differs from that doctrine at this point only in its completer Pelagianism. Like it, it conceives of man as persisting, under whatever curse it may allow the fall to have brought upon him, *in puris naturalibus*; and, in order to sustain this position, it denies moral character to all the movements of the human soul, deliberate volitions in view of moral inducements alone excepted.[71]

Thus, Warfield concludes that Finney's notion of sin is essentially the Pelagian doctrine of concupiscence and that especially his affectional movements such as love, hate, malice, and compassionateness without any moral character made him to fall into the "paradoxes which made him the easy mark of ridicule."

Depravity of Man

For Finney, the moral depravity of man is universal. He writes, "Subsequent to the commandment of moral agency, and previous to regeneration, the moral depravity of mankind is universal."[72] He teaches that a newborn infant is just a little animal without moral nature. Finney says, "Previous to moral agency, infants are no more subject of moral government than brutes are."[73] This means that infants cannot be moved to action through "inducements addressed to their moral judgment." With regard to the salvation of infants Finney teaches a proleptic salvation. He writes:

> All that can justly be said . . . is, that if infants are saved at all, which I suppose they are, they are rescued by the benevolence of God from circumstances that would result in certain and eternal

---

70. Warfield, *Perfectionism*, 188.
71. Warfield, *Perfectionism*, 189.
72. Warfield, *Perfectionism*, 179–80.
73. Warfield, *Perfectionism*, 180.

death, and are by grace made heirs of eternal life. But after all, it is useless to speculate about the character and destiny of those who are confessedly not moral agents. The benevolence of God will take care of them.[74]

To the above statements Warfield raises the following questions, "Are infants not moral beings? Does a man cease to be moral being every time he goes to sleep? Are we moral beings only when we are acting, but becomes unmoral and only brutes whenever we are quiescent?"[75] Warfield sums up Finney's doctrine, "Infants are at first just little animals; after a while they pick up a moral nature; at that very moment they pick up sin also. Thus, all men become depraved from the very first moment when moral agency begins with them."[76]

Despite the teachings in Romans 5:12–21, Adam has nothing to do with the moral depravity of man in Finney's doctrine. According to Finney, all men would inevitably have sinned whether Adam had sinned or not. The babies become depraved because of the habits formed before they had any knowledge. Finney explains the doctrine:

> The sensibility acts as a powerful impulse to the will, from the moment of birth, and secures the consent and activity of the will to procure its gratification, before the reason is at all developed. The will is thus committed to the gratification of feeling and appetite, when first the idea of moral obligation is developed. This committed state of the will is not moral depravity, and has no moral character, until the idea of moral obligation is developed. The moment this idea is developed, this committal of the will to self-indulgence must be abandoned, or it becomes selfishness, or moral depravity.[77]

Warfield sees in the above statements the substitution of the rationalistic account for the Augustinian one. Warfield points out Finney's mistake of making God equally responsible for human depravity and thus depriving him of all justification for attaching it to man. Warfield writes:

> It would still be open to fatal objections, but no longer to this one—that it represents God as arbitrarily creating the human race after a fashion which made it inevitable that every member of it should fall into hopeless moral depravity—at the first dawn

---

74. Warfield, *Perfectionism*, 181.
75. Warfield, *Perfectionism*, 181.
76. Warfield, *Perfectionism*, 181.
77. Warfield, *Perfectionism*, 182–83.

of moral agency—as if the kind of humanity which He desired, intended and provided was a totally depraved humanity.[78]

Regarding the free agency and temptation Finney says that "no motive to sin could be a motive or a temptation, if there were not a sinful taste, relish, or appetite, inherent in the constitution, to which the temptation or motive is addressed."[79] To this statement Warfield responds, "Finney, abandoning the simple formula of free-agency plus temptation, is himself compelled in the end to assume a bias to sin in order to account for the universality of sin."[80] Warfield clearly shows that Finney's concept of the acquired depravity of man, rather than the imputed depravity, is not the Augustinian orthodox doctrine. He writes, "It posits a bias to sin as distinct as that posited by the Augustinians. The difference is that the Augustinians posit a bias brought by every man into the world with him; Finney a bias created invariably for himself by every man in his first essays at living."[81]

Sanctification

As with New Divinity teachers, Finney rejects the doctrine of constitutional moral depravity but warns that they have lost sight of Christ as our sanctification also. He writes that they "have fallen into a self-righteous view of sanctification, and have held that sanctification is effected by works, or by forming holy habits."[82] He asserts man's dependence on Christ for sanctification and sanctification by faith rather than works. Finney writes, "That is, faith receives Christ in all his offices, and in all the fullness of his relations to the soul; and Christ, when received, works in the soul to will and to do all his good pleasure, not by a physical, but by a moral or persuasive working."[83] Warfield points out that the above statements are the key to Finney's entire teaching on sanctification.[84] He shows the difference

78. Warfield, *Perfectionism*, 185.
79. Warfield, *Perfectionism*, 187.
80. Warfield, *Perfectionism*, 187.
81. Warfield, *Perfectionism*, 187.
82. Warfield, *Perfectionism*, 207.
83. Warfield, *Perfectionism*, 207
84. Charles Finney's understanding of human psychology shows the influence of faculty psychology which was dominant in the nineteenth century. Franz Delitzsch's *A Systematic Biblical Psychology* published in the nineteenth century represents the milieu of psychological study during this era which tended to compartmentalize the nature of man. Delitzsch viewed man in the threefold nature of spirit, soul and flesh. This is also seen in John Laidlaw who expressed man's nature in terms of faculty psychology

between the New Divinity and Finney's view as whether the works are done under Christ's persuasion or not. Warfield explains, "So that the only conceivable distinction between the rejected view of the New Divinity and Finney's own must be thought to lie in the answer to the question whether the works, done in both views alike by the soul itself and only by the soul itself, are done under persuasion from Christ or not."[85]

Thus, Warfield raises a question whether Finney's view of sanctification is any different from the New Divinity's view, which he rejects. Warfield writes that they are essentially the same for "the New Divinity did not at all deny that the soul was influenced in its sanctifying walk by the persuasions of the Holy Spirit."[86] According to Finney, "we believe in Christ for our sanctification; he then acts persuasively in our souls for sanctification; under this persuasion we act holily; that is our sanctification." Warfield points out it is nothing but Pelagianism. He explains Finney's Pelagian view:

> It is all a sanctification of acts. We are not ourselves cleansed; but then there is no need of cleansing us, since we were never ourselves clean. We were only a bundle of constitutional appetites, passions, and propensities, innocent in themselves, which we have been misusing through a bad will. What needs correcting is only this bad will into a good one. And the appropriate, the only, instrument for the correction of our willing is persuasion. Moved by this persuasion we "make ourselves a good heart"—we "change our mind," as the phrase goes—and that is the whole of it.[87]

Thus, Warfield accuses Finney of making sanctification an easy do-it-yourself operation of correction of one's will. Warfield concludes that "as this ready making for ourselves a new heart, makes us a perfectly holy heart, it

---

in his *The Bible Doctrine of Man*. He wrote, "Under this general expression [spiritual factor in the human being] may be held as included spirit, who used to denote the nature of that factor; mind, as its intellectual or rational aspect; and heart, when it is regarded as the practical center or fountain of man's life." However, in the twentieth century psychology of human nature took the holistic approach to the study of man. The holistic approach to the study of human nature is seen in Herman Ridderbos' *Paul*. He writes, "Flesh(body) and spirit do not stand over against one another here as two 'parts' in the human existence or in the existence of Christ. There is no question here of a dichotomistic distinction in an anthropological sense." He again writes, "The fundamental structure of Paul's proclamation of redemption is the totalitarian character." Laidlaw, *Bible Doctrine*, 276; see also Ridderbos, *Paul*, 66, 265.

85. Warfield, *Perfectionism*, 207.
86. Warfield, *Perfectionism*, 207.
87. Warfield, *Perfectionism*, 208.

is with this ease and despatch[sic] that according to Finney's form of perfectionism we become perfect."[88]

Assessment of Warfield's Evaluation of Perfectionism

The evaluation of perfectionism by Warfield was based on the orthodox theology in the Augustinian, Calvinistic tradition. Employing this orthodox theology, he gave the most pungent and thorough evaluation of perfectionism in modern times. He focused on Oberlin perfectionism, chiefly on Charles Finney, for the evaluation of American perfectionism. He had few, if any, words of praise for the perfectionist theology. Page after page, Warfield pointed out the fallacies of the arguments of the perfectionists. And many times, he stressed that perfectionism was based on the Pelagian and humanistic teachings. In particular, he dissected the doctrines pertinent to perfectionism and showed them to be unscriptural and antiorthodox under close scrutiny.

There are especially two things that stand out in Warfield's response to perfectionism. First, he underscored the teaching that sanctification is by faith. Although the perfectionists, including Charles Finney, claimed the same statement, Warfield probed into their teaching and demonstrated that it actually was a Pelagian and humanistic concept. The perfectionists' teaching was essentially sanctification by man's efforts. As opposed to this perfectionist humanistic teaching, Warfield emphasized sanctification by faith. This is in the same line as in Berkouwer's statement, "The sola-fide is at the heart of justification but no less at that of sanctification."[89] The concept of sola-fide in sanctification preserves the theocentric point of view in the doctrine of sanctification. Ridderbos remarks that "the theocentric character of this new obedience is the central and repeatedly recurring concept of sanctification."[90]

Second, Warfield emphasized the progressive nature of sanctification, chiding the perfectionists' impatience in expecting immediate sanctification. For Warfield, sanctification always has the inherent progressiveness in the life of a believer. The life of a believer ends, not begins, with perfection. There is no such thing as perfection during the life of a believer. Warfield asserts that perfectionism is a humanistic way to taste and experience the final glory that is yet to come in the life of the believer. A similar thought is also expressed by Berkouwer in the following

88. Warfield, *Perfectionism*, 208.
89. Berkouwer, *Sanctification*, 33.
90. Ridderbos, *Paul*, 260.

statement, "Perfectionism is a premature seizure of the glory that will be: an anticipation leading irrevocably to nomism."[91]

Although perfectionism was severely criticized by Warfield for its Pelagian theology, the assessment of perfectionism for its positive contribution to Christianity is called for today. First, the immediate and instantaneous character of sanctification in perfectionism influenced the orthodox Christian church to examine Scripture for definitive aspect of sanctification. Warfield's evaluation of perfectionism was wholly based on the progressive aspect of sanctification without any reference to the definitive aspect of sanctification. As such, Warfield, even though he had the ablest refutation of perfectionism rendered by the Reformed theologian, lacked a fully balanced approach in his evaluation of perfectionism. The perfectionists' teaching of the immediate and instantaneous nature of sanctification impelled many Reformed theologians to reexamine Scripture to discern whether Scripture actually taught such a concept. As a result, Reformed theologians such as Herman Ridderbos and John Murray had the two aspects in their doctrine of sanctification. John Murray introduced the doctrine of definitive sanctification based on Romans chapter 6, and Ridderbos had the "already" and "not yet" concept in his doctrine of sanctification.

Second, the emphasis on Christ in sanctification by perfectionism gave the impetus to the orthodox theologians to stress the Christological character of sanctification as well as the pneumatological one. In his evaluation of perfectionism Warfield asserts that sanctification is the work of the Holy Spirit based on justification. Again, unlike Warfield, both Murray and Ridderbos accentuate the Christological character of sanctification along with the pneumatological one. Ridderbos writes, "Christ enters the picture by the Spirit as the author of sanctification."[92] Murray also repeatedly stresses the "believer under the reign of Christ" in Romans 6 in his doctrine of definitive sanctification.

In assessing Warfield's view on sanctification, his emphasis on the gradual process of sanctification should not be understood as that the concept of the "already" is absent in his understanding of salvation. Warfield affirms some definite changes that occur in the renewal of a man. He writes:

> From that moment of the first divine contact the work of the Spirit never ceases: while man is changing his mind and reforming his life, it is ever God who is renewing him in true

---

91. Berkouwer, *Sanctification*, 67.
92. Ridderbos, *Paul*, 261.

righteousness. Considered from man's side the new disposition of mind and heart manifest themselves in a new course of life.[93]

There is already some transformation in the man who is saved through faith by Jesus Christ. Warfield bases the gradual process of sanctification on an enabling act from God which is "the peculiarly immediate and radical nature" at the initial point. He writes, "At the basis of all there lies an enabling act from God, by virtue of which alone the spiritual activities of man are liberated for their work (Rom. 6:22, 8:2)."[94]

We may also see Warfield's concept of the "already" and the "not yet" in his exposition of the apostle Paul's doctrine of renewal even though his concept is not as clearly defined and elaborated as Murray's and Ridderbos's. Warfield explains this concept as it relates to the holiness of a believer. He writes:

> The process may be hard—a labor, a struggle, a fight; but the end is assured. No matter how far from perfect we yet may be, we are not in the flesh but in the Spirit if the Spirit of God dwells in us; and we may take heart of faith from that circumstance to mortify the deeds of the body and to enter upon our heritage as children of God. Here in brief compass is the Apostle's whole doctrine of renewal. Without holiness we certainly shall not see the LORD: but he in whom the Holy Spirit dwells, is *already potentially* holy; and though we see *not yet* what we shall be, we know that the work that is begun within us shall be completed to the end. The very presence of strife within us is the sign of life and promise of victory.[95]

Warfield thus shows the concept of the "already" and the "not yet" in the salvation of man.

Although Warfield hints the immediate operation of the Spirit at the initial point in sanctification, he primarily treats and explicates sanctification from the progressive perspective. Warfield states this point:

> For the essence of the New Testament representation certainly is that the renewal which is wrought upon him who is by faith in Christ, is the work of the Spirit of Christ, who dwells within His children as a power not themselves making for righteousness, and gradually but surely transforms after the image of God, not the stream of their activities merely, but themselves in

---

93. Warfield, *Theological Studies*, 369.
94. Warfield, *Theological Studies*, 369.
95. Warfield, *Theological Studies*, 372. The emphases are mine.

the very center of their being. The process by which this great metamorphosis is accomplished is laid bare to our observation with wonderful clearness in Paul's poignant description of it, in the seventh chapter of Romans. We are there permitted to look in upon a heart into which the Spirit of God has intruded with His transforming power.[96]

In these statements we see Warfield basically dealing with sanctification from the progressive aspect of transformation. We would have liked to see him going to Romans 6 before referring to the seventh chapter of the book. We feel that one has to exegete Romans 6 before Romans 7 in explicating the definitive aspect of sanctification.

Conclusion

The holiness movement in the nineteenth century was spearheaded by Oberlin perfectionism developed and taught by the Oberlin theologians as led by Charles Finney. Warfield responded to perfectionism by examining and criticizing the theology of the leaders of perfectionism. He especially examined the teachings of Asa Mahan, William Cochran, and Charles Finney. In particular, he concentrated on the critical evaluation of the theology of Charles Finney who was the dominant figure in perfectionism in the nineteenth century.

Warfield begins his evaluation of perfectionism with the examination of the teachings of Asa Mahan who is regarded as the key figure in the beginning of the development of the doctrine. He examines in detail Mahan's doctrines of sanctification, relationship between justification and sanctification, transformation in sanctification, and baptism of the Spirit and finds that Mahan's theology is basically unsound New Haven theology and is full of faulty logic.

The only praise given to the perfectionist teachers by Warfield goes to William Cochran who is credited for developing the doctrine of the simplicity of moral action. However, Warfield's evaluation of this doctrine is neither decisively positive nor negative. The importance of this doctrine for perfectionism is nevertheless clearly shown by Warfield in that it makes the doctrine of sanctification the supreme doctrine in salvation for perfectionism.

Charles Finney is the main object of Warfield's examination of perfectionism. Warfield dissects Finney's theology and exposes Pelagianism in his theology. He especially deals with Finney's doctrines of election, ability of man, sin, depravity of man, and sanctification, and exposes the

---

96. Warfield, *Theological Studies*, 371.

humanistic and Pelagian nature of these doctrines. Warfield dismisses Finney's teachings as false teachings and concludes that Finney's theology of perfectionism is simply Pelagianism.

Warfield's response to perfectionism in the nineteenth century is scriptural and thoroughly orthodox. However, his evaluation of perfectionism is primarily from the progressive aspect of sanctification. In his response to perfectionism the immediate and once-for-allness of sanctification taught in Scripture is not brought out plainly and clearly to evaluate perfectionism with the fully balanced approach to sanctification. Warfield, however, gives the ablest and most thorough refutation of perfectionism in his time.

Warfield, though his response was most comprehensive, was not the only Reformed theologian in America who responded to perfectionism in the late nineteenth and early twentieth centuries. It would be helpful for us to see the reaction of other Reformed theologians to perfectionism during this time. The responses of these theologians would give us a good description of the theological milieu about perfectionism during the era of the holiness movement.

Chapter 4

Other Reformed Theologians' Response to Perfectionism

B. B. WARFIELD RENDERED the ablest and most comprehensive response to perfectionism from the perspective of Reformed theology. However, many other Reformed theologians also expressed their evaluation of perfectionism. The views of some of these theologians are presented in this chapter. These theologians are Lyman H. Atwater, Charles Hodge, Archibald Alexander Hodge, James Henley Thornwell, Robert L. Dabney, William G. T. Shedd, and James Oliver Buswell. All of them are from the American Presbyterian tradition. Also, the views of Louis Berkhof and G. C. Berkouwer, as fellow Reformed theologians, from non-Presbyterian Reformed tradition are included. The theological views of these theologians would give us a good overview of how perfectionism was perceived by the Reformed circle in the nineteenth and early twentieth centuries.

Lyman H. Atwater

Lyman H. Atwater was a professor at Princeton College from 1854 to 1883.[1] He taught and wrote extensively on theology and apologetics. He published many articles on these subjects in the *Princeton Review*. In the nineteenth century, along with Charles Hodge he defended vigorously Old School Presbyterianism against such theology as Taylorism.

In 1877, Atwater published an article on Christian perfection. In this article he examined the teachings of perfectionism. As an Old School Presbyterian theologian, he rejected the teachings of perfectionism and affirmed the Reformed view of sanctification. He affirmed that "sanctification is a gradual work, growing with the growth, and promoted by the efforts, struggles and

---

1. Smith, "Atwater," 93.

prayers of the Christian; who, while in his predominating character holy, is yet never free in this life from the remains of sin."[2]

First, Atwater shows in the article that there is the constant confounding of sanctification with justification in perfectionism. Before showing the fallacy in perfectionism, he presents the orthodox position on the doctrine of justification and sanctification:

> Justification is instantaneous and complete upon the first act of faith in Christ or vital union to Him. In its nature, justification is entire, or not at all. "He that believeth shall no more come into condemnation, but hath passed from death unto life." There is indeed "no more condemnation to those that are in Christ Jesus, who walk not after the flesh, but after the Spirit." Sanctification, on the other hand, is begun in infantile yet prevailing strength at conversion, and advances by a gradual and progressive growth, in which the new-born soul goes forward, "having these promises, to cleanse itself from all filthiness of the flesh and spirit, perfecting holiness in the fear of God"; so always cleansing stains which, although thus growing less, yet still remain in this decreasing form to be a contended against till they are wholly expunged.[3]

Atwater asserts that the perfection "must relate to that which is at once made perfect by the offering of Christ, viz., justification." Citing the passage in 1 John 1:7–9, "That the blood of Jesus Christ his Son cleanseth us from all sin . . . if we confess our sins, he is faithful and just to forgive us our sins, and to cleanse us from all unrighteousness," Atwater writes that it obviously refers "to justification as the immediate and finished result of the application of this blood, and only indirectly to sanctification which accompanies justification, at first initial and germinant, but gradually carried forward to perfect sinlessness in heaven."[4] Thus, all promises of the washing away of sins consists in perfect justification, or a progressive cleansing of sin by gradual sanctification. Underscoring the progressive nature of sanctification, Atwater writes, "One source of obscurity and confusion on this subject, therefore, is the tendency of many of the High Life persuasion more or less to confound justification and sanctification."[5]

Second, Atwater accuses the perfectionists of treating the conflict between the flesh and spirit as unreal. In refuting the perfectionists' teaching,

2. Atwater, "Christian Perfection," 392.
3. Atwater, "Christian Perfection," 397–98.
4. Atwater, "Christian Perfection," 398.
5. Atwater, "Christian Perfection," 398–99.

he first quotes the passage in 1 John 1:8, "If I justify myself, mine own mouth shall condemn me: If I say I am perfect, it shall prove me perverse." Atwater contends that "this could not be true of the claims to any but sinless perfection, as other kinds of perfection are freely ascribed to the faithful servants of God."[6] Also citing the LORD's Prayer, he emphatically says that it is a Christian's duty always to pray, "forgive our trespasses, even as we forgive those who trespass against us."

To show the Christian conflict vividly, Atwater moves to Galatians 5:17 and Romans 7:14, 25, which in his mind constitute the proof of the conflict between the flesh and the spirit in a Christian. He stresses that the people whom Paul was writing to were the professed Christians. In Romans 7, the person depicted in this passage is a regenerated man who can say "O wretched man that I am! Who shall deliver me from the body of this death? I thank God through Jesus Christ our LORD." For Atwater, this person cannot be an unbeliever. He writes, "If this is the language of impenitent unbelievers, where shall we find what is distinctive of the newborn soul? Do we need more evidence that the flesh, and sin itself, as well as the outside world, are among the foes with which the Church militant must ever contend?"[7]

Third, Atwater calls the perfectionists' teachings antinomian. Atwater himself says this is a grave charge. He charges the perfectionists for lowering the perfect standard of the divine law. According to Atwater, though the perfectionists claim they are against antinomianism, they themselves fall into it. He writes:

> When we say that they are essentially Antinomian, we do not mean that their abettors call them such. Some of them, like John Wesley, even warn its adherents against Antinomianism. And many of them have no suspicion that the scheme logically or practically involves such a taint. What we maintain, however, is, that its advocates really take Antinomian ground; that they in one form or another lower the standard of perfect holiness below the only perfect and immutable standard of goodness—i.e., the divine law—to some vague and indeterminate level, depending on and varying with the subjective states of each person who supposes himself to be perfect.[8]

Therefore, for Atwater what perfectionism claims is not based on the law of God but some lower, yet undefined, standard level for man's depraved and fallen state. "What is undeniable," writes Atwater, "is that the perfection

6. Atwater, "Christian Perfection," 401.
7. Atwater, "Christian Perfection," 402.
8. Atwater, "Christian Perfection," 403.

maintained is below some requirements of the divine law known or unknown to its possessor."[9]

Taking the antinomian teachings of perfectionism to their logical end, Atwater shows that the perfectionists cannot take a uniform and consistent position on this subject and that there will not be the clear difference between the perfectly and the imperfectly sanctified believers. Not only the antinomian teaching makes sanctification meaningless, but also it renders a licentiousness in the Christian life. Atwater rejects the perfectionists' teaching and life with sharp remarks:

> It cannot be denied that the Antinomian feature of this system has strong logical and practical affinities for licentiousness: men who esteem themselves perfect are apt to make themselves, their own subjective exercises, experiences, judgments, desires, and appetites, the measure and standard of perfection; to make these the rule and measure of rectitude, rather than God's word; or rather to construe them as God's voice and word, speaking in and through them. They have often maintained that as Christ was living within them, their desires, and words and deeds were Christ's. This, of course, is the extreme of fanatical and blasphemous Antinomian pride and licentiousness.[10]

Charles Hodge

Charles Hodge was a professor at Princeton Seminary from 1822 to 1878 except for the two years from 1826 to 1828 during which he studied in Germany.[11] As the most prominent American Reformed theologian of the nineteenth century, he was the bulwark of the conservative Presbyterianism in his time. During his long teaching career at Princeton Seminary, Hodge published numerous books and articles on theology. His writings and teachings greatly influenced the Old School Presbyterianism of his time and the succeeding generations.

Hodge defines sanctification as the "maintenance and progression of a new life, imparted to the soul, by a direct agency of the Spirit of God, in regeneration or the new birth."[12] In his magnum opus *Systematic Theology*, Hodge comments on the doctrine of perfectionism. In particular, he finds

---

9. Atwater, "Christian Perfection," 406.
10. Atwater, "Christian Perfection," 419.
11. Mullin, "Hodge," 537.
12. C. Hodge, "Sanctification," 68.

the perfectionists' doctrines of man's ability, the nature of sin, and the extent of the obligation of the law to be Pelagian.[13]

First, Hodge repudiates the perfectionists' doctrine of man's ability. He asserts that bestowing upon a depraved man the ability to obey the commands of God to the degree of perfection is nothing but a Pelagian teaching. Responding to Charles Finney's statements that "men are able to resist the utmost influence that the truth can exert upon them, and therefore have ability to defeat the wisest, most benevolent, and most powerful exertions which the Holy Spirit can make to effect their sanctification," Hodge writes:

> Not only is truth the sole instrumentation in regeneration and sanctification, in Mr. Finney's opinion, but men have the ability to resist it when wielded with the utmost energy of the Holy Ghost. Surely this is a combination and carrying out of the worst errors in new school divinity, which should arouse those who remain halting between two opinions, to take a decided stand for the truth. So far as the argument for perfect sanctification rests upon the ground of the requisitions of God and the natural ability of man, (properly understood) it may be reduced to this statement: God commands men to be holy, they are accountable moral agents and ought to be holy, therefore some men are holy; which is clearly a non sequitur.[14]

Thus, for Hodge the perfectionists' doctrine of the ability of man is not only incorrect theologically but also is false logically. Accusing the perfectionists of destroying the distinction between natural and moral ability, Hodge calls the perfectionists' doctrine Pelagian, not Edwardsean. He rejects the perfectionists' claim that truth or motive is the only efficient cause in regeneration and sanctification, and yet man is able to resist the utmost influence of the truth. Hodge remarks concerning this inconsistent claim:

> No conclusions from such premises need surprise us, and if the Oberlin folly should open the eyes of the church to the real tendency of modern speculations and professed improvements in Theology, it will serve a valuable end and add another to the numerous illustrations of the truth, that God is able to bring good out of evil.[15]

Second, Hodge rejects the perfectionists' doctrine of sin and calls it Pelagian. The perfectionists' concept of the nature of sin stems from their

---

13. C. Hodge, *Systematic Theology*, 3:257.
14. C. Hodge, "Finney's Sermon," 234.
15. C. Hodge, "Finney's Sermon," 235.

doctrine of the ability of man. Hodge points out the fallacy of the nature of sin in perfectionism:

> It is not true, as our own conscience teaches us, that our obligation is limited by our ability. Every man knows that he is bound to be better than he is, and better than he can make himself by any exertion of his will. We are bound to love God perfectly, but we know that such perfect love is beyond our power. We recognize the obligation to be free from all sin, and absolutely conformed to the perfect law of God. Yet no man is so infatuated or so blinded to his real character as really to believe that he either is thus perfect, or has the power to make himself so. It is the daily and hourly prayer or aspiration of every saint and of every sinner to be delivered from the bondage of evil. The proud and malignant would gladly be humble and benevolent; the covetous would rejoice to be liberal; the infidel longs for faith, and the hardened sinner for repentance. Sin is in its own nature a burden and a torment, and although loved and cherished, as the cups of the drunkard are cherished, yet, if emancipation could be effected by an act of the will, sin would cease to reign in any rational creature.[16]

Hodge shows that one Pelagian doctrine naturally leads to another Pelagian doctrine, in this case the doctrine of man's ability to that of the nature of sin.

Hodge also points to the perfectionists' treatment of sin only in the overt sense. Perfectionists insist that nothing is sinful but the deliberate transgression of known law. There is no moral character in feelings and emotions according to the perfectionists. Hodge aptly points out that "the command to love God is an absurdity," because love has no moral character and "is not under the control of the will."[17]

Third, Hodge moves to the perfectionists' concept of the extent of the obligation of the law. Perfectionists argue that "the law of God levels its claims to our debilitated powers." Hodge calls this statement "the most startling proposition, upon which the doctrine of perfect sanctification is made to rest."[18] Perfectionists teach that man's natural powers were "debilitated in the fall, and have been subsequently weakened by transgression." They claim that the standard of Christian perfection has been elevated much above the demands of the law in its application to man in his present state of existence. In other words, the law levels its claims to man as he is and the correct

---

16. C. Hodge, *Systematic Theology*, 2:156.
17. C. Hodge, *Systematic Theology*, 2:156.
18. C. Hodge, "Sanctification," 241.

interpretation of this statement is indispensable to a right understanding of perfectionism. Hodge comments regarding the above statements:

> These views are doubtless a sufficient foundation for the doctrine of perfect sanctification, they are true. The idea of the adaption of the law to our wants has always been a pillar in the edifice of impenitence; it is the standing argument of legalists, and the oft repeated excuse of the dissolute. But what proof has Mr. Finney that the powers and the faculties which constitute man's accountability were debilitated in the fall, and have been progressively weakened by ages of intemperance, and by the continued abuse of the human constitution? It is not obvious, upon such a principle, that in this downward progress the time may come when all obligation will cease, and when sin shall have destroyed accountability? . . . How low has the law of God levelled its claims in regard to those inhabitants of the cities of the plain "who are set forth for the example, suffering the vengeance of eternal fire?"[19]

Hodge emphatically shows that the perfectionists' doctrines are full of errors and heretical teachings. He writes that "perfectionism levels downwards, and glorifies its followers at the expense of the law, and at the sacrifice of truth."[20] Drawing from the lessons of history, Hodge makes a prophetical comment as he closes the article on sanctification, "One great conclusion may be drawn from the history of this heresy, that departures from the standard of truth, however specious or apparently trivial, are like the fabled dragon's teeth, inert and harmless as they are cast into the earth, but presently producing a harvest of armed men."[21]

In his *Commentary on the Epistle To The Romans*, Hodge focuses on chapter 7 for sanctification and treats chapter 6 as the transition from justification to sanctification. Hodge writes that "in the sixth [chapter] . . . this doctrine of gratuitous justification, instead of leading to licentiousness, presents the only certain and effectual means of sanctification."[22] According to him, the believer's union with Christ is the source of sanctification. Romans 6 shows that this is how the effectual means of sanctification is to be understood. Hodge explains:

> The main idea of the section is, that such is the nature of the believer's union with Christ, that his living in sin is not merely

---

19. C. Hodge, "Sanctification," 242.
20. C. Hodge, "Sanctification," 250.
21. C. Hodge, "Sanctification," 250.
22. C. Hodge, *Romans*, 244.

> an inconsistency, but a contradiction in terms, as much so as to speak of a live dead man, or a good bad one. Union with Christ, being the only source of holiness, cannot be the source of sin.[23]

Hodge here describes the characteristic of the believer who has been united with Christ. However, he does not see the immediate aspect of sanctification in this chapter. He tends to interpret the once-for-all aspect of the change of a believer in the sense of justification.

Hodge moves to chapter 7 and treats it as the main explication of the doctrine of sanctification. Sanctification is primarily seen as the gradual process in which a believer struggles against indwelling sin and will eventually conquer it by the power of the Holy Spirit. He explains this struggle:

> This is precisely the bondage of sin of which every believer is conscious. He feels that there is a law in his members bringing him into subjection to the law of sin; that his distrust of God, his hardness of heart, his love of the world of self, his pride, in short his indwelling sin, is a real power from which he longs to be free, against which he struggles, but from which he cannot emancipate himself.[24]

The believer is not wholly freed from the power of sin in this life. There is no such one as the perfectly sanctified person in this life for Hodge. He concludes, "Paul merely asserts that the believer is, and ever remains in this life, imperfectly sanctified; that sin continues to dwell within him; that he never comes up to the full requisitions of the law, however anxiously he may desire it."[25]

Archibald Alexander Hodge

Archibald Alexander Hodge was a son of Charles Hodge and later succeeded his father as a professor of systematic theology at Princeton Seminary. He taught at Princeton Seminary from 1878 to 1886 during which time he defended conservative Presbyterianism and the Reformed worldview.[26]

A. A. Hodge describes sanctification as involving "both the gradual destruction of the old body of sin, and the quickening and strengthening of all the graces of the new man, and the inward purification of the heart

---

23. C. Hodge, *Romans*, 191.
24. C. Hodge, *Romans*, 230.
25. C. Hodge, *Romans*, 241.
26. Hoffecker, "Hodge, Archibald Alexander," 536–37.

and mind, as well as all those holy actions which proceed from them."[27] He continues, "It is never perfect in this life, but in every case, as in that of Paul, there remains more or less of the old 'law in our members,' warring against the law of our mind."[28]

First, Hodge refutes the perfectionists' denial of original sin and inherent corruption of nature in man that sin is only a voluntary transgression of known law, from which any man may abstain if he wills. Hodge asserts that a man has a depraved nature which cannot be totally eradicated until death. The moral state of the soul is the true source of the evil in the action. Thus, not only is the outward evil action sin, but also sinful is man's nature which lies far below the outward action. Hodge writes:

> All genuine Christian experience involves the same practical judgment. The main element in all genuine conviction of sin is, not simply that the thoughts, words, and feelings are wrong, but that, lying far below all exercises or volitions, the nature is morally corrupt. It is his deadness to divine things—blindness, hardness, aversion to God—which he is helpless to change, that chiefly oppresses the truly convicted man with a sense of sin; and in some degree the same conviction remains until death.[29]

Also, Hodge shows that the perfectionists' concept of sin is totally wrong. He shows the utter inconsistency in the teaching of perfectionism. Hodge writes:

> This theory denies that mistakes and infirmities resulting from the effect of original sin, are themselves sin, yet admits that they are to be confessed, forgiveness implored for them, and the atonement of Christ's blood applied to them, and that the more perfect a man becomes the more he abhors his own internal state. Surely this is a confusion of language, and abuse of the word sin.[30]

Second, Hodge rejects the perfectionists' claim that God adjusts the requirements of the divine law to suit man's ability. He asserts the immutableness of God's holy law and says that God's law has never been lowered to accommodate the weakened faculties of men. Hodge explains:

> Now, the truth is that this law has never been lowered, the principle of the law by which moral character is to be measured

---

27. A. Hodge, *Confession*, 194.
28. A. Hodge, *Confession*, 195.
29. A. Hodge, *Confession*, 199.
30. A. Hodge, *Outlines of Theology*, 538.

> having its norm in the absolutely perfect moral constitution of God himself. God's law is an utterance, it is an expression of God himself in the forms of human thoughts and language; it reveals to man the infinitely perfect moral nature of God himself. And when God's law is altered, and so altered and modified that God is compromised, that moral character has been modified and has been compromised in the very throne of the universe itself. It is true that the law has been satisfied for us for our justification, that the LORD Jesus Christ has been substituted in our place. But the law was not lowered—it was magnified, it was made honorable.[31]

Hodge shows the perfectionists' attempt at lowering God's standard to be theologically incorrect.

Third, Hodge tackles the means whereby the perfectionists claim that perfection may be attained. They contend that "they maintain the plenary ability of man's natural will to discharge all the obligations resting upon him, and they admit the assistance of God's grace only in the sense of the influence of the truth, and other propitious circumstances in persuading man to use his own power."[32] From these statements Hodge deduces that the means of the perfectionists' perfect sanctification are man's own volition, the study of Scripture, and "prudent avoidance of temptation."

Responding to the perfectionists' teaching on the means of sanctification, Hodge sets forth the means of sanctification as taught in orthodox theology. He presents there are inward and outward means of sanctification. The inward means of sanctification is faith. Hodge underscores the indispensable nature of faith as the instrument of man's justification and also of sanctification. Hodge writes:

> Faith is the instrument of our justification—and hence of our deliverance from condemnation and communion with God—the organ of our union with Christ and fellowship with his Spirit. Faith, moreover, is that act of the regenerated soul whereby it embraces and experiences the power of the truth, and whereby the inward experiences the power of the truth, and whereby the inward experiences of the heart and the outward actions of the life are brought into obedience to the truth.[33]

The outward means of sanctification, according to Hodge, are the truth revealed in Scripture, the sacraments, prayer, and the gracious discipline of

---

31. A. Hodge, *Popular Lectures*, 348.
32. A. Hodge, *Outlines of Theology*, 530.
33. A. Hodge, *Confession*, 195.

God's providence. The work of sanctification involves the destruction of the old body of sin as well as the growth of the new man implanted in regeneration. But this process is not instantaneous and immediate but goes on throughout the life of the believer. Hodge writes:

> That the whole body of death is not immediately destroyed in the instant of regeneration is plainly taught in the sixth and seventh chapters of Romans, in the recorded experience of many Biblical characters, and in the universal experience of Christians in modern times. It hence necessarily follows that the tendencies graciously implanted and sustained must come in conflict with the tendencies to evil which remain.[34]

The same concept is also expressed by Hodge in his article "The Ordo Salutis." He writes, "The change of relation to the law signalized by the term justification, involving remission of penalty and restoration to favor, necessarily precedes and renders possible the real moral change of character signalized by the terms regeneration and sanctification."[35] Thus, Hodge affirms the progressive work of sanctification and rejects the concept of immediate perfect sanctification. Hodge situates the perfectionists' doctrines in the Pelagian camp and rejects them as erroneous teachings.

James Henley Thornwell

James Henley Thornwell was the towering figure along with Robert L. Dabney in the southern Presbyterian church in the nineteenth century. He taught at Columbia College and Columbia Theological Seminary. He taught and defended Old School Presbyterian doctrines. During his time, Thornwell was known as a brilliant Old School preacher, Reformed theologian, and "perhaps the most influential Southern minister before the Civil War."[36]

In his *Collected Writings*, Thornwell delineates the doctrine of sanctification in the section "Christian Effort." Though he does not directly deal with perfectionism exclusively, his teachings on sanctification presented in his writings gives a good idea of how he stands with regard to perfectionism. Thornwell says that sanctification is the duty of the believers. The believers "must strive together for the faith of the Gospel." For Thornwell, there can be no separation between justification and sanctification. So, in

---

34. A. Hodge, *Confession*, 197.
35. A. Hodge, "Ordo Salutis," 311.
36. Freundt, "Thornwell," 1174.

the life of the believers as the followers of Christ sanctification is an indispensable element. He writes:

> There can be no cordial acceptance of Christ for righteousness without a cordial acceptance of Him for sanctification. He cannot be divided. No man can receive Him as a priest who does not at the same time receive Him as a king. The general idea of the Apostle, therefore, is that Christians should strive together for the purpose of promoting the success of the Gospel in themselves and others.[37]

According to Thornwell, one of the important objects held up before the believer demanding his efforts is sanctification.

Thornwell teaches that the believer cannot be satisfied with only justification by the redeemer. His desire should be a well-ordered life and holiness to glorify his God. Thornwell explains the progressive nature of sanctification by showing the long process of conforming to the image of Christ:

> He[believer] cannot be content with a bare hope that he has passed from darkness to light, but he strives and prays and labours that the body of sin may be mortified in him, and that he may day by day become more conformed to the image of Christ. His regard is fixed on holiness, his hatred is directly against sin, and he can neither be content nor at rest until he is freed from every vestige of corruption and indwelling sin, which will only be when he awakes from the sleep of death in his Redeemer's likeness.[38]

Thornwell shows that perfect holiness is not possible in this life. The believer's sanctification takes a long process in this life and only after death does the believer become perfect conforming to the image of Christ.

Although sanctification involves efforts of the believer, the holiness in his heart "can be obtained only through the faith of the Gospel." Sanctification is the work of the Holy Spirit. Thornwell writes:

> Christ by His Spirit sanctifies the soul, and the Christian must be found resting upon Christ and looking to Christ for every blessing of the Covenant of Grace. "Without Me ye can do nothing;" and hence the faith of the Gospel is peculiarly dear to him who hungers and thirsts for holiness of heart. There alone we

---

37. Thornwell, *Writings*, 397.
38. Thornwell, *Writings*, 398.

see our strength—that strength of Christ which is imparted to us through the medium of faith.[39]

He clearly rejects, though indirectly, the perfectionists' teaching of having man's ability involved in sanctification as the primary source of sanctification.

Thornwell affirms the progressive nature of sanctification and faith as the means of sanctification of the believer. Though his writing on sanctification was not directly addressed to the perfectionism of the nineteenth century, it is clear that Thornwell followed the tradition of Reformed teaching on sanctification.

Robert L. Dabney

Robert L. Dabney was a southern Presbyterian theologian and educator. He taught philosophy and theology at the University of Texas and Austin Theological Seminary, respectively. His theology was Reformed in line with the nineteenth-century Old School Presbyterianism taught at Princeton by such a theologian as Charles Hodge. Dabney dealt with difficult theological issues and made his own critical observations in his systematic theology.[40]

Dabney explicitly deals with perfectionism in his writing. He shows that the perfectionists argue that it is scriptural to obtain perfection in this life. He summarizes the perfectionists' teachings:

> 1. The means provided by God are confessedly adequate to this complete result, should He please to bless them. . . . 2. He has actually commanded us to pray for entire sanctification. Ps. cxix:5, 6. . . . 3. Not only has He thus encouraged, but commanded us to seek perfection. See Matt. v:48. Unless obedience were possible, the command would be unjust. 4. Perfect sanctification is nowhere connected with the death of the body by explicit texts. . . . As to the involuntary imperfections which every man, not insanely vain, must acknowledge, they are not properly sin; for God does not hold man guilty for those infirmities which are the inevitable results of his feeble and limited nature.[41]

Responding to these teachings, Dabney points out the faults and sins of the saints in the Bible. He writes, "As if to refute the idea of their sinless perfection, Scripture in every case records of them some faults, drunkenness of Noah, lying of Abraham, adultery and murder of David, unbelief of

---

39. Thornwell, *Writings*, 398.
40. Freundt, "Dabney," 336–37.
41. Dabney, *Lectures*, 667.

Zechariah, Luke 1:20, while Job concludes by saying, 'I abhor myself, and repent in dust and ashes.'"[42]

Also, Dabney asserts that the believers are made perfect in holiness at death. He shows that Scripture teaches the progressive nature of sanctification and that this is the way God designed it for the benefit of the believers:

> It is not Gnosticism, but Scripture and common sense, to attribute some obstacles to entire sanctification to the continuance of the animal appetites in man. While God's omnipotence could overcome those obstacles, yet it is according to His manner of working, that He has seen fit to connect the final completeness of His work of grace in the soul, with this last change. Hence, when the Scriptures show that this is His plan, we are prepared to believe it so.[43]

What makes perfectionism most objectionable to Dabney is its Pelagianism. He asserts that the perfectionists' insistence, especially that of the Wesleyans, of viewing sin only as a volitional outward action is Pelagian. Dabney explains:

> But the Wesleyan, acknowledging remainders of concupiscence in his "complete" saint, and yet asserting that his prevalently godly acts are perfect acts, has unconsciously adopted the false Pelagian philosophy, in two points: that "concupiscence is not itself sinful;" and that the "moral quality resides exclusively in the act of soul." Again: when the Wesleyan says that an act, to which the good man is hurried by a gust of temptation so sudden and violent as to prevent deliberation; an act which is against his prevalent bent and purpose, and which is at once deplored, is an infirmity, but not a sin; he is pelagianizing.[44]

Dabney also rejects the perfectionists' Pelagian teaching of "directing the attention." This doctrine teaches that "if, in perpetrating crime, the direction of the intention is to a right end, this makes the act right, because the act which is prevalently right is wholly right."[45] Dabney maintains this kind of teaching of the perfectionists loathsome and even dangerous: "The abominations to which this Pelagian dogma led, in Jesuits' hands, were such, that they contributed to their suppression. It is not charged that Wesleyans

---

42. Dabney, *Lectures*, 668.
43. Dabney, *Lectures*, 670.
44. Dabney, *Lectures*, 669.
45. Dabney, *Lectures*, 670.

countenance any of these immoral and loathsome conclusions: but their premises are dangerous, as appear from these results."[46]

Moving on to the perfectionists' teaching on the ability of man, Dabney finds their doctrine of the ability of man totally unacceptable. He contends that man's impotence is an inability of will. Thus, the standards of the divine law in man should not be lowered. Dabney elaborates:

> Our inability to keep God's whole law perfectly is not physical. It began in man's sin. By that sin we lost none of those faculties which, when Adam's will was right, enabled him to keep God's command without sin. Our impotency is an "inability of will." Hence, it ought not to alter the demands of God's justice on His creatures. It is right in God to require perfection of us, and instruct us to seek it, because His own perfect nature can accept no less. Did God allow an inability of will to reduce His just claims on the creature, then the more sinful he became, the less guilt would attach to his shortcomings. A creature need only render himself utterly depraved to become completely irresponsible.[47]

Dabney shows the utter fallacy in the perfectionists' teaching on man's ability in perfectionism.

Refuting the perfectionists' claim of immediate sanctification, Dabney argues that sanctification is never complete in this life. He sets forth his four reasons for asserting his view. First, Scripture teaches that remains of sin exist in the believers also. Dabney gives Scripture passages such as 1 John 1:8, James 3:2, 1 Kings 8:46, and Proverbs 20:9 as proof texts. Second, according to the Scriptures there is the perpetual warfare between the flesh and the spirit in the life of a believer. "It is no avail," writes Dabney, "for the Wesleyan to attempt evading this picture of Rom. viii: as the language of Paul convicted but not yet converted; for other similar passages remain, as Rom. viii:7; Gal. v:17; Phil. iii:13; 1 Tim. vi:12 etc. Now, as long as the contest lasts, there must be an enemy."[48] Third, Dabney argues that "the impossibility of a perfect obedience by ransomed men" is taught in Scripture. He cites Psalm 119:96 and Acts 15:10. He states, "It is true, that in the latter place the ceremonial law is more immediately in Peter's view; but the whole law is included, as is obvious from his scope; and if either could be perfectly kept, surely the ceremonial would be the easier."[49] Fourth, Dabney asserts that the LORD's Prayer teaches the believers to pray for the

---

46. Dabney, *Lectures*, 670.
47. Dabney, *Lectures*, 670.
48. Dabney, *Lectures*, 671.
49. Dabney, *Lectures*, 671.

forgiveness of sin. This command would not be universally appropriate if the doctrine of perfectionism were true. Dabney writes:

> And if human experience can settle such a point, it is wholly on our side; for those who are obviously most advanced in sanctification, both among inspired and uninspired saints, are most emphatic in their confessions of shortcoming; while those who arrogantly claim perfect sanctification, usually discredit their pretentions sooner or later, by shameful falls.[50]

Dabney asserts that the perfectionism taught among the Christians in the nineteenth century is not perfectionism at all. He also expresses his personal concern over the spreading of perfectionism in the Reformed churches. Dabney states:

> Wesleyans sometimes say, that their doctrine of perfect sanctification, as defined by them, amounts to precisely the same with our statement concerning those better Christians, who, with Caleb and Joshua, (Num. xiv:24), "followed the LORD fully," and who enjoy an assurance of their own grace and salvation. Our objection is, that a dangerous and deluding statement is thus made of a scriptural truth. All Christians should be urged to these higher spiritual attainments; but they should not be taught to call that "perfection," which is not really perfect, nor to depreciate their remaining sins into mere "infirmities." A form of virtual perfectionism has become current recently, among Christians whose antecedents were not Arminians, but Reformed. They call themselves advocates of the "Higher Christian Life." This stage, they say, is reached by those who were before Christians, by a species of second conversion.[51]

Dabney concludes by affirming the scriptural and Reformed teaching on sanctification:

> The picture of the Christian's militant life, which we ever see portrayed in Scripture, is that of an imperfect, but progressive faith uniting him to his Saviour, always finding Him faithful to His promises, and always deriving from Him measures of grace corresponding to the vigour of its exercise, yet always leaving room for farther advances.[52]

---

50. Dabney, *Lectures*, 671.
51. Dabney, *Lectures*, 672.
52. Dabney, *Courses*, 673.

William G. T. Shedd

William G. T. Shedd was a Calvinist theologian in the Old School Presbyterian tradition and a church historian in the nineteenth century. Shedd was one of the eminent theologians of his era. He taught at Auburn Theological Seminary and later at Union Theological Seminary in New York for twenty-eight years. He was firmly committed to Reformed theology and opposed the revision of Westminster Standards.[53]

Shedd's view on sanctification follows the conservative Reformed view. In his writings he does not directly deal with perfectionism in his treatment of the doctrine of sanctification. But it is certain that he was very much aware of the perfectionism of his time as one of the reference works he used in the study of sanctification was John Wesley's *Christian Perfection*.

Shedd follows the definition of sanctification set forth in the Westminster Shorter Catechism, "Sanctification is the work of God's free grace, whereby we are renewed in the whole man after the image of God, and are enabled more and more to die unto sin, and live unto righteousness." The four elements of Shedd's view on sanctification from his writings are presented here, in order to show that his view on sanctification is clearly opposed to the teachings of perfectionism in the nineteenth century.

First, Shedd teaches that sanctification is gradual.[54] Referring to Romans 7:14—8:28, he points out the conflict and victory over indwelling sin in the life of the believer. In his *Commentary on Romans*, Shedd explains the ongoing struggle in the life of the believer as described in Romans 7:14–25:

> Verses 14–25 contains still further proof that the law, in its own nature, is neither sin nor death, by a reference to the experience of the believer. Having evinced this, in the preceding section, by examining the experience of the unregenerate, both as unconvicted and convicted, St. Paul now turns to the experience of the regenerate. The sudden and striking change, in verse 14, and continuing through the entire section, from the past to the present tense, together with ποτέ in verse 9, indicates this.[55]

Shedd teaches that the believer is imperfect, yet a saint. He reminds the readers of Paul rebuking the Corinthian Christians for their sins before God yet calling them saints.[56]

---

53. Pointer, "Shedd," 1081.
54. Shedd, *Dogmatic Theology*, 555.
55. Shedd, *Romans*, 189.
56. Shedd, *Sermons*, 302.

Second, Shedd shows the means of sanctification are internal and external. The internal means of sanctification are faith, hope, joy, and peace, whereas the external means are the Scriptures, prayer, God's providential discipline, and the sacrament of the Supper. In supporting this view Shedd quotes the Scripture passages of Romans 5:5; 1 Peter 1:8–9; Philippians 4:7; John 17:17; 1 Peter 1:22–23; John 14:13–14; Acts 2:42; John 15:2; and Hebrews 12:5–11.

Third, Shedd asserts that sanctification is progressive and is not complete in this life. The Christian life is a journey of progress toward the perfection at death as Shedd further expounds:

> In order to understand this truth, and feel its impression, we must remember that the Christian life upon earth is a race and a fight, and consequently cannot be a rest and a paradise. The Scriptures uniformly represent the course and career of a believer, this side of the grave, as one of conflict, toil, and effort. "Except a man take his cross daily, he cannot be my disciple. In the world, ye shall have tribulation." These are the declarations of the Founder of Christianity, and they enunciate the real nature of his religion, as it must exist in a world that is sinful, full of temptation, and unfriendly to holiness. "We are troubled on every side; we are perplexed; we are persecuted; we are cast down." We continually bear about in the body, the dying of the LORD Jesus.[57]

For Shedd, Christian life consists of toil and struggle to pursue holiness. He resoundingly rejects the idea of perfection in this life.

Fourth, Shedd holds that sanctification, once it begins, is never wholly lost. It may fluctuate with the faithfulness of the believer but never falls back into the state of the unregenerate man. The ongoing work of sanctification is true in the life of the believer, not because of man's effort, but because of the work of the Holy Spirit. Shedd explains:

> Exhortations to struggle with sin, and warnings against its insidious and dangerous nature, are one of the means employed by the Holy Spirit to secure perseverance. The decree of election includes the means as well as the end. Now if success in the use of means is certain, there is the strongest motive to employ them; but if success is uncertain, then there is little motive to use them. St. Paul employs the certainty of success as a motive

---

57. Shedd, *Sermons*, 317.

to struggle. "Fight the good fight of faith; lay hold on eternal life, whereunto thou art called," 1 Tim. 6:12.[58]

Emphasizing perseverance as an important part of struggle for holiness in this life, Shedd rejects the perfectionists' teaching of immediate entire sanctification of the believer in this life.

James Oliver Buswell

James Oliver Buswell was a Presbyterian minister and educator of Reformed theology. He taught theology at Wheaton College, Covenant College, and Covenant Theological Seminary.[59]

James Oliver Buswell, though born in the late nineteenth century, belongs more to the twentieth century than to the nineteenth century. Buswell is included in this chapter to show the general attitude of Reformed believers toward perfectionism in the early twentieth century. Buswell starts the discussion on sanctification by quoting Question 35 of the Westminster Shorter Catechism, "What is sanctification? Sanctification is the work of God's free grace, whereby we are renewed in the whole man after the image of God, and are enabled more and more to die unto sin, and live unto righteousness."

Buswell, citing passages from Galatians, Ephesians, and Colossians, sets forth his view on the doctrine of sanctification. He shows that Scripture teaches the progressive nature of sanctification in the life of a believer:

> Those who are born again are born as little children in spiritual things. They need to be taught patiently and carefully the implications of the walk of the Christian life. If it were true that regeneration and the indwelling presence of the Holy Spirit automatically produce holy living without detailed ethical instruction, then the Apostle Paul was very wrong in extensive passages of his epistles which he wrote, under the guidance of the same Holy Spirit, for the churches which had recently come out of heathenism into the light of the Gospel.[60]

After setting forth his view of sanctification, Buswell refutes the perfectionists' teaching of sinless perfection. Although the goal of the Christian is sinless perfection, he does not achieve this goal in this life. The Christian is in the process of growth in holy living while in this life. Buswell states:

58. Shedd, *Dogmatic Theology*, 557.
59. Carpenter, "Buswell," 204.
60. Buswell, *Systematic Theology*, 201.

> If it is true that born again people will by the continuous work of the Holy Spirit, and by the agencies employed by the Spirit, grow in holy living, it is equally true that while we live in this life in the flesh here upon earth, we do not attain sinless perfection. Perfection is the standard which God has set before us and which we shall reach when we see our LORD face to face (1 John 3:2). To use a mathematical expression, we approach sinless perfection asymptotically. In quasi-mathematical language, we might say, "The limit of growth in sanctification, as the Christian life advances, is absolute sinless perfection."[61]

Buswell does not dispute God's command of perfection to the believers. It is only consistent in God's attributes that he sets the standard of perfection for his children. But that does not necessarily mean that they achieve this standard in this life. It is only the goal to which every Christian has to strive for in this life. Buswell explains:

> When we stop to consider, it would be completely illogical for us to think that God would set before us any other standard than perfection. How preposterous would it be if the Scriptures said, "Stop ninety percent of your stealing, lying, etc.!" It is the tenth commandment, "Thou shalt not have evil desires," which is the most exacting. Nevertheless how absurd it would be if the Bible said, "Thou mayest entertain evil desires so long as thou dost not commit the outbreaking act!" What an immoral psychology that would imply![62]

Buswell then moves to assert the time process of the sanctification of the believer. Believers are not perfectly holy even at their best. He teaches that even though "all the potentialities for complete sanctification" are already provided in Christ, it is God's decree that "it shall take time" for the believers to grow in sanctification. He explains his position by referring to Romans 8:

> One of the clearest expressions of the time involved in sanctification is found in the eighth chapter of the epistle to the Romans, verses 18–25. Paul has just explained, "If indeed we suffer together [with Christ] it is in order that we may be glorified together." He continues, "For I reckon that the sufferings of this present time are not of any account in view of the future glory to be revealed in us."[63]

---

61. Buswell, *Systematic Theology*, 202.
62. Buswell, *Systematic Theology*, 202–3.
63. Buswell, *Systematic Theology*, 203–4.

Thus, believers are to continue the fight of faith faithfully. In this process the Holy Spirit helps and energizes believers to continually walk the life of growth and development. Yet the perfection is not reached by believers in this life. Buswell shows that Scripture clearly refutes the perfection of the believer in this life:

> That sinless perfection is not attained in this life is made crystal clear by verses 22 and 23, "We know that the entire creation groans together and pains together until now. Now only so, but we ourselves, we who have the first fruits of the Spirit, we ourselves groan within ourselves waiting for the fullness of sonship the redemption of our body." These words in the first person plural are descriptive of regenerate Christians, including the Apostle Paul himself, as he writes the eighth chapter of the epistle to the Romans.[64]

Buswell reminds believers that they still live in bodies which are corrupted by sin. All the "God-given instincts for self-preservation" become the evil desires at the time of the fall, so that the only way man becomes perfect is by the grace of Christ at the time of his resurrection in the LORD.

Commenting on the perfectionists' doctrine of the baptism of the Holy Spirit, Buswell flatly rejects their idea of a second work of grace after regeneration. He asserts that the phrase "baptism of the Spirit" is used for the initial work of grace in the Scriptures:

> The phrase "baptism of the Spirit" as used in the New Testament always refers to the initial work of grace making men members of the body of Christ. The reader is referred to an exhaustive concordance. It will be seen in the context of every case where the baptism of the Spirit is referred to that this is the initial work of the Spirit in the life of a child of God and not any work subsequent to his conversion.[65]

A crisis the believer may go through after regeneration is not the second work of grace. The believer goes through many crises, big or small, throughout the Christian life. Buswell contends that the filling of the Spirit is a progressive process and that many believers experience the filling of the Spirit through many means throughout the Christian life:

> The idea of the Christian life is expressed in the words, "Be ye being filled with the Holy Spirit" (Ephesians 5:18). There ought to be a constant infilling of the Holy Spirit as the heart

---

64. Buswell, *Systematic Theology*, 204.
65. Buswell, *Christian Life*, 106.

and life of a Christian enlarge and grow, as his interests and knowledge expand, as he takes in new territory, new areas of experience. Actually, however, growth does not take place in a perfectly smooth upward curve. There are plateaus, and sometimes there are valleys. The filling of the Spirit, a progressive process in the grace of God, frequently takes place in crises. Many Christians have experienced a special time of abundant blessing, some crisis in which the power of the Holy Spirit is particularly manifested.[66]

Thus, the Holy Spirit constantly works in the life of the believer. This is exactly what Scripture teaches—the process of sanctification. Buswell concludes, "It would be a mistake to overemphasize the crisis nature of the filling of the Spirit. Each regenerate person should constantly maintain the attitude of openness toward the influence and the power of the Holy Spirit under all circumstances."[67]

Louis Berkhof

Louis Berkhof and G. C. Berkouwer are the non-Presbyterian Reformed theologians. Berkhof is an American Reformed theologian and Berkouwer a Dutch Reformed theologian. The presentation of Berkhof's and Berkouwer's views on perfectionism would give a broader view on the evaluation of perfectionism by Reformed theologians.

Louis Berkhof was a theologian of the Christian Reformed Church in the early twentieth century. Born in the Netherlands in 1873 and educated in America, he taught biblical studies and systematic theology at Calvin Theological Seminary for thirty-eight years. He became best known for his *Systematic Theology* which has been widely used as a textbook in systematic theology. During his life Berkhof set forth the "riches of the Reformed theology" in contrast to various theologies of his time.[68]

According to Berkhof, the perfectionists teach that "it is possible for believers in this life to attain to a state in which they comply with the requirements of the law under which they now live, or under that law as it was adjusted to their present ability and needs, and, consequently, to be free from sin."[69] He starts by refuting the teaching of sinless perfection of the

---

66. Buswell, *Systematic Theology*, 210.
67. Buswell, *Systematic Theology*, 211.
68. Klooster, "Berkhof," 135.
69. Berkhof, *Systematic Theology*, 538.

perfectionists. The idea of perfection in Scripture has nothing similar to the actual sinless life claimed by the perfectionists. Berkhof writes:

> If the Bible occasionally speaks of believers as perfect, this does not necessarily mean that they are without sin. They can be called perfect in Christ, or perfect in principle, or perfect in the sense of fullgrown, I Cor. 2:6; 3:1, 2; Heb. 5:14; II Tim. 3:17. The Bible contains no examples of believers who led sinless lives. Even the men mentioned as examples fell into grievous sins, Gen. 9:21; Job 3:1; II Chron. 16:7ff. And the statement found in the Epistle of John that he who is born of God does not sin evidently means either that the new man as such does not sin, or that the believer does not live in sin. Moreover, this statement of John would prove too much for the Perfectionist, namely, that the believer actually never sins. Even the Perfectionist does not maintain that. Consequently it proves nothing to the point.[70]

Berkhof objects to the teaching of perfectionism and gives four reasons for his position against it. First, he asserts that perfectionism is against the teachings of the Bible. Berkhof writes, "In the light of Scripture the doctrine of perfectionism is absolutely untenable. The Bible gives us the explicit and very definite assurance that there is no one on earth who does not sin, 1 Kings 8:46; Prov. 20:9; Eccl, 7:20; Rom, 3:10; Jas. 3:2; 1 John 1:8."[71] He finds that it is impossible for those who believe the Bible as the infallible word to hold the teaching of sinless perfection in this life.

Second, citing the passage in Romans 7:7–26, Berkhof asserts that there is an ongoing struggle between the flesh and the Spirit in the life of a believer. Even the most mature believer is striving for perfection in his life. Berkhof writes, "According to Scripture there is a constant warfare between the flesh and the Spirit in the lives of God's children, and even the best of them are still striving for perfection."[72] He also cites Galatians 5:16–24 and Philippians 3:10–14 to show a struggle that characterizes the children of God in this life.

Third, Berkhof argues that Scripture teaches that confession of sin is continually required in the life of a believer: "Jesus taught all His disciples without any exception to pray for the forgiveness of sins and for deliverance from temptation and from the evil one, Matt. 6:12, 13."[73] First John 1:9 also

---

70. Berkhof, *Manual of Christian Doctrine*, 270.
71. Berkhof, *Systematic Theology*, 540.
72. Berkhof, *Systematic Theology*, 540.
73. Berkhof, *Systematic Theology*, 540.

teaches the confession of sins by believers. He also shows that the saints in the Bible are constantly involved in confessing their sins.

Fourth, Berkhof attacks the fallacy of the perfectionists' doctrines of law and sin. He points out the perfectionists' attempt to lower the standard of the divine law and to treat sin as only outward action. Berkhof writes, "The Perfectionists themselves deem it necessary to lower the standard of the law and to externalize the idea of sin, in order to maintain their theory."[74] He also points out the inconsistency in their formulation of the doctrine. Berkhof writes:

> Moreover, some of them have repeatedly modified the idea to which, in their estimation, believers can attain. At first the ideal as "freedom from all sin"; then, "freedom from all conscious sin," next, "entire consecration to God," and, finally, "Christian assurance." This is in itself a sufficient condemnation of their theory. We naturally do not deny that the Christian can attain to the assurance of faith.[75]

Thus, Berkhof finds perfectionism unscriptural, illogical, and unorthodox in its doctrines.

G. C. Berkouwer

G. C. Berkouwer was a Dutch Reformed theologian in the twentieth century. He taught theology for many years at the Free University of Amsterdam. His teaching and writings influenced greatly the Dutch Reformed theology in his time. His teachings on Reformed theology also influenced Reformed groups in America as his works were translated into English.

Berkouwer's representative work on sanctification is *Faith and Sanctification*. In this work he deals with perfectionism from the European, Continental background of Reformed theology. Although the object of Berkouwer's study of perfectionism is Wesleyan perfectionism, much of his analysis applies to American perfectionism since it has roots in Wesleyan perfectionism.

Berkouwer starts the discussion by stating the perfectionists' teaching that "it is possible for the believer, even before death, to attain perfection."[76] According to Berkouwer, perfectionism brings to our attention the "problem

---

74. Berkhof, *Systematic Theology*, 540
75. Berkhof, *Systematic Theology*, 540.
76. Berkouwer, *Sanctification*, 49.

of sin of those who are justified and whose sanctification is Christ himself," the problem which cannot be lightly dismissed. He further construes:

> A faulty reaction to Perfectionism would be to assert that the implication of human life is a matter of course. One cannot fob off Perfectionism by saying "In many things we all stumble" (James 3:2) or "Wretched man that I am! who shall deliver me . . . ?" (Romans 7:24), for these utterances are not excuses for sin but confessions of sin.[77]

After commenting on the importance of the problem perfectionism addresses, Berkouwer begins examining the perfectionists' teachings theologically. He points out nomism and synergism in perfectionism. Regarding Wesley's tendency of nomism, Berkouwer maintains:

> For again and again there comes to the surface in his Perfectionism a strong nomistic tendency. Wesley did not fail to warn against a facile overestimate of self, but an insidious nomism he did not entirely escape. As Lerch says, "Not only our reflection but also the subsequent course of the Holiness movement shows that there is here the threat either of legal rigorism or of overestimating the strength of one's own footing."[78]

Berkouwer then expresses his serious concern toward Wesley's synergism. Wesley treats *Sola-fide* and the process of sanctification as a power and its effects. This kind of thinking in Wesley inevitably leads to the breakage between *Sola-fide* and sanctification and ends in synergism. Berkouwer writes:

> Since Wesley proceeded emphatically from the justification of the ungodly, his synergism is a serious warning. The Sola-fide doctrine is subject to frequent misunderstanding. One can assume it as one's starting-point, as did Wesley, and subsequently view the process of sanctification in terms of a dynamic category—a power plus its effects—without taking account of the bearings which faith always sustains toward divine grace. Sola-fide becomes a point of departure and breaks its connections with sanctification. Here lies the cause of Wesley's tendency toward synergism, in spite of his adherence to Sola-fide. This tendency is not a count against Sola-fide but a warning against misconceiving its all-important significance.[79]

---

77. Berkouwer, *Sanctification*, 49.
78. Berkouwer, *Sanctification*, 52.
79. Berkouwer, *Sanctification*, 52–53.

After pointing out nomism and synergism in perfectionism, Berkouwer refutes the teachings of perfectionism by citing a German Reformed confession. He quotes Heidelberg Catechism's LORD's Day 44, 51, and 21 to refute the perfectionists' teaching. LORD's Day 44 denies the teaching of perfectionism. Berkouwer writes:

> Let us first of all consult our Confession. LORD's Day 44, for instance, is openly hostile to the central thesis of Perfectionism. "But can those who are converted to God keep these commandments perfectly?" —that is the question, and we know what Perfectionism replies to it. But this is the answer of the Catechism: "No; but even the holiest men, while in this life, have only a small beginning of this obedience; yet so that with earnest purpose they begin to live, not only according to some but according to all the commandments of God."[80]

Also referring to LORD's Day 51 and 21, Berkouwer says that believers, though washed in the blood of the redeemer, still struggle against evil desires in them all their life, "In LORD's Day 21 the believer admits his sinful nature against which, he says, he must struggle all his life long."[81]

Berkouwer then moves to the Scriptural response to perfectionism. He contends that the interpretation of Romans 7 is pivotal in the discussion of the sanctification of a believer. He asks, "Who is the subject speaking in the verses 14 and 25?"[82] Berkouwer finds in Romans 7 the believer who is constantly embroiled in a conflict between the flesh and the Spirit. In taking this view he basically follows Calvin's interpretation of the subject in Romans 7. Berkouwer writes:

> The conflict here depicted by Paul is found only in the recipient of the Holy Spirit. The man who is left to his own natural devices is a stranger to this conflict. Calvin protests against the philosopher who describe the human mind in terms of this conflict and contraposes with this view the Scriptural doctrine of the evil heart. He recalls the sophists who appealed to Romans 7 to fortify their conception of free will. In the natural man, says Calvin, there is never any hatred of sin.[83]

Thus, Berkouwer sees in Romans 7 the believer who is in tension between the flesh and the Spirit, who is going through the process of sanctification

---

80. Berkouwer, *Sanctification*, 53.
81. Berkouwer, *Sanctification*, 55.
82. Berkouwer, *Sanctification*, 55.
83. Berkouwer, *Sanctification*, 58.

and will obtain the victory over sin in the LORD at the end of this life. He sets forth his view on Romans 7 clearly:

> The subject of Romans is not the natural man as seen by the believer, but the believing child of God as by the grace of God he has learned to see himself. From this knowledge is born his confession of guilt. From this knowledge, too, springs his daily tussle with himself. It is surely not a tussle without tension. Woe to him who would rest upon grace as upon his laurels and forget the law of sin in his members! Whatever hope there is must be of faith.[84]

Berkouwer, in fact, uses the term spiritual "warfare" which must be "waged only from the incentives of Romans 7: humility and gratitude."

Moving on to the perfectionists' teaching of a "second blessing," Berkouwer says that it makes sanctification independent of justification. The perfectionists' teaching of the second blessing creates the two classes of Christians: those who are advanced in their Christian life and those who are not. This is tantamount to a denial of the unity of the church and the reality of sin in the believer. Berkouwer remarks, "Perfectionism could not therefore escape the bane of activism and nomism. The perfection of which it spoke was a rational inference from the doctrine of justification and hence the possibility of moral perfection and of a "second" blessing bore a speculative character."[85]

As he concludes his discussion on sanctification Berkouwer underscores that nowhere in the Bible is taught the possibility of attaining perfection before the "great consumption." In the grace of God, the believer is involved in the struggle to be more like the image of Christ in each day of his life. He concludes with the following statements:

> To speak of the Church is to speak of the struggle to remain children of God in communion with him and to live gratefully in virtue of the forgiveness of sin. This life of sanctification proceeds in weakness, temptation, and exposure to the powers of darkness. Hence the life of the believer is fenced in with admonitions: "Ye have not yet resisted unto blood, striving against sin" (Heb. 12:4). Or in the incisive words of Paul: "Neither give place to the devil" (Eph. 4:27), or of James: "Resist the devil" (James 4:7).

---

84. Berkouwer, *Sanctification*, 63.
85. Berkouwer, *Sanctification*, 64.

All these admonitions are expressions of divine grace. Grace prompted Paul to rage against the sins of the Corinthian Church, against such fornication as is not even among the gentiles (1 Cor 5:1), against pride (1 Cor 5:2), against greed and irreverence (1 Cor 11:21).[86]

Conclusion

Some responses to perfectionism by Reformed theologians have been presented in this chapter. Many of them are from American presbyterian tradition and others are from non-Presbyterian Reformed faith.

Lyman H. Atwater, a Reformed theologian at Princeton, examined the teachings of perfectionists and accused them of confounding sanctification with justification in their teaching. He sharply criticized them for teaching antinomianism and licentiousness in perfectionism. Another theologian from Princeton, Charles Hodge, also examined the perfectionists' teachings such as man's ability, sin, and the extent of the obligation and concluded that perfectionism is full of errors and heretical teachings. He rejected the immediate and once-for-all aspect of sanctification and perfectionism. In his exegesis of Romans 6, Charles Hodge interpreted the immediate aspect of transformation in the sense of justification and primarily saw sanctification in the progressive aspect which he said was depicted in Romans 7. His son, A. A. Hodge, closely followed his father's view on sanctification. A. A. Hodge especially emphasized the means of sanctification and affirmed the progressive nature of sanctification.

Southern Presbyterian theologians with Reformed faith, James Henley Thornwell and Robert L. Dabney, were also against perfectionism. Thornwell viewed sanctification as the gradual process involving the believer's work. Dabney specifically dealt with the teachings of perfectionists and dismissed them as Pelagianism. He rejected the immediate aspect of sanctification. Dabney gave the harshest criticism of perfectionism in saying that the perfectionists' teaching was loathsome and dangerous.

William G. T. Shedd, also a Presbyterian theologian, viewed sanctification as a gradual process in the believer's life. He saw sanctification totally in the progressive aspect. James Oliver Buswell also taught sanctification as a progress in the believer's life. God's standard for man is perfection but man is never perfect in this life. Thus, both Shedd and Buswell rejected perfectionism in this life.

In the non-Presbyterian Reformed circle, generally the same response to perfectionism was found as represented by Berkhof and Berkouwer.

86. Berkouwer, *Sanctification*, 66–67.

Berkhof briefly stated the doctrine and then refuted it. Though Berkouwer likewise rejected the teaching of perfectionism, he expressed that the problem the perfectionists addressed to—the problem of sin of those who are justified and whose sanctification is Christ himself—required the earnest and Scripturally sound response from the Reformed church.

It is seen in this chapter that the Reformed theologians in America rejected the immediate and once-for-all aspect of sanctification taught by the perfectionists and taught the progressive nature of sanctification. Berkhof and Berkouwer likewise rejected perfectionism, but Berkouwer made the keen observation that hinted that the response to perfectionism had to involve more than repeating the progressive nature of sanctification and dismissing it as a theologically irrelevant teaching by the Reformed church.

The acrimonious response by the Reformed theologians, especially B. B. Warfield as seen in chapter 3, did not dampen the holiness movement in America. As the holiness movement branched out into several small movements in the late nineteenth and early twentieth centuries, they took their own theological characteristics and persuasions. One of these smaller movements, sensing the accusation of Pelagianism from the Reformed theologians, took mild Calvinism into its teaching and attracted many people from the Presbyterian and Reformed churches. This movement was called Keswick in which many notable and respected ministers from various denominations were involved for spreading its own teaching on sanctification.

Chapter 5

Keswick's View of the Victorious Christian Life

THE STRONG OPPOSITION BY Reformed theologians against perfectionism did not abate the current of the holiness movement in America in the late nineteenth century. At the turn of the century perfectionist teachings were modified by various groups receptive to the ideas and goals of the holiness movement. Two prominent groups emerged, the Keswick and the Pentecostal-Charismatic, for the furtherance of the holiness movement. Unlike the Pentecostal-Charismatic movement, the Keswick movement with a mild Calvinism attracted many ministers and lay Christians from the Presbyterian and Reformed churches. As many believers from these churches were involved in or influenced by the Keswick teaching either directly or indirectly, it became incumbent to examine Keswick for its theology and method for the ministry.

The History of Keswick

The Keswick movement started from England in 1875. Its purpose was to promote the holy or victorious life of Christians. It exerted a considerable influence on the holy life of Christians in the late nineteenth and early twentieth centuries. Today, the annual Keswick Convention still attracts many people from the world who desire the victorious Christian life.

British Keswick

Although the Keswick movement was started in the British Isles, its genesis is owed to the American evangelists, Mr. and Mrs. Robert Pearsall Smith. Robert Pearsall Smith, a Quaker from Philadelphia, arrived in London in the spring of 1873 and stirred the town with his message that a devout Christian can and should lead the higher Christian life. During the next two years Robert and Hannah Smith traveled around England teaching about the higher Christian life. In the audience at one of the meetings was Canon Harford-Battersby. At first, he was skeptical about the teaching but was moved by the message of a London clergyman, Evan Hopkins. Canon Harford-Battersby describes what happened in him at the meeting: "I said to myself, Has not my faith been a seeking faith when it ought to have been a resting faith? And if so, why not exchange it for the latter? And I thought of the sufficiency of Jesus and said, I *will rest* in Him—and I did rest in Him."[1] Harford-Battersby confesses that after this experience he felt the overwhelming sense of the presence of the LORD Jesus and became fully consecrated to his Christian life and ministry with a new effectiveness. As it turned out, this experience of Harford-Battersby became a classic "Keswick experience."

In 1875, Harford-Battersby organized a meeting to promote the higher Christian life at the town of Keswick in England. Robert Pearsall Smith was scheduled to speak at the meeting but became ill and returned to America immediately. The meeting was nevertheless held as planned and several ministers spoke at the meeting instead of Robert Pearsall Smith. The result of the meeting proved to be so successful that many people went home with a great spiritual blessing. Harford-Battersby explains after the first Keswick meeting:

> We have had a time of extraordinary blessing. More, far more, than our weak faith enabled us to grasp beforehand . . . I can only account for it by the fact that we were so entirely thrown upon the LORD. It has been a lesson of great value to myself and my faith has been much strengthened in consequence.[2]

People at the first Keswick meeting were so blessed by God that they decided to hold the meeting there annually. Keswick meetings continued every year except during the world wars and still continue today.

The Keswick movement quickly forged strong links between Christians of different denominations and attracted many able ministers from various denominations. In the early years the Keswick leaders included Canon Harford-Battersby, Evan H. Hopkins, and Handley C. G. Moule, the Principal of Ridley Hall, Cambridge, and later Bishop of Durham. Other leaders included Andrew Murray, a Dutch Reformed minister from South

---

1. Pollock, *Keswick*, 27.
2. Pollock, *Keswick*, 46.

Africa, Theodore of Monod of France, George H. C. Macgregor, H. W. Webb-Peploe, F. B. Meyer, W. H. Griffith Thomas, W. Graham Scroggie, and G. Campbell Morgan. These Keswick leaders were among England's best-known ministers, and they influenced the world greatly in the matter of the holy life of a Christian. Timothy L. Smith writes, "In ten years Keswick became the chief center of holiness teaching in England. It was in some ways a British equivalent of the national camp meeting movement."[3]

American Keswick

Keswick teaching came to America through the ministry of Dwight L. Moody. In 1891, Moody invited F. B. Meyer, one of the British Keswick leaders, to his Northfield Conference. In spite of the initial skepticism by the American audience, Meyer's message made an inroad among the American Christians regarding the higher life of a Christian. Many American Christians who were turned off by the emotional emphasis and the Arminianism of perfectionism and who were seeking practical guidance on holiness, turned to Keswick teaching. Keswick teaching was conveyed so as to bridge the gulf between the Wesleyan and Reformed traditions on the teaching of holiness. Following F. B. Meyer, such Keswick leaders as Andrew Murray, H. W. Webb-Peploe, and G. Campbell Morgan spoke at the Northfield Conference after 1894.[4]

Keswick teaching gathered a considerable following among the American millenarian groups. After the various Bible conferences an American Keswick organization led by Robert C. McQuilkin from Philadelphia was formed in 1913. Robert C. McQuilkin was a member of the North United Presbyterian Church of Philadelphia. McQuilkin confesses that he experienced repeated failures in his Christian life. He wrestled with sins of commission, failure in Bible study and prayer, and a lack of miracles in his Christian life.

In 1911, McQuilkin attended a conference on spiritual victory in the Christian life. At this meeting he went through an experience which gave him a new commitment and attitude in the Christian life. He confesses that "there was nothing between my LORD and me."[5] McQuilkin came out of the conference with the firm belief that his life was now consecrated to the purpose of the LORD Jesus.

---

3. T. Smith, *Called Unto Holiness*, 24.
4. Sandeen, *Fundamentalism*, 178–81.
5. R. C. McQuilkin, *Victory in Christ*, 18.

In 1913, the first American Keswick Conference organized by McQuilkin was held at the United Presbyterian Church in Oxford, Pennsylvania. About seventy-five people attended the meeting and Henry W. Frost, the home director of the China Inland Mission, and W. H. Griffith-Thomas were the main speakers. The assembly grew larger and larger each year and they moved to Keswick Grove, New Jersey in 1923.[6] Today, the town of Whiting, New Jersey is the home of American Keswick which has exerted a great influence on the holy life of Christians in America.

The two institutional heirs of Keswick's victorious message are Nyack College, established by Albert B. Simpson, and Columbia Bible college, founded by Robert C. McQuilkin. These two schools and many others influenced by the victorious life message still teach the Keswick message in their theological education. The aim of Keswick teaching was well-described by the leaders in 1916. They wrote that the aim of these conferences was "to bring men and women into a life of communion with God, victory over sin, and fruit-bearing, through the presentation of the Bible message concerning the life that is Christ."[7]

In 1952, there came good news for Keswick followers who did not really have an official doctrinal statement, or textbook representing their teachings. It came from a man named Steven Barabas, then-assistant professor of theology at Wheaton College, with the book titled *So Great Salvation*. Barabas's book was hailed by Keswick leaders as a textbook on Keswick teachings which had been taught and practiced by Keswick advocates. Fred Mitchell, Chairman of the Keswick Convention Council, 1948–51, praises Barabas's book:

> It was with great joy, therefore, that one received Dr. Barabas' manuscript. It is a book which is faithful and accurate; it is well annotated with sources of his information; it is saturated with an appreciative spirit, for he himself has been so much helped by Keswick. The book will form a text-book and a reference book on this unique movement which has been reproduced with more or less similarity in every continent.[8]

True to Mitchell's words, Barabas's book became a textbook for many years even until today for those who want to study Keswick's teachings.

There may be several factors which contributed to the great growth of the Keswick movement in America in the twentieth century. C. Melvin

---

6. Shelley, "Pietistic Fundamentalism," 74.
7. Shelley, "Pietistic Fundamentalism," 74
8. Barabas, *So Great Salvation*, ix–x.

Loucks attributes Keswick's growth to three reasons.[9] First, Keswick provided a large easily accessible interdenominational center in the East when there were very few evangelical conference centers in the northeast of the United States. Second, Keswick's positive message of victory appealed to many people in a day of turmoil and uncertainty. Third, Keswick provided excellent evangelical speakers at each meeting who exerted a great influence on the followers of the Keswick movement. These speakers include A. W. Tozer, Stephen Olford, Harry A. Ironside, Lewis Sperry Chafter, James O. Buswell III, John Walvoord, Charles Ryrie, Robert C. McQuilkin, Harold J. Ockenga and many others.[10]

The Method of Keswick

Since the teaching at Keswick conferences is unique in style, it is important to observe Keswick's methods which are no less important than the teaching itself. There are five methods that are employed by Keswick to inculcate its teachings at the conference.

Bible-Centered Teaching

Perhaps the most important Keswick's method is a Bible-centered method of teaching. Keswick has no formal denominational theology. Everyone attending the conference believes that the Bible is the true word of God. Interpretation of a particular passage may be different, but everyone agrees that the Bible is what God says. Barabas describes this characteristic method of Keswick:

> One of the first things that strikes a person who hears or reads the addresses given at the Convention is the evident effort of the speakers to make the Bible alone their criterion of what is true. One may agree or disagree with their interpretation of the Scriptures under consideration, but there is never any doubt that central in their thought is what God has to say.[11]

Since Keswick's aim is to promote practical holiness, the Bible is the textbook for this purpose. As such, the Bible is a practical book, not just a textbook for doctrines, which can revolutionize man's life when taken seriously. Every word and every passage of the Bible are taken seriously by

---
9. Loucks, "Theological Foundations," 87.
10. Loucks, "Theological Foundations," 88.
11. Barabas, *So Great Salvation*, 29.

Keswick because each word in the Bible is God's word that has the power to transform and revolutionize man's life.

This is one of the reasons Keswick was well-received by fundamentalist groups which espoused the literal interpretation of the Bible. Especially at the turn of the century when Presbyterian churches were attacked by German rationalism and the higher criticism of the Bible, Keswick's Bible-centered teaching with its emphasis on holiness attracted many conservative and fundamentalist Christians.

A Spiritual Clinic

The typical Keswick conference, unlike other Bible conferences, is held as a spiritual clinic. Keswick treats sin as a spiritual disease and a sinner as a spiritual patient. So, Keswick in a sense, is a spiritual hospital where the sinner, who is spiritually sick, comes for the healing of a spiritual disease, sin. Just as a soldier has to be physically healthy in order to fight the enemy, in the same way then "so Keswick, in its diagnosis of the state of the Church, finds it in a dangerously unhealthy condition, and looks upon the Convention as a place where health may be maintained."[12] Thus, the goal of the Keswick conference is the spiritual cure of soul.

In this method is seen the Wesleyan concept of sin and Phoebe Palmer's application of a technique to cure this spiritual "disease." Keswick took it a step further by making the "healing center" institutionalized to cure the "disease." The physical and tangible concept of sin brought about the practical and tangible method to deal with it.

A Witnessing Platform

At the Keswick convention the speakers are not chosen to teach doctrinal or theoretical truth but to share their own personal testimonies of the spiritual life. The founder of Keswick, Canon Harford-Battersby, expresses the importance of the personal testimony as the seal of a blessing by God:

> Yes, personal testimony is often demanded by God as the seal of a blessing, and as a real preparation for further usefulness. He who is not willing to make the little sacrifice which it demands, how shall he make the much more difficult sacrifices which are involved in teaching and in living the life of Holiness?[13]

---

12. Barabas, *So Great Salvation*, 31.
13. Harford, *Keswick Convention*, 53.

So, from the inception of the Keswick convention the speakers are invited to the convention to share their personal testimony on the holy life with others. Canon Harford-Battersby elaborates:

> Our desire is to let those speak to us and lead us, not who are able to make the most eloquent speeches, but whom God has manifestly led into the secret of the divine life, and who are willing to be nothing, and let Him speak through them; men who will be faithful with us and not spare us, but set forth very plainly our sins, and the things that hinder our full enjoyment of God's peace and growth in holiness.[14]

Barabas observes the distinctiveness of Keswick's style of teaching or sharing the truth. He writes, "Keswick stands for a peculiar type, both of spiritual teaching and living, and to this all else is consistently subordinated. Those who by conviction hold these truths, and by experiment have tasted them, are asked to take part, and no others."[15]

Although Keswick claims that the speakers are not involved in teaching but in sharing their testimonies, it nevertheless involves teaching as Barabas himself uses the term "spiritual teaching." Spiritual teaching inevitably involves doctrines. Thus, Keswick is involved in teaching their own doctrines on spiritual matters. Doctrinal teachings are used to show people their wrongs and direct them to the correct way.

Progressive Order of Teaching

A Keswick convention usually has five specific topics, one allocated for each day respectively. The first day emphasizes the subject of sin. An effort is made on the first day to focus on sin and to encourage Christians to abandon it immediately.

On the second day the theme of God's provision for a victorious Christian life is presented. Keswick stresses that the finished work of Christ provides more than justification. Drawing from the teaching of the union with Christ, as taught in Romans 6, God's provision for the Christian's victorious life is found not only in the work of Christ but also in the "inner work of the Holy Spirit." Thus, Keswick emphasizes the importance of the work of the Holy Spirit in the believer for the victorious life. A Keswick advocate, J. Robertson McQuilkin, underscores this point:

---

14. Pierson, *Keswick Movement*, 46–47. Cited by Barabas, *So Great Salvation*, 33.
15. Barabas, *So Great Salvation*, 33.

> Of the members of the Trinity, it is He [Holy Spirit] who sanctifies the believer, He works to counteract the downward pull of sin. He does not eradicate the susceptibility to sin, nor does He displace human responsibility to believe and choose. Rather, the Spirit exercises a counterforce, enabling the surrendered and trusting believer to resist successfully the spiritually downward pull of his or her natural disposition.[16]

Thus, the secret of maintaining a consistent victorious Christian life is taught on the second day of the convention.

On the third day consecration is the theme, wherein the followers are taught to acknowledge their own failure and inability and to surrender themselves to God unconditionally. They are taught to see their utter inadequacy and miserableness before surrendering themselves to God.

The fullness of the Spirit is the topic on the fourth day. Here the people are taught to seek a life filled with the Spirit, which Keswick teaches is the birthright of every Christian. The importance of being "filled with the Spirit" is emphasized since the Holy Spirit is God's provision for the victorious Christian life.

On the fifth day the subject is Christian service, which is presented in its practical and social implications. It is designed to turn the attention of consecrated Christians toward serving God and others in the power of the Holy Spirit. Naturally, missions is the major emphasis for this theme. The Christians are encouraged to dedicate their lives for the cause of world evangelization.

Positively speaking, Keswick in this method may be said to be involved in the progressive order of teaching. However, it sounds more like the believer is going through an assembly line in a factory in order to be assembled into a final product. Holiness is not a packaged product. Keswick's method to attain holiness for the believer sounds much like a manmade and mechanical method.

Unity of Spirit

In all Keswick conventions the unity of Christians in Jesus Christ is stressed. Regardless of the different background and denominations, the unity of the Christians is exercised in brotherly love and fellowship at Keswick conventions. Barabas observes, "The unity of Spirit that prevails at the Convention is one of its most impressive features. When it is

---

16. J. R. McQuilkin, "Keswick Perspective," 155.

remembered that the speakers come from many different denominations, this is a remarkable fact."[17]

To preserve the unity of the Christians at the convention, it is generally agreed in Christian spirit that the speakers are not to speak about the topics that may be controversial. In spite of the possible differences in some doctrines among the speakers at the convention, they all agree that they are there to share one and the same goal, promotion of the holy life of the Christians by the power of the Holy Spirit.

The main reason that Keswick could maintain the unity of the Christians at the convention is that the Holy Spirit is exalted at the convention. The Holy Spirit is regarded by all the people at the conventions as the real leader of the convention.[18] Thus, all the speeches and meetings are organized as being led by the Holy Spirit. Minor differences and disagreements among the people at the convention are discarded as they all sense the strong bond of unity in the Holy Spirit for the cause of the gospel.

Keswick's emphasis on the unity of Spirit is commendable. However, maintaining silence and ignoring the differences among the people do not resolve the differences. This method is good as far as it goes. But eventually Keswick will have to deal with the differences among people in an honest and theological manner. Otherwise, Keswick's teaching will turn into a mysticism or a shallow teaching.

Keswick's Teaching on the Victorious Christian Life

Although Keswick claims that their conventions are organized not to teach doctrine but to share spiritual truth, the method of spreading Keswick's message is by teaching, and the content of the message certainly embodies doctrines in one form or another. In this section, the teachings of Keswick are presented to show the emphasis and uniqueness of Keswick's message. Keswick's teachings presented here are their understandings of sin, sanctification, faith, consecration, and a Spirit-filled life.

Sin

Sin is what caused the separation between man and God, bringing all miseries of man including the death. The sin problem is at the core of theology. How one views sin of man usually determines the solution to that

---

17. Barabas, *So Great Salvation*, 34–35.
18. Barabas, *So Great Salvation*, 37.

sin, the doctrine of salvation. Thus, it is important to examine Keswick's teachings on sin first, in order to understand the overall approach to the salvation of man by Keswick.

Definition of Sin

The definition of sin is one of the most crucial expressions in Christian theology because one needs to identify the problem as exactly as possible before finding the solution for the problem. Undoubtedly, sin is *the problem* of man and salvation in Christ is the solution for him. Since Keswick lacks definite statements of their doctrines, it is difficult for us to find a succinct definitive statement on sin such as one might find in Charles Hodge's or Louis Berkhof's *Systematic Theology*. However, Keswick advocates expressed their views on the nature of sin in man. H. W. Webb-Peploe states that the word "sin" means that "everything that lacks the thoroughness and glory of the standard that God lifts up, is sin. What are we to say to this?— everything coming short of the perfection of God, is sin!"[19] Another advocate of Keswick, Evan H. Hopkins defines sin negatively. He says that sin is not "an inseparable adjunct to our human nature" or "a necessary constituent of our moral progress."[20] He then goes on to say that the character of sin is correctly understood only when man's sin is seen in relation to God. After expressing the inherent theological character of man's sin, Hopkins defines sin in six ways.[21]

First, Hopkins defines sin as an offense against God. Sin is "rebellion against the purity and goodness and majesty of God." Man deserves punishment in rebelling against God's holy law. The law of God is understood here as "not only the Mosaic law of the Old Testament, but also the law of the New Testament, and by Him explained in the word and exhibited in the life, as the law written in man's heart for his special direction."[22] Sin is thus rebellion against the sovereignty and authority of God. Hopkins explains this point:

> Sin is an offence, because it is rebellion against the sovereignty of God, a contradiction to His nature, an insult to His holiness. It stands related to law—not merely to the law of reason, or of conscience, or of expediency, but to the law of God. Sin consists

---

19. Webb-Peploe, "Sin," 37.
20. Hopkins, *Law of Liberty*, 3–4.
21. Hopkins, *Law of Liberty*, 11–29. Described by Barabas *Salvation*, 42–51.
22. Hopkins, *Law of Liberty*, 12.

essentially in the want of conformity to the will of God, which the law reveals; it is lawlessness—a breach of law.[23]

God's holy law reveals the awfulness of sin. It also reveals man's rebellion against God's sovereignty and authority. "Man is therefore guilty before God who created him, and his sin has to be punished and atoned for."[24] On this point Hopkins is generally in line with the orthodox and Reformed view of sin.

Second, sin is a ruling principle in man. It is a power that takes hold of the entire being of man and rules it according to its sway. Hopkins writes, "Sin is a power that has entered into the central citadel of a man's being, and, establishing itself there, has brought every part of his nature under its sway."[25] Sin is a principle that is opposed to God and has taken the place of the ruler in man's being instead of God. In sinning, man has become a slave to sin. Referring to Romans 6, Hopkins points out the believer's present condition in reference to sin. Christ has set man free from the authority of sin. The believer is now free and under the authority of the LORD Jesus Christ. Hopkins explains Paul's purpose in writing Romans 6:

> The purpose of the Apostle, in this sixth chapter, is to show how completely the believer is identified with Christ when "He died unto sin." To enter fully into the meaning of that death is to see that Christ has emancipated us from any further dealings with our old master sin. The believer is privileged thus to take his place in Christ, who is now "alive unto God." From that standpoint he is henceforth to regard sin. He is now and forever free from the old service and the old rule. The Cross has terminated the connection once for all, and terminated it abruptly. It has effected a definite and complete rupture with the old master, sin.[26]

Sin is a powerful ruling principle which cannot be severed from man by anyone, except by Jesus Christ.

Hopkins' reference to Romans 6 in defining sin as a ruling principle or power in man is very important. Keswick's concept of crisis sanctification centers around this concept. Also, it plays a critical role in defining John Murray's doctrine of definitive sanctification as the response to Keswick's sanctification.

---

23. Hopkins, *Law of Liberty*, 13.
24. Barabas, *So Great Salvation*, 43.
25. Hopkins, *Law of Liberty*, 12.
26. Hopkins, *Law of Liberty*, 15.

Third, sin is seen as moral defilement which makes man unclean and unfit for God's presence. Hopkins generally refers to the Book of Leviticus. The book describes the defilement of the Israelites by indwelling evil. Referring to the man who is defiled and washes away the pollution physically, Hopkins writes, "The body in these types stands as an image of the soul. Ceremonial defilement and cleansing represented spiritual pollution, and the purification revealed to us in the gospel."[27] Sin as the spiritual, moral defilement can be washed away only by the atoning blood of Jesus Christ. Hopkins writes, "To be cleansed from any impurity is just to be separated from it [sin's defilement]. Nothing can separate any person from sin except the death of Christ."[28] Even unbelievers have the innate sense of the unwashable pollution of sin. It is interesting to note that Barabas quotes Lady Macbeth's cry in *Macbeth* after murdering the king, "Not all the perfumes of Arabia can sweeten this little hand."[29]

Hopkins' definition of sin as moral defilement is valid as far as it goes. In his arguments we sense that he is moving toward the physical concept of sin. He is setting a stage where he can deal with sin in a physical and tangible way. In fact, this is exactly where he is heading as he goes on to his fourth definition of sin.

Fourth, Hopkins states that sin is a spiritual disease in the soul. He says, "The effect of disease on our physical organism is just a picture of what sin produces on our spiritual nature."[30] Just as disease makes the physical body impaired and devoid of the power and freedom of the body, so does sin make the soul powerless and without freedom. After describing the effect of paralysis on the physical body which is rendered with the loss of the power of voluntary muscular motion, Hopkins shows sin's effect on the soul:

> Sin has precisely the same effect on our souls. Though there is spiritual life, there may be lack of spiritual vigour. The effects of sin may be traced in the impairment of voluntary power, and in the enfeebling of all moral energy, as well as in the hardening and deadening of the spiritual sense. And the result is the whole tone of the spiritual life is lowered. Sin thus robs us of the power by which we are able to perform the functions that belong to our renewed being. And it not only undermines our strength, it hinders our growth.[31]

---

27. Hopkins, *Law of Liberty*, 17.
28. Hopkins, *Law of Liberty*, 19.
29. Barabas, *So Great Salvation*, 45.
30. Hopkins, *Law of Liberty*, 20.
31. Hopkins, *Law of Liberty*, 20–21.

According to Hopkins, sin especially robs man of his power of hearing and speaking. Sin robs man of his power of hearing the voice of God, and it robs the believer of the willingness to listen to the voice of God. Sin also robs man of the power of praising God or of calling upon him in prayer. It also deprives him of the power to speak for God to men.

Hopkins' definition of sin here clearly depicts Wesleyan influence on Keswick. John Wesley himself used this term "spiritual disease" specifically in defining sin. Now, Keswick appropriates this concept and is moving toward providing a "clinic" to get rid of it. As W. Ralph Thompson points out in his article there are many similarities between Wesleyan perfectionism and Keswick's teaching.[32] This Wesleyan concept of sin as a spiritual disease left a lasting imprint on Keswick's teaching.

Fifth, sin is an acquired habit. Hopkins says that habit is "an acquired power, and is the result of repeated action. It is often like a second nature."[33] Sin therefore is an acquired evil habit. Hopkins here distinguishes between the sin tendency and the sinful habit:

> It is clear from this that we are not born with habits, though we inherit that which gave rise to them. Evil habits must not therefore be confounded with those sinful tendencies with which every child of Adam comes into the world. We are born with the sinful tendency, but we are not born with the sinful habit.[34]

Hopkins asserts that every sinful habit has to be laid aside in order to be delivered from the power of any habit. Citing Ephesians 4:25–32, Hopkins lists examples of sinful habits: "Falsehood, theft, corrupt speech, bitterness, wrath, anger, clamour, railing, malice—all these are to be laid aside, not subjugated or kept under, but altogether put away, as things with which the believer has nothing more to do, and from which he is to be actually separated."[35] Barabas says that this aspect of sin by Keswick is often overlooked by church today.

Contrary to Barabas' assertion, this is exactly the concept of sin the church has been teaching believers to be separated from. Barabas's claim that the church has been teaching the subjugation rather than elimination of this sin is not correct. What underlies Barabas's statement is that the church has not viewed sin in a physical sense so that it may be washed away completely from the believer.

32. Thompson, "Appraisal of the Keswick," 13.
33. Hopkins, *Law of Liberty*, 23.
34. Hopkins, *Law of Liberty*, 23.
35. Hopkins, *Law of Liberty*, 24.

Sixth, sin is an indwelling tendency in man. Every man has the tendency to sin. "Even Adam in his original sinless and innocent condition was not free from the liability to sin."[36] In order to show the ever present tendency to sin in every man even after being cleansed by the blood of Christ, Hopkins gives a hypothetical illustration:

> But there are some who seem to think we may be freed in this life from all *tendency* to sin. There are some who seem to maintain that the blessing of being "pure in heart" is a state of purity, rather than a *maintained condition* of purity. The distinction is important. It may be made clear by an illustration. Let us suppose a natural impossibility; namely, that by passing a lighted candle through a dark room, such an effect is produced by that *one act*, that the room not only becomes instantly lighted but *continues* in a *state* of illumination. If this were possible, the room would not be dependent on the continued presence of the lighted candle for its light, though it would be indebted to the candle in the first instance for the state of light introduced into it. Such is not, we maintain, the nature of the cleansing which Christ bestows upon us.[37]

Hopkins insists that the tendency to sin is never completely eliminated in this life. But the tendency to sin can be counteracted by the Holy Spirit in the believer's life. Hopkins writes, "The very fact that 'the law of the Spirit of life in Christ Jesus' must be ever in force as a continual necessity, is a proof that the tendency to sin is not extinct, but is simply counteracted."[38] Man is never absolutely free from the presence of evil; "the tendency to sin and death is ever with us."[39]

Hopkins's claim that sin is an indwelling tendency to sin is an ambiguous one. If it is understood as moral corruption, then his conception is not much different from orthodox teaching. But he makes a great jump by equating the "tendency to sin" with the "liability to sin" as in the case of Adam. Then Hopkins's statement does not make a sense because what he in fact says is that Adam had sin even before he fell into sin. Here Hopkins is greatly confused by confounding the tendency to sin which arises from moral corruption with the liability to sin. But the exact theological definition does not seem to be a great concern for Hopkins and Keswick

---

36. Hopkins, *Law of Liberty*, 25.
37. Hopkins, *Law of Liberty*, 25. All emphases are Hopkins's.
38. Hopkins, *Law of Liberty*, 27.
39. Hopkins, *Law of Liberty*, 27.

advocates, because whatever it is, as long as it is counteracted by the power of the Holy Spirit the believer is in a good spiritual condition.

It is seen from the Keswick's definition of sin that Keswick's teaching is a mixture of various theological teachings. Keswick has in its teaching some orthodox and Reformed doctrines, some Wesleyan teachings and even its own inventions. Therefore, some people see a mild Calvinism in Keswick while Wesleyans claim many similarities between Keswick and Wesleyan perfectionism. The obvious result of this kind of teaching is inconsistency and confusion. Anthony A. Hoekema expresses this concern, "I have major problems with . . . the definition of sin."[40] Another example of this inconsistency is the Keswick's view of sin as a disease which is to be washed away by elimination in one place and its teaching of counteraction by the Holy Spirit for controlling sin in the believer in another place. Keswick's definition of sin is at best a hodgepodge of several theologies.

Sin in the Believer

Keswick's focus is sin in the believer. Keswick calls the believer who is under the power of sin a carnal Christian. It is Keswick's aim to transform this carnal Christian into the one who lives a victorious life.

THE CARNAL CHRISTIAN

Keswick distinguishes between carnal Christians and spiritual Christians. McQuilkin refers to 1 Corinthians 3:1–3 to show that carnal Christians believe in the same manner as unconverted people and that spiritual Christians are dominated by the Holy Spirit.[41] The aim of Keswick at this point is to transform carnal Christians to spiritual Christians.

Andrew Murray describes the marks of the carnal Christian.[42] The first mark of the carnal Christian is a protracted infancy. In other words, they are spiritual babies. They are fed with the spiritual food of milk when they should be taking in the spiritual food of meat by themselves. As spiritual babies they are always dependent upon someone else. They cannot help themselves or others. The carnal Christians are totally dependent on others and are selfish. Murray speaks of the Corinthian Christians as the typical carnal Christians:

40. Hoekema, "Response to McQuilkin," 187.
41. J. R. McQuilkin, "Keswick Perspective," 160.
42. A. Murray, "Carnal Christian," 84.

Corinthian Christians. They continued babies. Now, what are the marks of a babe? They are specially two marks: a babe cannot help itself, and a babe cannot help others. A babe cannot help itself; and that is the life of many Christians. They make their ministers spiritual nurses of babes. It is a solemn thing that these spiritual babes keep their ministers occupied all the time in nursing them and feeding them, and they never want to grow to be men, and they never help themselves. They do not know themselves how to feed on Christ's Word, and the minister must feed them. They do not know what contact with God is; the minister must pray for them. They do not know what it is to live as those who have God to help them; they always want to be nursed.[43]

The second mark of the carnal Christians is that sin is the master in their lives, according to Murray. Sin has the upper hand in their lives. The lives of the carnal Christians are dominated by selfish acts and desires such as envy, strife, greed, and others. Murray says that these selfish desires and acts are contrary to the first fruit of the Holy Spirit, love. Thus, every unloving act is from the flesh and is the mark of the carnal Christians. Murray elaborates:

> Every touch of unlovingness is nothing but the flesh. Most of you know that the word *carnal* is a form of the Latin word for *flesh*, and all unlovingness is nothing but the fruit or work of the flesh. The flesh is selfish and proud and unloving; therefore, every sin against love is nothing but a proof that the man is carnal.[44]

The carnal Christian serves sin as the master by living a selfish and unloving life.

Although Andrew Murray was a well-respected Christian leader in his time, his teaching on this point has to be refuted. He teaches here that a carnal Christian who has been saved by Jesus Christ is still under the power of sin. This is contrary to the teaching of Romans 6 and to the doctrine of definitive sanctification. If this Christian is still under the power of sin, what difference has the work of Jesus Christ made upon his life? The so called "carnal" Christian may be under the influence of sin but cannot be under the power of sin.

Third, the carnal state of the Christian can coexist with great spiritual gifts. A Christian with great spiritual gifts does not necessarily mean that he is

---

43. A. Murray, "Carnal Christian," 85.
44. A. Murray, "Carnal Christian," 86.

a spiritual Christian. Murray explains, "Remember, there is a great difference between spiritual gifts and spiritual graces, and that is what many people do not understand. Among the Corinthians, for instance, there were very wonderful spiritual gifts."[45] A Christian may have great spiritual gifts and still be ruled by sin in his life. The Corinthian Christians were blessed with many great spiritual gifts such as prophecy and speaking in tongues, but they were rebuked by the Apostle Paul for their carnal state. Murray gives a warning to Christians not to confuse spiritual gifts with spiritual graces:

> It is a very solemn thing for us to remember that a man may be gifted with prophecy, that a man may be a faithful and successful worker in some particular sphere among the poor and needy, and yet by the sharpness of his judgment and the pride that comes into him, and by other things, he may give proof that while his spiritual gifts are wonderful, spiritual graces are too often absent.[46]

Murray, in this argument, makes the believer to be under the dominion of sin and of grace at the same time. What is described of the Corinthian Christians by Murray is true, but they were not under the dominion of sin. They were much influenced by the power of sin, yet they were under the dominion of grace as they were believers who had been separated from the darkness of sin once and for all.

Another mark of the carnal Christian is that it is impossible for him to receive spiritual truths. The carnal state hinders the reception of spiritual truth. So the carnal Christian is robbed of spiritual food and spiritual growth is absent in his Christian life. Murray emphasizes that the carnal Christian should be lifted out of the carnal state into the spiritual state by receiving a blessing at the Keswick convention. He continues, "The only evidence that you get a blessing at Keswick is that you are lifted out of the carnal into the spiritual state. God is willing to do it, and let us plead for it, and accept it."[47]

Though Murray and Keswick advocates make much out of the separate states of carnal and spiritual Christians, 1 Corinthians 3:1–3 describes immature Christians or mere infants in Christ, but not carnal Christians as a different kind from spiritual Christians. Carnality was a behavioral problem of the Corinthians. Scripture does not make a distinction between carnal and spiritual Christians as described by Murray. Hoekema affirms my position:

45. A. Murray, "Carnal Christian," 87.
46. A. Murray, "Carnal Christian," 87.
47. A. Murray, "Carnal Christian," 88.

> There is no biblical basis for the distinction between "carnal" and "spiritual" Christians. The New Testament does distinguish between people who have been born again and those who have not (John 3:3, 5), between those who believe in Christ and those who do not (v. 36), between those who "live according to the flesh" and those who "live according to the Spirit" (Rom. 8:5), and between the "unspiritual man" and the "spiritual man" (1 Cor. 2:14–15). It never speaks of a third class of people called "carnal Christians."[48]

Keswick's attempt to make carnal Christians out of believers is not supported by Scripture. The classification is important for Keswick advocates because they want to put every Christian who has not had Keswick's crisis sanctification into this category.

The Insipid Christian

In Keswick's teaching the insipid and defeated Christians are classified as carnal Christians. But they are a special kind of carnal Christians Keswick focuses on and aims to transform into spiritual Christians. According to Keswick, the insipid Christians are those who are spiritually lukewarm. Drawing from Revelation 3:16, W. W. Martin defines the insipid or lukewarm Christians, "In other words they were insipid Christians, those who would attract no attention in the crowd, Christians of the same temperature as the crowd, of whom it would never be said that they burned for God; just warm; whose religious life was unmarked by enthusiasm or zeal."[49] Martin reveals that the Christian's spiritual state can be varied from hot to lukewarm and that it is a serious matter. The cause of this lukewarmness in the spiritual life is spiritual inactivity. Unwillingness to change one's life and idleness are believed to be the major causes of the spiritual inactivity. Martin writes, "In view of the call for labourers for the harvest, are you standing about in the market place with a greatcoat on, resting in cold self-complacency? You have forgotten the harvest field, the field overripe for harvest. Idleness, indolence, are tragic."[50]

Martin especially points to the two sources where the lukewarmness comes from. First, it stems from unanswered prayer. Some Christians, after praying for some time, lost the zeal for praying. Unanswered prayers lead to a lost zeal for praying which in turn leads to lukewarmness in the

---

48. Hoekema, "Response to J. R. McQuilkin," 189.
49. Martin, "Insipid Christians," 133.
50. Martin, "Insipid Christians," 135.

spiritual life. Second, lukewarmness comes as the result of "long-drawn-out opposition." Problems and oppositions that creep into the Christian's life can lead to the spiritual inactivity. Martin construes, "You went forth full of zeal; you felt you had faith that could remove mountains; but this meeting of the old problems and old persecutions, and ridicule day after day, has made your outlook on life change, and you have lost the zealous character of your witness for God."[51]

Is lukewarmness sin? Martin says, "Yes." It is the sin that cripples the Christian's spiritual life and makes him useless for God. Martin further expounds:

> Lukewarm! He is a man at Bethesda's hospital; once he was enthusiastic, but he had been there for thirty-eight years, and had lost all hope. Why? *Sin*! "Go thy way and sin no more"—the present tense. All those many years he had been sinning; and if there is one sin, whether large or little—it is probably little—that you are hugging, and still indulging in your life, and upon which God has put His finger and said "This is the thing which is crippling your spiritual life," if there is that one sin, and you retain it, you will become a lukewarm Christian, an insipid Christian that the world despises and is of no use to God.[52]

It is true that the lukewarmness of a Christian should be changed into a zeal and a love for the LORD Jesus Christ. However, Martin's identification of lukewarmness with sin is not correct. Lukewarmness is a result of sin or a symptom of sin rather than sin itself. Martin's teaching of the insipid Christian is not built upon a theological definition. Problems with the Keswick movement arise with a teaching such as this where its advocates fabricate practical or functional definitions which seem to suit their own way of teaching a certain doctrine.

THE DEFEATED CHRISTIAN

The defeated Christians are, according to Keswick, those who tried to get rid of their sins and to achieve holiness with their own strength. Canon Harford-Battersby confesses his frustration and disillusion in his defeated spiritual life:

> I am just in the condition of the person described in Romans vii. This is my habitual state, however much I may realise[sic] at

---

51. Martin, "Insipid Christians," 136.
52. Martin, "Insipid Christians," 136.

> times the blessedness of peace and justification; and thus being anxious about myself, not being whole within, it is impossible that I can have leisure or abstraction of mind enough to treat the diseases of others, or to enter upon my work heartily.[53]

Thus, he ascribes the description of Romans 7 to the defeated Christian. In seeing the experience of the defeated Christian in Romans 7, Keswick closely follows the Arminian and Wesleyan views on this chapter.

The experience of the defeated Christian life is not unique to Harford-Battersby. Hudson Taylor, the founder of the China Inland Mission, shares a similar experience:

> Well, dearie, my mind has been greatly exercised for six or eight months past, feeling the need personally and for our Mission of more holiness, life, power in our souls. But the personal need stood first and was the greatest. I felt the ingratitude, the danger, the sin of not living nearer to God. I prayed, agonized, fasted, strove, made resolutions, read the Word more diligently, sought more time for meditation—but all without avail. Every day, almost every hour, the consciousness of sin oppressed me.[54]

Thus, Keswick teaches that the experience of the defeated Christian life is not only present in the rank and file Christians but also in those who are considered as "spiritual giants" such as Harford-Battersby and Hudson Taylor. Harford-Battersby suggests that humiliation and prayer are to be exercised in order to achieve victory over the defeat in the spiritual life. He says, "It is only when we have got down upon our faces before God, when we are humbled before Him, and we have shut out the voice of the world, that we can hear the LORD's voice. But let us remember that humiliation is not enough. When the voice comes, it is a call to action: 'Get thee up; search out the sin; bring it out; bring out the cause of failure before me.'"[55] So for Keswick, the cause of the defeated Christian life is sin, unsubdued or hidden, which also includes attempting to achieve holiness by one's own effort.

Keswick's identification of Romans 7 with the experience of the defeated Christian is crucial to its teaching. Keswick's purpose is to give the victory in Christ to the Christian whose experience is such as the one described in Romans 7. Man's effort to achieve sanctification will result in defeat every time. Thus, Keswick introduces its own way of achieving sanctification. Keswick's view closely follows the Arminian and Wesleyan

---

53. Harford-Battersby, *Memoirs*, 146.
54. Taylor, *Spiritual Secret*, 113.
55. Harford-Battersby, "Defeated Soldier," 114.

view except that Keswick also sees the Christian who is defeated trying to achieve sanctification with his own efforts. Incredibly, Herman Ridderbos, a Reformed theologian, renders his interpretation of Romans 7 which closely resembles Keswick's view.[56]

Sanctification

Keswick distinguishes between the "wrong" way and the "correct" way of sanctification. Naturally, Keswick's approach to sanctification is regarded by the followers as the "correct" way of achieving holiness.

Wrong Ways of Seeking Sanctification

Keswick claims that the defeated Christian life is often the result of the Christian's effort to seek sanctification in "wrong" ways. Keswick shows that there are generally four "wrong" ways the Christians seek sanctification.

Regarding Sanctification as a Matter of Course

One of the "wrong" ways to seek sanctification is to regard sanctification as a matter of course. It means that the Christian does not need to trouble himself about it because he will achieve it automatically in his Christian life. A belief in this "wrong" way of sanctification leads the Christian to idleness and carelessness in his Christian life. Not only is this kind of Christian life "wrong" in seeking holiness but also it is even dangerous because it eventually leads the Christian to his downfall in his spiritual relation to God. A Keswick advocate, J. E. Cumming explains:

> The New Testament continually warns Christians to "give all diligence" to "make their calling and election sure," to "watch and pray," "to give earnest heed" to the things they have heard, to "hold fast that which they have, that no man take their crown": and to "fear lest haply a promise being left of entering into His rest, any one should seem to have come short of it." Let every Christian beware of the folly of sitting down in unconcern and leaving his reward soul to take care of itself! The lusting of the flesh "will in that case soon assert itself to his downfall."[57]

---

56. Ridderbos, *Paul*, 127.
57. Cumming, *Spirit*, 113.

If sanctification is taken as a matter of course by the Christian, he will never achieve holiness in this life, and will disobey the teachings of the word of God which exhort the Christians to be holy in their lives.

Keswick's emphasis on this point is commendable. Perhaps the Christian church has not been teaching the importance of sanctification enough to Christians. However, Keswick's labeling it as a "wrong" way of seeking sanctification is not correct. It is more being ignorant or not seeking rather than seeking it in a wrong way. A lack of emphasis on the zealous holy life of the Christian may have resulted from the overemphasis on the Calvinistic perseverance and security of the believer at the expense of the believer's earnest effort for the holy life.

Regarding Sanctification as a Gradual Process

According to Keswick, the second "wrong" way to seek sanctification is to regard sanctification as a gradual process. Sanctification is traditionally taken as a gradual process which is not to be stopped or hindered or accelerated by any effort on the part of the Christian. Barabas cites Cumming concerning two perceived harmful effects resulting from this view, "It leads Christians to expect no positive holiness for a long period of years; and it prevents them from taking any definite steps toward holiness that would lead to an improvement in their condition."[58] Evan H. Hopkins also depreciates the gradual process of sanctification and says that God's work is never complete according to this view:

> Our sanctification can never in this life reach a point beyond which there is to be no further progress; it can never therefore be said to be complete. So long as there is room for a full manifestation of the Divine image the work cannot be said to be complete.[59]

Keswick points out that sanctification is misconstrued if it is taken as a gradual process. Then, the spiritual growth is treated as same as the physical growth such as is seen in the vegetable and animal kingdoms. Whereas the physical growth is gradual and slow, the spiritual growth may be fast and even instantaneous. By eliminating sins in the believer's life, the spiritual growth is accelerated to achieve holiness in a short time, even instantaneously.

Barabas includes the interesting statement regarding this point in an effort to clarify Keswick's position on this view. "It must not be thought that

---

58. Barabas, *So Great Salvation*, 70.
59. Hopkins, *Law of Liberty*, 64.

Keswick denies that sanctification is progressive and a matter of growth. It denies only that growth is necessarily imperceptibly slow and it cannot be retarded or hastened by anything the believer may do."[60]

According to Barabas, Keswick does not say that sanctification is not progressive in some sense. It is against the traditional way of viewing sanctification only as a slow gradual process. Then, it seems that the difference between the traditional and Keswick's way of sanctification is the speed of sanctification. According to Keswick, the speed of sanctification can be varied by applying Keswick's way of achieving it.

Regarding Sanctification as Gained through Suppression of the Old Nature

Keswick teaches that one of the "wrong" ways to seek sanctification is by suppressing the old nature of the believer. The believer cannot be freed from the dominion of sin by trying to conquer the old nature. He cannot achieve sanctification by bringing himself under spiritual discipline. Evan Hopkins calls it "a kind of sanctification of the flesh." Hopkins turns to Romans 7 to show the wrong way of trying to achieve sanctification and God's remedy for it. He first points out the wrong interpretation and misuse of this chapter:

> Practically, we know that too often this seventh chapter of Romans has been used as a refuge by those who are leading an inconsistent life; and our spiritual enemy would lead us to use this passage as a warrant for expecting defeat. Is it not true that too often it has been used, shall I say, as an excuse for sinning? At all events, many of God's children have come to this chapter for comfort and encouragement while pursuing a course of failure. Surely this was not the purpose of the apostle in writing the passage.[61]

Hopkins sees in this chapter the believer who tries to achieve sanctification by his own efforts. The consequence of this self-effort sanctification is frustration and defeat in the spiritual life of the believer. Thus, Romans 7 does not describe the normal spiritual life of the believer but shows the experience of struggle and defeat when the believer tries to achieve sanctification by conquering the old nature with his own efforts.

Hopkins moves to Romans 8 to show God's remedy for this problem. In Romans 8, not only the believer is saved by the death of Christ, but he

60. Barabas, *So Great Salvation*, 71.
61. Hopkins, "Law of Sin," 157.

is also delivered from sin to abide in Christ. Hopkins writes, "But we are brought to understand God's remedy in the meaning of that little word 'in.' To be 'in Christ' is *not only union, but fellowship.*"[62] The law of the Spirit of life in Christ has made the believer free from the law of sin and death. He explains this principle:

> Let us suppose that I place my rod with the lead and cork into a little life-belt, and I put them into the table of water. The rod now does not sink. Why? Because it is in the life-belt. There is sufficient lifting-power in it to keep it from sinking; but it is only as it is in the life-belt that it has the benefit of that law. It is the power of a superior law counteracting the other law. The lead is not taken away, but the rod has the benefit of a stronger power so long as it abides in the life-belt.[63]

Thus, Hopkins argues that the believer cannot achieve sanctification by trying to suppress the old nature by his own efforts. Rather, he can achieve sanctification by abiding in Christ because the Holy Spirit counteracts the law of sin by his superior power.

Although I agree with Keswick that sanctification is not achieved through suppression of the old nature by man's efforts, I deny Keswick's implication that the orthodox church including the Reformed church has been teaching that sanctification is achieved through suppression of the old nature by man's efforts. The orthodox church has never taught this view. Sanctification always involves the work of the Holy Spirit as well. The orthodox view is that sanctification involves man's efforts guided by the Holy Spirit, never man alone. If Keswick equates the orthodox view with this wrong way, then it is grossly misrepresenting the orthodox view.

Regarding Sanctification as Gained through Active Christian Service

Keswick also attempts to refute the idea that sanctification may be achieved through active Christian service. True sanctification would necessarily involve Christian service, but that service is not the divine means of sanctification. Evan Hopkins distinguishes between the "work of the Christ for the believer" and the "work of the Spirit in the believer." The work of the Spirit in the believer, Christian service, is not the means of the work of the Christ

---

62. Hopkins, "Law of Sin," 160. The emphasis is Hopkins's.
63. Hopkins, "Law of Sin," 161.

for the believer, sanctification. Rather, the Holy Spirit carries out his work in the believer in connection with Christ's work for him.

Sanctification cannot be achieved by active Christian service which is just another way of trying to achieve sanctification by human efforts. Nor can it be gained as a reward from God for the Christian's diligent service. For Keswick, W. Graham Scroggie says that the experience of such Christian is "too often, one of disgrace, of joylessness, of prayerlessness, of worldliness, and of defeat."[64]

Keswick is right in saying that sanctification is not achieved through active Christian service, an element of man's efforts. However, there is a problem in Hopkins's differentiation between the "work of the Christ for the believer" and the "work of the Spirit in the believer." He equates the former with sanctification and the latter with Christian service. This is arbitrary and theologically unsound. Sanctification involves the work of the Spirit in the believer. Keswick advocates' teaching like this reveals that their teachings are created to accommodate practical needs of their ministry.

Keswick's Approach

Keswick affirms the biblical meaning of sanctification "set apart to God." The setting apart of a man to God involves removing sin from him because God is holy. According to Keswick, this removal process of sin is sanctification. God's desire for the believer's holiness involves sanctification. Having stated the meaning of sanctification, Keswick presents its approach to sanctification. For its approach to sanctification Keswick reveals its view on the aspects, elements, ground, agent, and limits of sanctification.

ASPECTS OF SANCTIFICATION

Keswick views sanctification in three aspects: process, crisis, and gift. Sanctification is first seen as a process in that a divine work is wrought in the believer by the Holy Spirit after justification. Unlike justification, which is instantaneous, sanctification is progressive and goes through a prolonged process. Evan Hopkins writes, "We learn, for instance, that it is gradual and progressive, from such passages as 2 Corinthians 3:18. Our spiritual transformation is there described as still going on."[65] So the change described here is a "gradual assimilation to Christ which takes place during this

---

64. Scroggie, "Keswick's Distinctive Message," 81.
65. Hopkins, *Law of Liberty*, 63.

present life." Since sanctification is a progressive and gradual development, the sanctification of the believer is seen as never being able to reach a point in this life where there is no further progress.

In viewing sanctification as a process in this way Keswick is not different from the Reformed view. However, Keswick views process sanctification as inferior to their crisis sanctification whereas the Reformed church views process sanctification as the normal pattern of sanctification. Keswick's statement of process sanctification seems to be only a formal declaration while their real emphasis lies on crisis sanctification.

Second, Keswick views sanctification from the perspective of crisis. Keswick advocates say that many believers do not make progress in sanctification because their spiritual growth is often hindered and halted. Many believers often do not make real progress in sanctification until they come to a crisis in life. Faced with a crisis, the believers surrender their unsubdued sins to God and make considerable progress in a short time. Evan Hopkins gives a biblical example of a man in crisis from Genesis 32:25. With his human resources exhausted, Jacob is in a crisis. "The power of resistance—which is self-will—being broken, the strength to cling—which is faith—is now brought into exercise."[66] Jacob's crisis in this passage parallels a crisis of believers in this life. Oftentimes believers leap into the maturity of sanctification through the crisis of life.

Keswick's primary focus is on crisis sanctification. The progress of sanctification is usually hindered by some obstacles in the believer's life. Crisis in the believer's life gets rid of these obstacles and helps him to make a giant jump in sanctification. Thus, in a sense, Keswick views progressive sanctification without crisis as an abnormal phenomenon. For Keswick, the crisis sanctification is the superior sanctification which makes the believer to achieve sanctification in a short time.

Third, sanctification is seen as a gift. It is a gift of God to the man who abides in Christ. As salvation is a gift of God, so is sanctification. They are all included in Christ. "Christ Himself is made of God unto us sanctification as well as righteousness, many of God's children fail to understand. One of God's greatest gifts—bound up in His 'unspeakable Gift'—is that of holiness."[67] Thus, sanctification cannot be achieved by the struggles of a man. Sanctification as a gift of God is one of the important teachings of Keswick. Barabas underscores this point:

> Again and again Keswick speakers emphasize that sanctification is a gift of God's love, in the same way that salvation itself is. It

---

66. Hopkins, *Law of Liberty*, 65.
67. Hopkins, *Law of Liberty*, 69.

is not something for which we have to struggle or strive; it is something that we are to receive as a free gift of God's grace. God does require holiness of His creatures, but what He requires He first provides. Sanctification is primarily and fundamentally neither an achievement nor a process, but a gift, a divine bestowal of a position in Christ.[68]

Sanctification as a gift is God's gracious blessing on every believer.

Keswick's view of sanctification as a gift of God is nothing new to Reformed theology. Sanctification is certainly a gift of God to a believer. But the difference between the two positions comes in when Keswick emphasizes this teaching at the expense of the involvement of man's efforts in sanctification. Keswick's overemphasis on this point naturally leads to passivity and quietism. J. I. Packer points out this weakness, "The point is plain. Passivity, which quietists think liberates the Spirit, actually resists and quenches him."[69]

Elements of Sanctification

Keswick teaches that the removal process of sin, sanctification, involves three elements, or sometimes called "three stages." These three elements are positional, experiential, and complete sanctification.[70]

The first element of sanctification is positional sanctification. In positional sanctification the sinner is set apart from his sin for the "purpose of becoming God's own possession." The positional sanctification involves the forgiveness of sin. Since man is forgiven of his sins, eternal punishment is also taken out of his life. It also includes justification. As the justified person, man's guilt and guilty record are removed from his life. God now sees the man as a pure and clean individual who has been washed and purified by the blood of Jesus Christ. Thus, positional sanctification is judicial as the sinner is forgiven of his sins and is declared righteous before God. Furthermore, positional sanctification includes setting the sinner free from the authority of a sinful disposition. J. Robertson McQuilkin explains what happens to the believer positionally as he enters the union with God:

> Sin is the prevailing characteristic of persons who live apart from God. They do not have the desire or power to choose consistently the right or to change their condition. Upon union with

---

68. Barabas, *So Great Salvation*, 88.
69. Packer, *Keep In Step*, 157.
70. J. R. McQuilkin, "Keswick Perspective," 159.

> God the process is reversed, and right begins to prevail. A new life-force has been introduced that has power to prevail against a sinful disposition. Christians may not behave in this way, but such is their true condition and potential.[71]

According to Keswick, in positional sanctification the believer has been sanctified through the death of Christ and has been made holy before God. Such is the condition of every believer in God.

Although much of what Keswick teaches about the believer's position is true, Keswick here really displays its bad theology by confounding sanctification with justification. Actually, Keswick puts justification inside of sanctification and makes too much of sanctification. It seems that in Keswick's theology there is no need for the doctrine of justification. For Keswick advocates, sanctification is the central doctrine in their teachings. And its emphasis on the doctrine of sanctification at the expense of other important doctrines is clearly seen here.

The second element of sanctification is experiential sanctification, according to Keswick. Experiential sanctification involves the "outworking of one's official position in daily life." So it involves the process of sanctification which realizes each day more and more a legal standing before God. It means the believer is delivered from sinful attitudes and actions in his life. All believers go through experiential sanctification. It is the day-by-day transformation of the believer into the image of Christ and is progressive in nature. It begins at conversion, continues throughout the life, and never ends in this life.

Keswick teaches that in order to have the victorious life the experiential sanctification should involve crisis sanctification. A crisis or traumatic experience of the believer is what expedites the process of experiential sanctification. Although Keswick uses the term "process sanctification" here, we should keep in mind that Keswick's experiential sanctification has the variable time factor including the instantaneous moment.

The third element of sanctification is complete or permanent sanctification. Complete sanctification occurs when the believer is entirely transformed into the image of Jesus Christ. Keswick's complete sanctification may be equated with the Reformed concept of glorification in which the believer is no longer tainted with sin.

Although Keswick differentiates sanctification into the above three elements, their main concern lies in the second element, experiential sanctification—how to experience freedom from sinful thoughts and deeds in daily life.

71. J. R. McQuilkin, "Keswick Perspective," 159.

Ground of Sanctification

Keswick teaches that the ground of the believer's sanctification is his identification with Christ in his death to sin. Christ died for the believer to save him from sin. Because of the death of Christ for the believer, God remembers his sins against him no more. The important truth here is that when Christ died on the cross to sin, believers were identified with him in that death to sin. In other words, the believers died with him on the cross. By virtue of the union of the believer with Christ in his death, he is freed from the "penalty of sin and emancipated from the power of sin." Thus, believer's sanctification rests upon the atoning work of Jesus Christ. Barabas writes, "The cross of Christ is the efficient cause of deliverance from the power of sin. Freedom from the dominion of sin is a blessing we may claim by faith, just as we accept pardon."[72] Therefore, sanctification is also one of the benefits of the work of Christ, and is "just as much our inheritance as is the forgiveness of sins."

What Keswick actually teaches here is the orthodox position on sanctification. Union with Christ is foundational for the believer's sanctification. This has been the Reformed view on sanctification. John Calvin, Charles Hodge, and B. B. Warfield taught this truth as well regarding sanctification.

For Keswick, the most important passage in the New Testament on this teaching is Romans 6, which has been called the Magna Charta of the Christian. One of the key verses in this chapter is verse 6, "For we know that our old self was crucified with him so that the body ruled by sin might be done away with, that we should no longer be slaves to sin." Evan Hopkins defines "old self" as the "unregenerate man" and "body ruled by sin" or "body of sin" as "our natural body used by sin."[73] Romans 6 teaches the believer's identification with Jesus Christ in his death. Hopkins explains the meaning of believer's identification with Christ in his death:

> In my unconverted state, I was identified with Christ on the Cross. That is a fact. It is one thing to see that our sins were laid upon Him: it is another thing to see that we ourselves have been nailed upon the Cross with Him. That is a fact accomplished. It does not come to you and me first of all as an experience, but it comes to us, first, as that which is judicially true of all believers, without exception. That is the fact, then.[74]

---

72. Barabas, *So Great Salvation*, 89.
73. Hopkins, "Our Old Man," 173–74.
74. Hopkins, "Our Old Man," 175.

Hopkins's identification of "old self" with the "unregenerate man" is important here in that Keswick shows the radical change that occurs in the believer. John Murray in his doctrine of definitive sanctification also takes this view departing from the traditional Calvinistic interpretation of "old nature" taken by John Calvin and Charles Hodge.

The result of the identification with Christ is that the believer can now say that the body of sin, as such, does not exist. The guilt of sin is no longer upon the believer and he is free from sin's claim. The purpose of the identification with Christ is the emancipation of the body from sin's legal claim. The believer serves sin no more in his actual daily life. Hopkins writes, "The fact is always in Christ. Then comes the faith in you, and the experience follows."[75] He continues, "Your experience is not a fact. Faith cannot rest upon that which does not exist. The fact is in Christ. You died with Christ, and this body which sin has claimed and used has ceased to exist, as such, and now you need not serve sin."[76]

The actual experience of freedom from sin comes by appropriating the truth. It is by faith, by the reckoning of faith. Hopkins asserts that by the claiming of faith the privilege of freedom from sin's authority has been secured to the believer in virtue of Christ's death, and in virtue of the believer's identification with that death. Hopkins illustrates the difference between the legal and actual freedom of man:

> In America the Deed of Emancipation which set free millions of slaves was first executed before a single slave could know practically what freedom meant.... The news came to him that the Deed of Emancipation had been executed. But he is still in bondage; he is under the power of a cruel master. It is not a question of struggling out of his power, but of simply claiming his right. He is legally set free; by faith he claims that privilege; then comes the practical experience.[77]

Sanctification is grounded on that which is true of all believers—their identification with Christ in his death to sin.

In Keswick's view the ground of sanctification is not realized until the believer claims it by reckoning faith. So there is the possibility of losing this wonderful blessing forever unless one appropriates it by going through the reckoning process. Thus, Keswick makes sanctification ultimately dependent on man.

---

75. Hopkins, "Our Old Man," 175.
76. Hopkins, "Our Old Man," 175.
77. Hopkins, "Our Old Man," 175–76.

Agent of Sanctification

For Keswick, the Holy Spirit is the agent of sanctification whereas the cross of Christ is the ground of sanctification. It is the Holy Spirit who makes the work of Christ true in the believer's practical life. Just knowing the theological knowledge of union with Christ and freedom from the dominion of sin is not enough to achieve sanctification. This freedom is only potential in the believer. The potential has to become a reality in the believer's life. The Holy Spirit works in the believer to accomplish this purpose. Keswick thus teaches that Christ is our sanctification and the Holy Spirit is our sanctifier. Barabas writes, "Unless the Holy Spirit is given His rightful place in the life of the Christian, then even though historically and judicially he was crucified with Christ, the experience of the 'wretched man' in Romans 7 will be the result."[78]

In sanctification, the work of the Holy Spirit is always built upon the work of Christ. The cross of Christ is foundational for the work of the Holy Spirit. The Holy Spirit works in the believer in order for him to experience the freedom from the dominion of sin, the truth that has been accomplished by the work of Christ. The work of the Holy Spirit in sanctification is never separated from the cross of Christ. Christ purchased for the believer the freedom from sin's dominion and the Holy Spirit imparts the freedom to the believer.

Reformed theologians also have been teaching that the Holy Spirit is the agent of sanctification. However, the Spirit's involvement in sanctification as the agent does not mean that there is no struggle in sanctification for the believer. Keswick tends to interpret the spiritual struggle in sanctification as a defeat in the Christian life.

Keswick also teaches that the principle of counteraction is God's method of sanctification in the believer. It means that the work of the Holy Spirit in sanctification is counteraction, not suppression or eradication. It is seen in Romans 7 that the "law of sin" is working in the believer. The only way to be free from the law of sin is to counteract this negative drive with the more powerful positive force such that the positive force rules the life of the believer. This positive force in the believer is the law of the Spirit of life in Christ Jesus. Keswick advocates frequently go to Romans 8:2 to support this view, "because through Christ Jesus the law of the Spirit who gives life has set you free from the law of sin and death." Griffith Thomas illustrates this principle, "If I drop this book, by the law of gravitation it falls, but as it falls I put forth my hand and catch it and stop it from falling. That is to say,

---

78. Barabas, *So Great Salvation*, 94.

the lower law of gravitation is counteracted by the higher law of my will, and the book does not fall to the ground."[79]

Keswick asserts that the law of sin is always operative in our life and is never eradicated. The deliverance of the believer from the law of sin comes by the law of the Spirit of life which counteracts the law of sin with a mightier force. The power of the law of the Spirit of life is just as real as the law of sin in the believer's life but is mightier than the drive of the law of sin. Robert McQuilkin writes about his experience concerning this teaching:

> I realized that in myself I was as weak as ever. There were the same desires, the same temptations, the same possibility of sin—nay, the certainty of sin, apart from the grace of the LORD. But this new secret was that I could look to the LORD in faith and expect a power not my own to take hold and give victory, as I yielded and trusted him.[80]

The principle of counteraction by the Holy Spirit against the law of sin is one of the fundamental teachings of Keswick. It is also different from the Reformed teaching of eradication by the Holy Spirit in the believer. Keswick advocates then are in a dilemma as to whether the law of sin is to be eliminated in glorification or the believer goes into the presence of God with the law of sin in him. They would choose the former, in which case they need to explain why the eradication of the law of sin takes place only in glorification when the Holy Spirit has been working in the believer just the same way throughout the life. In asserting this view, Keswick implies that there is no inherent change in the believer in the process of sanctification throughout the life. This is one of the weakest doctrines of Keswick.

Limits of Sanctification

Are there limits of sanctification for the believer in the present life? Keswick advocates seem to reply "yes" to this question. Alexander Smellie says, "Our answer to the query must be, Never so far as absolute sinlessness, till even sin in us is eradicated and destroyed, till within and without we wear only the spotless glory of the Son of God; never to that ultimate end beyond which nothing remains to be coveted."[81]

According to Keswick, sanctification is perfect from God's side, but there will be imperfect holiness in the believer because of the imperfect

---

79. Thomas, *Victorious Life*, 40.
80. R. C. McQuilkin, "Victory in Christ," 608.
81. Smellie, *Lift up Your Heart*, 90.

receptivity of a fallen man. The believer can experience a continual emancipation from the dominion of sin by the power of the Spirit, but he is not yet delivered from sin's presence. He still has to reckon with the flesh everyday. "He no longer lives in the sphere of the flesh, but the flesh is in him, and just so far as its 'infection' is there, he needs every moment the conquering counteraction of the Holy Spirit."[82]

Barabas asserts that Keswick does not teach perfectionism. He argues that the believer even in sanctification is under the possibility of falling into temptation or of committing sin. He writes, "It is not taught that the believer's crucifixion with Christ implies that sin is dead or that it is eradicated. It *is* taught that in Christ he is brought positionally into such a relationship to sin that he is beyond the reach of sin's dominion and lordship."[83] Thus, it seems that according to Keswick the believer may be potentially perfect but is not perfect in his practical life. But Barabas continues and seems to give an inconclusive answer to this discussion, "If he walks in the Spirit that which is positional may be made experimental."[84] Thus, on the limits of sanctification, Keswick teaches on the one hand that the believer is not perfect in holiness in the present life, but on the other hand, that there is possibility of achieving perfect holiness in this life.

Faith

For Keswick, faith is the key to appropriating God's provision for a powerful Christian life. Faith is the difference between a powerless and a powerful Christian life. In studying Keswick's teaching on sanctification, it is important to study its view of faith which Keswick advocates believe acts as the switch which releases the current of divine power in the believer's life.

Definition of Faith

In defining faith, J. Robertson McQuilkin cites Charles Hodge's statement, "Faith is the persuasion of truth founded on testimony." Here the persuasion is based on the evidence of testimony. In the case of Scripture, the evidence of testimony includes the testimony of the prophets and the apostles. The evidence of testimony along with the work of the Holy Spirit compels acceptance. J. Robertson McQuilkin writes, "Faith is a miraculous

---

82. Barabas, *So Great Salvation*, 100.
83. Barabas, *So Great Salvation*, 100.
84. Barabas, *So Great Salvation*, 100.

gift that confirms the evidence and even carries one beyond the evidence if necessary."[85]

For Keswick, faith is both the gift of God and man's responsibility. Man must respond in obedience to God's word in order to receive his blessings. So, from the perspective of man, faith is a willing choice of man to commit himself to God. McQuilkin gives the practical definition of faith for the purpose of Keswick's teaching, "Faith is a choice to commit all of oneself unconditionally to the person of God, who is revealed in the Bible and witnessed to by the Holy Spirit."[86] Although Keswick's definition of faith is generally correct, Keswick advocates seem to prefer a practical definition over a theological definition in relation to sanctification.

Faith as Means of Sanctification

Keswick teaches that sanctification comes by faith. The believer believes certain divine truth; he believes and acts upon it; then the truth becomes reality in his daily life. Sanctification becomes reality in the believer's life only through faith. Trumbull writes, "The final secret of victory . . . is not in praying for it, but in taking it by faith. There is a great deal of prayer in the life of victory; but we can pray, and pray, and pray, and not have victory."[87]

Keswick advocates claim that the faith they teach here is not the same as quietism. It is not effortless passivity. The believer has an abundant work to do in praying, self-examination, confession, studying God's word, and many other sacred ordinances. The believer is actively involved in sanctification by exercising faith in God.

But the active participation of the believer in sanctification does not mean that sanctification is achieved by his own works. Rather, God requires a complete surrender of the believer before exercising faith. Surrender is defined by Keswick as follows:

> It is . . . a complete yielding, loosening, relaxing; a falling in conscious and gladly acknowledged helplessness at the feet of Jesus Christ, and asking him to finish the even then incomplete work of surrender by putting us completely to death, crucifying us with himself, and then replacing our wrecked, helpless, worthless, dead self with himself, so that hereafter Christ shall

---

85. J. R. McQuilkin, "Keswick Perspective," 168.
86. J. R. McQuilkin, "Keswick Perspective," 169.
87. Trumbull, "Faith," 104.

be literally and personally our life as well as our Master and our Saviour.[88]

Surrender must be fulfilled by the faith of the believer in order to experience the victorious Christian life. Keswick uses the "let go" for surrender and the "let God" for faith in pursuing the holiness.

Although Keswick advocates here try very hard to separate itself from both quietism and sanctification by works, they inevitably falls into both of them. Keswick's concept of the "let go" for surrender means that you don't do anything, which is identical to passivity and quietism. Also, Keswick's concept of "let God" for faith means that you make sure God does it for you which is the same as sanctification by man's work.

Activities of Faith

In Keswick's teaching about faith two activities of faith are emphasized. First, faith requires a conscious and continuous looking to Christ as one's holiness. The conscious and continuous looking to Christ involves an occupation with Christ, his person and his work completely in one's Christian life. Christ is the proper object of faith. For such a person, Christ is not the only the source of the victorious life but also the life itself. Griffith Thomas asserts:

> I am not a prophet nor the son of a prophet, but I will make bold to prophesy this morning that if you and I are occupied each day with the LORD Jesus Christ we shall never become degenerate. If we live on what we learned yesterday or the day before about Jesus Christ we shall find it will not last, but if every day we are occupied with the Person and work of Christ we shall not only not go back but shall go forward.[89]

As the believer exercises a complete trust in Christ, he experiences what Keswick teaches is "the rest of faith." Andrew Murray explains this concept, "Faith is always repose in what another will do for me. Faith ceases to seek help in itself or its efforts, to be troubled with its need or its weakness; it rests in the sufficiency of the all-sufficient One who has undertaken all."[90] Faith then turns into a passive resting from the active seeking.

Keswick, in this way, sees faith as involving both active seeking and passivity rather than perceiving it as a gift of God. For Keswick, a certain amount

88. Trumbull, "Let Go," 442.
89. Thomas, "Christ," 142.
90. A. Murray, *Holiest*, 144.

of active seeking of faith is necessary in order to go into the "resting" stage of faith. The reason Keswick advocates separate faith into two elements in a temporal sequence is that they seek to emphasize the notion of a "resting faith." However, it would inevitably promote passivity and quietism.

The second activity of faith involves "the principle of reckoning." It is based on Paul's letter to the Romans 6:11, "In the same way, count(reckon) yourselves dead to sin but alive to God in Christ Jesus." The important word for Keswick here is "reckoning." It means to count, compute, and calculate. So the principle of reckoning involves taking God at his word. W. H. Aldis explains:

> We begin with the assumption that God is able and willing to meet our every need according to His riches in glory by Christ Jesus; and we act upon that assumption, and regard it as a word eternal truth. Unless we are prepared to do this, we shall find little joy in thinking of God's provision for cleansing equipment, and we shall always be in danger of regarding such truths as ideals which are beyond our attainment. Consequently, at every stage of the pilgrimage, we must learn to say: "LORD, I believe; help Thou my unbelief."[91]

The principle of reckoning operates in the believer's identification with Christ. The believer's identification with Christ is taught in Romans 6:4, "We were therefore buried with him through baptism into death in order that, just as Christ was raised from the dead through the glory of the Father, we too may live a new life." Because the believer is united by faith to the LORD Jesus and reconciled to God through him, he has been crucified to sin and raised with him in newness of life. This is the heart of the reckoning process. Aldis explains:

> By faith, the believer is enabled to see that through the death of Christ he has been delivered completely from the penalty of sin; but he is enabled to see, also, that through his identification with Christ in that death he is delivered from the power of sin as a ruling principle, and is enabled to live a victorious life in the mighty energy of the Resurrection.[92]

Thus, Keswick teaches that death to sin and being alive to God must be reckoned by faith in the believer in order for him to enter into the victorious Christian life.

---

91. Aldis, *Message of Keswick*, 51.
92. Aldis, *Message of Keswick*, 54–55.

Keswick seems to teach that the believer needs something more than faith to achieve sanctification. Keswick teaches that reckoning involves a superior faith—the faith which is supposedly better than the ordinary faith a believer exercises every day—in order to achieve sanctification. There is no biblical support for the teaching that sanctification involves reckoning faith while other elements in the *ordo salutis* involve something less than this faith.

Consecration

Consecration is an important part of Keswick's teaching in promoting practical holiness. At Keswick conventions believers, having accepted Jesus Christ as Savior, are exhorted to make a complete surrender to the master and crown him as the LORD. This is the dedication of the self to God. Aldis says that dedication is the act of the believer whereas consecration is the act of God.[93] Thus, from man's point of view, consecration involves dedication and full surrender of the self. And God consecrates what one is willing to dedicate. In the study of consecration taught by Keswick, the nature and effect of consecration in Keswick's teaching are presented.

Nature of Consecration

According to Keswick, consecration involves the dedication and full surrender of the self to God. The nature of consecration involves three elements: taking Jesus as LORD, crisis and process, and absolute surrender.

First, Keswick teaches that in order to enter into consecration one must accept Jesus not only as savior but also as the LORD. Jesus Christ is first our savior and then our LORD, our master. In order to achieve sanctification through consecration the believer needs to accept Jesus Christ as his LORD, the master of his life, as well as his savior. There is a place in man's heart that is called a "throne," which is the center of control of man's life. Someone always occupies this place. It may be the self or it may be the Christ. Until man turns this place of throne over to Christ man occupies the throne as the master of his life. Receiving Jesus Christ as the LORD means that man yields this throne to Christ as he lets him occupy the place of the throne as the LORD and master to rule his life. Evan Hopkins explains this teaching:

> This wonderful little world within us, the realm of thought, of desire, of volition—you cannot manage it. If you try to manage yourself, you have confusion, conflict, chaos, anarchy. There is

---

93. Aldis, *Message of Keswick*, 63.

only One that can bring peace into that little kingdom, and that is the Prince of peace, the Christ; and to sanctify Christ as LORD is to enthrone Him as King. He is to be the Master of your whole life. He is to make your place and mark out your future.[94]

Keswick here is making sanctification a second blessing in salvation. Keswick advocates teach that man is saved by receiving Jesus Christ as savior, but he needs to go further in receiving him as the LORD in order to achieve sanctification. However, Jesus Christ cannot be separated into the savior and LORD in the believer's life. He is always the savior and LORD for the believer. Keswick advocates here make a serious error in teaching that man may be saved in a partial salvation which does not include the blessing of sanctification.

The second element of the nature of consecration is crisis and process. Is sanctification a single act or a continual process? Keswick attempts to give an answer to this question by the crisis and process approach to sanctification. It is commonly said by Keswick advocates that sanctification is a process beginning with a crisis. The sense of the all-sufficient grace of Christ comes to the believer instantaneously. But it is followed by an experience of progressive growth in the spiritual life. Evan Hopkins describes this teaching:

> Sanctification in the sense of conformity to the life and character of Christ is a process, a gradual process, a continuous process, an endless process. But sanctification, in the sense of a definite decision for holiness, a thorough and whole-hearted dedication to God, the committal of the whole being to Him, is a crisis; and the crisis must take place before we really know the process. Before you can draw a line you must begin with a point. The line is a process, the point is the crisis.[95]

Thus, for Keswick, consecration is both crisis and process. The process succeeds the crisis. It is important to know what Keswick means by "crisis" in order to understand Keswick's view of consecration. Crisis "refers to the decision by which a believer commits himself wholly to his LORD, pledging himself henceforth to be obedient unto him in all things; a decision which initiates, not the process of sanctification, for that began at regeneration, but sanctification in real earnest."[96] Crisis removes that which hinders sanctification as a normal process. It is like the removal of rocks which hinder a natural flow of

---

94. Hopkins, "Christ Our LORD," 267.
95. Hopkins, "Crisis and Process," 332.
96. Barabas, *So Great Salvation*, 115.

water. Whenever crisis occurs, it marks a turning-point in the believer's life. It can be either climactic or gradual in one's Christian life. For some people, it is a climax comparable to the crisis of regeneration. For others, on the other hand, it is a gradual yielding to God's rule.[97]

Keswick's insistence that crisis precedes process in sanctification is critical to their teaching. In other words, according to Keswick, one cannot have a genuine progressive sanctification without having the crisis first in his life. While Keswick has a notion of process sanctification, it actually treats crisis sanctification as a superior sanctification. Also, Keswick's implication that believers who have not had a crisis are not in a genuine process sanctification, should be dismissed totally. Keswick's teaching here eventually leads to promoting a spiritual pride among believers. Is the crisis to be repeated? Keswick answers affirmatively to this question. Crisis is to be repeated in the believer's life in a twofold sense. To those who slipped back, it is to be repeated in the sense of restoration. To other believers it is to be repeated in the sense of confirmation. Hopkins construes:

> "In that sense I did give myself wholly to the LORD yesterday, or last week, and now I discover fresh things, and pass them on at once, immediately." In that sense the crisis is repeated—but it is an act of confirmation. See that, every morning, and every day, and many times during the day, you can say, "Amen" to the fact that you have handed yourself wholly to Him. In that sense it is repeated, and you need not backslide in order to do it over again.[98]

Therefore, one can have the first, second, third, and even n^{th} crisis in his Christian life.

The logical consequence of the promotion of the crisis sanctification by Keswick is n^{th} crisis sanctification. What Keswick has to admit eventually is that the more the crises, the better the sanctification of the believer. It would be ideal for the believer to have continuous crises in his life, which would theoretically give him a higher sanctification in a shorter time by eliminating the slow process of progressive sanctification. So Keswick's teaching turns into a theory which bears absurdity and nonsense.

Third, Keswick also teaches that the nature of consecration involves an absolute surrender of the self to God. It means that we and all that we

---

97. Keswick does not precisely define a crisis theologically. Some argue that every vicissitude in the Christian life may be taken as a crisis. In this sense Keswick's description of crisis is relative. Although Keswick does not have the absolute scale to distinguish the "real" crises, it seems that Keswick's view of crisis is a situation in which a believer is completely depleted of his human strength and resources such that his only hope is the complete surrender of himself to God.

98. Hopkins, "Crisis and Process," 337.

have are God's. W. H. Aldis comments, "That is a full, unreserved consecration. It means everything: my lips, my hands, my feet, my time, my talents, my thoughts, my money, my property, my heart, my will, my all."[99] This absolute surrender is not without a price. It takes the sacrifice of one's life. Aldis continues, "Beloved, it must be costly; it may mean the reversal of all the plans that you have for your life—I do not know—but it is going to be a costly thing if we come to this full and absolute surrender and consecration to our LORD."[100]

Although what Keswick teaches on this point is generally true, Keswick's meaning of an absolute surrender is ambiguous. Can anyone render an absolute surrender of himself to God? Keswick's meaning of the absolute surrender is vague and the standard of the absolute surrender is arbitrary. Even if man is able to give an absolute surrender to God, the ensuing question would be, "Does God use only the men who give absolute surrender to him?" We think not. Scripture clearly shows that God uses all believers although the magnitude and degree of usefulness may be different from person to person.

Effect of Consecration

The effect of full consecration is that the believer now has the solid ground to experience sanctification as a process. Through consecration the believer goes into the position where progressive sanctification is possible to a degree that it has never been attainable before. Keswick advocates often describe consecration as the adjustment of a spiritual dislocation that is responsible for hindering the progress of sanctification. Barabas illustrates, "A man may be an excellent runner, but if a bone is out of joint or if he is out of condition, he can never win a race. So if a Christian's will is out of adjustment with the will of God, he will be so crippled that he cannot make any spiritual progress."[101] So, consecration is an adjustment of a spiritual condition. Having adjusted the spiritual condition, one has an open path for progressive sanctification.

Having removed the hindrances to sanctification, the believer's faith will grow exceedingly experiencing a fullness and richness of the promises of God. His heart will be filled with gladness for God's word which becomes fresh to him. His mouth will be filled with praise because Christ has become most precious to him. Thus, Keswick teaches that the believer comes out of

99. Aldis, "Surrender," 292–93.
100. Aldis, "Surrender," 293.
101. Barabas, *So Great Salvation*, 121.

the subnormal or abnormal progressive sanctification into the accelerated progressive sanctification.

Spirit-Filled Life

The message of the Spirit-filled life is the central theme of Keswick's teaching. The Spirit-filled life affords the believer a "sense of nearness, of childlike confidence, of constant and entire dependence on the LORD."[102] Hopkins makes the distinction between being "full of" and being "filled with" the Spirit. He explains, "The first indicates an abiding or habitual condition, the latter a special inspiration or illapse—a momentary action or impulse of the Spirit for service, at particular occasions."[103] The fullness of the Spirit denotes the abiding characteristic—men who have been filled with and are habitually full of the Holy Spirit. The filling of the Spirit points to a sudden impulse for a special occasion. "The 'fillings' come just when God sees they are needed; and then it is that the soul overflows with those 'rivers of living water' which our LORD declared should be the characteristic of Pentecostal days."[104] Keswick asserts that to be filled with the Spirit is not an optional matter for the believer but is an obligation that rests upon all believers. In this section, four topics about the Spirit-filled life are presented: the nature of the blessing, the subjects of the blessing, the way to obtain the blessing, and the result of the blessing.

The Nature of The Blessing

Keswick acknowledges that all Christians have the Holy Spirit. Evan Hopkins asserts, "All Christians have the Holy Spirit. They have not only been brought under His influence, they have received the Holy Spirit Himself. 'If any man have[sic] not the Spirit of Christ, he is none of His' (Rom. 8:9)."[105] Barabas repudiates the accusation that Keswick teaches the baptism of the Spirit as a second blessing subsequent to regeneration. He asserts, "The gift of the Spirit, or the baptism of the Spirit, is not, therefore, a blessing which the believer is to seek and receive subsequent to his experience of conversion."[106]

---

102. Hopkins, *Law of Liberty*, 118.
103. Hopkins, *Law of Liberty*, 117.
104. Hopkins, *Law of Liberty*, 119.
105. Hopkins, *Law of Liberty*, 116.
106. Barabas, *So Great Salvation*, 131.

Keswick emphasizes that to have the Spirit is not the same as being filled with the Spirit. While every Christian has the Spirit, not every one of them is filled with the Spirit. "To be filled with the Spirit means the complete possession and guidance of the believer by the Spirit."[107] Not every Christian claims to have had this experience. Evan Hopkins cites the Gospel of John to highlight this point, "We know from what is recorded in St. John's Gospel (20:22) that even before the Ascension the Holy Ghost had actually been given to the disciples, that Christ breathed upon them the Holy Ghost. But on the day of Pentecost they were filled with the Holy Ghost."[108]

Keswick's position on this point is ambiguous. It first denies a second blessing subsequent to regeneration, but then it shows the filling with Holy Spirit as a subsequent blessing to regeneration. Keswick tries to separate itself from the Wesleyan view of the second blessing, but it does not fully succeed.

According to Keswick, the Spirit-filled life is taught in the New Testament as the normal condition of the believer. It is not a special experience reserved only for a few privileged believers. The Spirit-filled life is needed for living a normal consistent Christian life. Barabas clarifies this point:

> A Spirit-filled Christian will not necessarily be used of God to perform miracles in the realm of nature or to do spectacular things in the realm of the Spirit, but he will lead a normal, consistent Christian life; and without the Spirit that would be impossible. In such a life God is in full control, and is thus able to work out His purposes.[109]

According to Keswick, all believers must be filled with the Spirit in order to live the victorious and powerful life God intended for them to live. It is often said by Keswick advocates that the experience of the fullness of the Spirit is emphasized not in order to work miracles, but to make Christians a living miracle.

The fullness of the Spirit, according to Keswick, is a definite experience. The experience of the fullness of the Spirit may be separable from regeneration, but not necessarily separated from it. One may experience regeneration and the fullness of the Spirit simultaneously whereas others may receive the fullness of the Spirit after regeneration. For many believers, there are varying intervals between regeneration and the reception of the fullness of the Spirit. These believers are encouraged by Keswick advocates to obtain the fullness of the Spirit as soon as possible after regeneration.

---

107. Barabas, *So Great Salvation*, 132.
108. Hopkins, *Law of Liberty*, 116.
109. Barabas, *So Great Salvation*, 133.

A modification of the Wesleyan view of the second blessing is seen in Keswick's teaching here. Wesleyan perfectionism says that every believer needs to have the second blessing whereas Keswick teaches that only those who have not had the experience of the fullness of the Spirit with regeneration need to have the second blessing. Therefore, while Keswick advocates deny that they teach a second blessing subsequent to regeneration, it becomes apparent that their teaching clearly involves the second blessing to some believers.

Keswick also teaches that, unlike regeneration, the reception of the fullness of the Spirit is not a once-for-all experience. One may lose this blessing by disobedience, unfaithfulness, rebellion or other ungodly characteristics. If one loses the blessing of the fullness of the Spirit, it may be restored by a new yielding of the life to the Spirit. Thus, one may have many succeeding infillings of the Spirit throughout his Christian life. Barabas writes, "The fulness of the Spirit must be a continuous experience, and new fillings may be had time and time again as new needs arise. Not only is there a second blessing, but a third, and a fourth, and so on, as long as life shall last."[110] In order to live a victorious life, the fullness of the Spirit "must be maintained with diligence, by watchfulness, prayer, and obedience." Keswick teaches that one can have as many experiences of the fullness of the Spirit as the crises in life. In Keswick's teaching, the experience of the filling of the Spirit is closely tied to crisis sanctification.

The Subjects of the Blessing

The fullness of the Spirit is for every believer. It is not for a select few such as ministers and missionaries. God desires to fill every believer with the fullness of the Spirit. But certain conditions as described in consecration have to be met before this blessing becomes a reality in the believer's life. It is an obligation for every believer to be filled with the Spirit of God. A real, normal Christian life is impossible without this experience.

In asserting this point, Keswick presupposes that the believer who has not had the fullness of the Spirit lives a subnormal Christian life. Keswick invents two kinds of Christians out of those who believe in Christ.

The Way to Obtain the Blessing

Perhaps the most important question asked by those who seek holiness is how one can be filled with the Spirit. Evan Hopkins delineates three steps

---

110. Barabas, *So Great Salvation*, 136.

that one can follow in order to be filled with the Spirit. First, the believer needs to recognize that he has the Spirit. He needs to realize that he is the temple of God. Referring to 1 Corinthians 3:16 "Don't you know that you yourselves are God's temple and that God's Spirit dwells in your midst?," Hopkins writes, "Let us begin where God would have us begin: recognize that fact. It is a grand thing to stand upon God's facts."[111]

Second, the believer needs to put every evil thing away from him. "All untruthfulness, all evil tempers and dispositions, all dishonesty, all impurity of thought or word and all evil speaking" must be put away just like a man takes off his coat and puts it away. All the evil habits must be rooted out of the believer's life in order to be filled with the Spirit. Hopkins further explains, "We heard this morning about the sycamore tree, and it was taken to indicate an unforgiving spirit. It had to be rooted out, and evil habits have to be rooted out, absolutely rooted out. The LORD can do it."[112] He exhorts the believers again, "Put away from you, therefore, every evil thing. You want the fulness of the Spirit. Well, now, this is God's way. We have to clear the way."[113]

Third, the believer needs to praise and thank God that he has done it. He needs to realize this blessing not through feeling but through faith. God gives him faith through which he realizes that he is filled with the Spirit. "God says, 'Now I give you believing instead of feeling'—and you have to begin to believe that He has done it. Now praise Him; go away from this tent praising Him. By and by you will find that it begins to work, that it is a reality."[114]

Keswick thus provides practical steps for believers to experience the fullness of the Holy Spirit. The believer can be filled with the Spirit simply by following the prescribed steps Keswick lays out for him. For Keswick, there is nothing mysterious about being filled with the Spirit. Just by following Keswick's practical steps it would give the believer the experience of being filled with the Spirit. Therefore, Keswick makes the fullness of the Spirit a man-made experience in the believer's life.

The Result of the Blessing

The result of being filled with the Spirit is the victorious Christian life. Having been filled with the Spirit, the believer now can live the victorious life

---

111. Hopkins, "Fulness of the Spirit," 461.
112. Hopkins, "Fulness of the Spirit," 462.
113. Hopkins, "Fulness of the Spirit," 463.
114. Hopkins, "Fulness of the Spirit," 464.

God intends for him to live. The victorious lfe of the believer is seen in three aspects of his life. First, in relation to God he lives an obedient life. He is fully committed to God's will and his work. Second, in relation to himself he has inner joy because he is consistently victorious over sin. His words and deeds are holy and powerful empowered by the Holy Spirit. Third, he has love toward everybody and has a burning desire to witness to unbelievers. The love he possesses is so broad and deep that it touches the hearts of many people. The victorious life is a desire of every believer. Keswick claims to make this desire within easy reach of every believer.

Conclusion

Keswick's brief history, method, and teachings have been presented in this chapter. Keswick started in the British Isles, however, its genesis is owed much to the American evangelists, Mr. and Mrs. Robert Pearsall Smith. In the early twentieth century, Robert McQuilkin started organized Keswick meetings in America. Keswick attracted many Christians from various denominations as it tried to combine the Wesleyan and Calvinistic teachings in its doctrines. Keswick's method was also unique in that it tried to cure the "spiritual disease" of the believer by following its own prescribed practical steps.

But what was most important about Keswick was its teaching on sanctification and the way to achieve it. Barabas provided the definitive presentation of Keswick's teaching. Evan Hopkins, often called the theologian of Keswick, and other Keswick advocates also presented Keswick's important doctrines.

Keswick gave six ways to define sin. In Keswick's definition of sin, we saw Keswick's attempt to combine Wesleyan teachings with Reformed doctrines. While sin was in one sense defined as an offense against God, it was also defined as a spiritual disease in the soul. Keswick also differentiated between carnal and spiritual Christians. Keswick focused on carnal Christians, especially insipid and defeated Christians, who should have experienced Keswick's sanctification in order to become spiritual Christians.

In sanctification Keswick displayed the "wrong" and "right" ways of achieving sanctification. Keswick advocates showed that regarding sanctification as a matter of course, regarding sanctification as a gradual process, regarding sanctification as gained through suppression of the old nature, and regarding sanctification as being gained through active Christian service are "wrong" ways of achieving sanctification. In asserting Keswick's way of sanctification, they explicated the aspects, elements, ground, agent, and limits of sanctification. Though some elements of Keswick's teaching on these subjects sound orthodox and Reformed, much of Keswick's teaching was connected to Wesleyan Arminian teachings. Keswick's sanctification emphasized crisis sanctification. In emphasizing crisis sanctification, it made progressive sanctification inferior to crisis sanctification.

What is important in Keswick's teaching is that Keswick advocates did not deny progressive sanctification. They presented another aspect of sanctification, crisis sanctification. Thus, Keswick came back with this subtle teaching after Charles Finney's perfectionism was severely criticized by B. B. Warfield and other Reformed theologians from the primarily progressive aspect of sanctification.

On the teaching of faith, Keswick advocates assumed a posture of passivity and quietism. And on the subject of consecration, they denied a second blessing subsequent to regeneration in spite of its insistence of the necessity of this blessing for some believers. What Keswick eventually ended up with was more than a second blessing, the nth degree blessing of the believer. They also made the experience of the fullness of the Holy Spirit a mandatory experience for every believer. In asserting this point Keswick differentiated believers into normal and subnormal categories of Christians.

It has been seen in this chapter that Keswick's doctrines do not appear outrageously Pelagian as Charles Finney's perfectionism. Many of the perfectionists' teachings have been modified by Keswick advocates, such that its teaching is sometimes called mild Calvinism. But only the appearance of Keswick's teaching looks Calvinistic while their teaching is really rooted in Wesleyan Arminianism with certain Pelagian elements sprinkled in.

Keswick's Calvinistic and the Reformed appearance of its theology attracted many Christians from the Presbyterian and Reformed churches in America in the early twentieth century. A critical and theological evaluation of Keswick's teaching by a Reformed theologian was called for. John Murray took the task of evaluating Keswick's teaching on sanctification in an effort to render a Reformed response to this offspring of the holiness movement in America. His task was to respond to Keswick's sanctification not only from the progressive aspect but also from the definitive aspect of sanctification, thus rendering a fully balanced approach to the doctrine of sanctification.

Chapter 6

John Murray's Response to Keswick's Sanctification

THE ORGANIZED FORM OF Keswick's teaching was presented by Barabas in his book *So Great Salvation*, in 1952. Upon the publication of the book, John Murray, then a professor of systematic theology at Westminster Theological Seminary, penned the first Reformed response to Barabas's book in the form of a book review in 1953. In a seven-page book review, Murray evaluated Keswick's teaching on sanctification as presented in its definitive form by Barabas. He examined the book and presented the strengths and weaknesses of Keswick's teaching on sanctification.

In this chapter, John Murray's evaluation of Keswick's sanctification documented in *So Great Salvation* is presented in the first part followed by Murray's formulation of the doctrine of definitive sanctification in the second part. For definitive sanctification, the historical background of formulation, explication, and importance of the doctrine are presented in detail. Definitive sanctification serves as the Murray's alternative position to Keswick's teaching on the immediate aspect of sanctification in the believer's life.

John Murray's Evaluation of Keswick's Sanctification

Murray's seven-page book review of Barabas's *So Great Salvation* in the *Westminster Theological Journal* is more like a medium-size article than a short book review. In this book review he presents the strengths followed by the weaknesses of Keswick's teaching on sanctification. He lists Keswick's strengths in three categories and the weaknesses in five categories.

Commendations of Keswick's Teaching

Murray begins the commendations of Keswick's teaching by stating that "certain emphases which Keswick propounds call for special commendatory mention."[1] He explains:

> Keswick has evinced a renewed appreciation of the implications for *sanctification* of the union of the believer with Christ. In this respect Romans 6 may be said to be the key passage, and Keswick has focused attention on the once-for-allness of the victory over sin secured for the believer in virtue of his union with Christ in the efficacy of his death and power of his resurrection.[2]

In his book, Barabas underscores the importance of the believer's union with Christ for sanctification, "When the Holy Spirit, on the condition of faith, baptizes a man into Christ and joins him permanently and eternally to Him, he becomes a man 'in Christ,' in union both with the person and the work of Christ. . . . He is identified with Christ in His death, in His resurrection unto new life in God."[3]

On the teaching of sanctification Barabas especially focuses on Romans 6 for its importance on this subject. For him it is *the* chapter in Scripture for the doctrine of sanctification. He contends:

> The place in the New Testament where the truth of the believer's identification with Christ in His death and resurrection is most clearly set forth is the sixth chapter of Romans. It would not be possible, I think, to exaggerate the importance of this chapter for the doctrine of sanctification. It has rightly been called the Magna Charta of the soul and the Emancipation Proclamation of the Christian.[4]

It may be admitted that American Reformed theologians have not given due consideration to Romans 6 in their treatment of the doctrine of sanctification. For example, Charles Hodge in his *Systematic Theology* has only two references in passing to Romans 6 on the subject of sanctification.[5] Barabas expresses his amazement at this finding:

> It is astonishing that theologians have not seen this, and have passed by the chapter almost as though it did not exist. One

---

1. Murray, Review of *So Great Salvation*, 79.
2. Murray, Review of *So Great Salvation*, 79.
3. Barabas, *So Great Salvation*, 103–4.
4. Barabas, *So Great Salvation*, 104.
5. C. Hodge, *Systematic Theology*, 3:227–28.

has only to examine the sections on "sanctification" in the systematic theologies of such standard theologians as Charles Hodge, William Shedd, Henry B. Smith, J. J. Van Oosterzee, and Louis Berkhof to see that they make scarcely any reference to it. This is really astonishing! Only since Keswick first called attention to the vital significance of this chapter to the whole question of sin and sanctification have theologians even begun to give it its proper place.[6]

While it is not fair to say that the theologians mentioned above made scarcely any reference to Romans 6 since Berkhof made more than half a dozen references and Charles Hodge two references to that chapter, it is acknowledged that the full import and magnitude of the teaching in Romans 6 on sanctification have not been fully propounded by them.

Murray commends Keswick for bringing out the importance of Romans 6 for the once-for-all aspect of sanctification. He especially notes Keswick's focus on the believer's union with Christ for its implications for sanctification. It may be said here that Keswick's focus on Romans 6 for sanctification not only elicited a commendation from Murray but also played an important instrumental role for the formulation of his doctrine of definitive sanctification as the response to Keswick's sanctification in later years.

A second commendation of Keswick by Murray is that "Keswick recognizes that sanctification is a process in connection with which the believer's responsibility is to be fully exercised."[7] In promoting practical holiness Keswick teaches the gradual and continuous process of sanctification which entails the exercise of the believer's responsibility. In the gradual aspect of sanctification, Keswick affirms the active participation of the believer in the process. For this emphasis Murray commends Keswick's teaching on sanctification.

However, another side of Keswick's teaching on sanctification needs to be brought out before a commendation is given to this part of Keswick's teaching without qualification. Keswick also teaches the passivity of the believer for sanctification. This characteristic of the believer in sanctification is expressed in such terms as "let go" and "surrender" as shown in the previous chapter. While Keswick's emphasis on the passivity of the believer for sanctification cannot exactly be termed as a traditional quietism, it cannot escape from the camp of quietism in the broader sense. Keswick's brand of quietism has the believer in full control of the process

---

6. Barabas, *So Great Salvation*, 104.
7. Murray, Review of *So Great Salvation*, 79.

but everything regarding sanctification was done for him. J. I. Packer aptly brings out this point:

> If I do anything to defeat sin, sin will defeat me; but if I do nothing beyond appealing to the Spirit to defeat it for me, instantaneous victory is assured. The Spirit's work of repelling the assaults of sin in my heart is thus *vicarious* in exactly the same sense as was Christ's work of bearing the penalty of sin on His cross. In each case what I was bound to do is done in my stead by Another, and in each case my cooperation is absolutely excluded. This is express quietism, but it differs from other forms of quietism in that the whole process is represented as being under my control.[8]

Third, Murray commends Keswick for stressing the importance of the work and presence of the Holy Spirit, "There is the recognition of, indeed constant stress upon, the work and presence of the Holy Spirit in the heart and life of the believer; the 'Spirit-filled life' is the 'central, dominating theme of the Convention.'"[9] It is a fair commendation and assessment of Keswick which at least endeavored to highlight the ministry of the Holy Spirit for the church in a state of lethargy. Murray laments the fact that the evangelical church in his time fell into the low point of dormancy. This may be true for the church in our time, and, in fact, in much of Christian history. For the church that is inactive, unproductive, and lethargic any group or movement that tries to stir up the spirituality of the church by focusing on the ministry of the Holy Spirit as taught in Scripture should certainly be commended or even applauded. Keswick advocates at least cannot be blamed for their endeavor to revitalize the church by emphasizing the ministry of the Holy Spirit in the believer's life.

The practical aspect of Keswick's importance in this matter cannot easily be discounted. J. I. Packer in his *Keep in Step with the Spirit* acknowledges the usefulness of Keswick in this practical aspect of the Christian life:

> Teachers of Keswick type have regularly spoken of being "filled with the Spirit." . . . But the summons to consecration that Keswick teachers have issued to slack Christians has always been strong and searching, and there is no question that in thus calling for full commitment they have ministered effectively to many double-minded, halfhearted, world-dominated, sin-indulging believers at the precise point of their spiritual blockage.[10]

---

8. Packer, "Keswick," 161.
9. Murray, Review of *So Great Salvation*, 79.
10. Packer, *Keep In Step*, 150.

Oftentimes in Christian history some aspect of Christian life demands a doctrinal formulation based on Scripture in order to describe and define the concept and nature of a certain experience in the Christian life. It may be said that Murray's doctrine of definitive sanctification falls into this category. While many holiness groups including Keswick were pushing for the once-for-all aspect of sanctification in their ministry to people, with the doctrine of definitive sanctification Murray supplied a doctrinal explanation for this aspect of the Christian life from a Reformed perspective.

Problems of Keswick's Teaching

Although many respected and honored Christian leaders such as Handley Moule, Webb-Peploe, Andrew Murray, and A. T. Pierson were involved in this movement, John Murray confesses that he needs to bring out what is not theologically and biblically sound in Keswick's teaching. Murray delineates five problematic areas of Keswick's teaching on sanctification. In his criticism of Keswick's teaching, germinal ideas of Murray's doctrine of definitive sanctification are seen at many points.

Murray's first criticism of Keswick is its view of sin. He states, "Keswick has not been successful in delivering itself from one of the greatest liabilities of its predecessor, the Higher Life Movement. While Keswick stresses the gravity of sin, there is still an understanding of the consequence for the believer of remaining indwelling sin, of what Keswick itself calls the tendency to sin."[11] What also displeases him is Keswick's differentiation of "known sin." Murray exposes Keswick's shallow and superficial view of sin:

> But it is just here that what we are compelled to censure as the superficiality of Keswick's conception of the consequence of remaining indwelling sin appears. Indwelling sin is still sin and the believer ought always to be conscious of it as such. To fail to be conscious of it amounts either to hypocrisy or self-deception. To have sin in us and not to be conscious of it is itself grave sin; it is culpable ignorance or culpable ignoring. As long as sin remains there cannot be freedom from conscious sin for the simple reason that in the person who is sensitive to the gravity of sin and to the demands of holiness this sin that remains is always reflected in consciousness.[12]

---

11. Murray, Review of *So Great Salvation*, 80.
12. Murray, Review of *So Great Salvation*, 80.

In exposing the superficiality of Keswick's view of sin, Murray touches the heart of Keswick's problem. Keswick treats sin as a manageable physical disease. For Keswick, as long as a wound outwardly appears to be manageable the disease is cured. Murray calls this a self-deception. Keswick minimizes the understanding of sin and claims to find the solution for that sin which actually is a small image of what sin really is.

The only way to fight sin is by a counteraction of the Holy Spirit, according to Keswick. Murray expresses an objection to this view: "If we are to use any of the terms mentioned above with reference to the grace of God as it is brought to bear upon the corrupt nature, namely, suppression, counteraction, eradication, the last is the only proper one."[13] According to Keswick's view, there is not an inherent change at all in the corrupt nature of a person from his unregenerate life to the last day of his regenerate life. Thus, Murray asserts eradication of the corrupt nature rather than counteraction over sin. In criticizing Keswick's poor understanding of sin, Murray generally affirms the Reformed position and follows Warfield's criticism of the holiness movement's teaching.

Second, Murray points out a shortcoming in the interpretation and application of Romans 6 by Keswick. He begins the criticism with "While Keswick maintains in commendable fashion the implications for sanctification of union with Christ in his death and resurrection and places a much-needed emphasis upon Paul's teaching in Romans 6, there is at the same time shortcoming in the interpretation and application of this passage and of others of like import."[14] Of the five criticisms of Keswick by Murray the germinal ideas for definitive sanctification are found most here.

It is seen from the previous chapter that Keswick has three stages of sanctification, positional, experiential, and permanent; and maintains that Romans 6 teaches positional sanctification. Murray asserts that Romans 6 teaches the actual possession rather than positional sanctification of the believer. He explains further, "The freedom from the dominion of sin of which Paul speaks is the *actual* possession of everyone who is united to Christ. It is not merely *positional* victory which every believer has secured."[15] In this statement is seen the germinal idea of his doctrine of definitive sanctification. It is the once-for-all gift of God in the believer's union with Christ in his death and resurrection. Murray continues, "But it is not simply positional, far less is it potential; it is actual. And because it is actual, it is experiential."[16]

---

13. Murray, Review of *So Great Salvation*, 81.
14. Murray, Review of *So Great Salvation*, 81.
15. Murray, Review of *So Great Salvation*, 81.
16. Murray, Review of *So Great Salvation*, 81.

But Murray does not explain in what sense this once-for-all victory is actual in the believer's life, nor does he make himself clear as to the exact difference between Keswick's positional victory and his concept of actually victory in Christ. Whether Murray sufficiently and convincingly elaborates this point is seen in the second part of this chapter which includes the explication of the doctrine of definitive sanctification.

Murray strongly underscores the teaching in Romans 6 of the believer's once-for-all and decisive breach with sin, which basically is not different from Keswick's teaching. Keswick teaches that the believer's positional victory can become experiential by "reckoning," or that the victory is secured by the "reckoning." Murray refutes this teaching. For him, since the believer's victory in Christ is actual it is experiential; there is no need to go through the reckoning process to experience it. Murray continues, "Reckoning ourselves to be dead indeed unto sin but alive to God is not the act of faith whereby victory is achieved; this reckoning is the reflex act and presupposes the deliverance of which Paul speaks in Romans 6:14."[17]

Third, Murray exposes Keswick's inaccurate interpretation of Romans 7:14–25 as depicting the experience of the abnormal or defeated Christian. Although he agrees with Keswick seeing the experience of the believer in Romans 7:14–25, he emphatically states that there is no sufficient evidence to describe Romans 7:14–25 as the experience of a defeated Christian:

> It is to be appreciated that the Keswick leaders, as a rule, interpret Romans 7:14–25 as depicting the experience of one who is a believer. But when they maintain that the experience of struggle and defeat here described is not the God-intended normal experience of Christians, but shows what happens when any person, regenerate or unregenerate, tries to conquer the old nature by self-effort, then we must dissent.[18]

The experience of struggle depicted in this passage is an experience of a normal Christian. "Anyone imbued with sensitivity to the demands of holiness and who yearns to be holy as the Father in heaven is holy must experience the contradiction which Romans 7:14 ff. portrays. A believer without this tension would be abnormal."[19] There is a tension in the

17. Murray, Review of *So Great Salvation*, 82. The "reflex act" is understood as an action that takes places in the believer automatically in response to union with Christ. The difference between Keswick and Murray is that for Keswick the believer has to claim consciously the blessing of the once-for-all aspect of sanctification by going through the reckoning process whereas Murray says that the believer automatically has this blessing when he is joined in union with Christ.

18. Murray, Review of *So Great Salvation*, 82.

19. Murray, Review of *So Great Salvation*, 83.

believer between the flesh and Spirit, between sin and righteousness and this tension is normal in the believer. Murray accuses Keswick of ignoring the reality of the tension in the believer. He concludes, "It is only by evading the realities of sin and grace that we can escape from the stern realism of the conflict of Romans 7. There is a grand candour in this passage, the candour of inspired utterance."[20]

Murray's position on Romans 7:14–25 is in the line of the orthodox and Reformed tradition regarding this passage. It is told that Alexander Whyte, whenever he received a new commentary on Romans, immediately turned to the seventh chapter. And if the commentator set up a man of straw in the seventh chapter, he immediately sent the book back to the publisher. Keswick, on this passage, tries to walk on a tightrope between Wesleyan and Reformed interpretations. Murray, however, rejects Keswick's interpretation of this passage.

Fourth, Murray points out that Keswick is too caught up with the psychology of sin rather than really understanding what sin is. Keswick, in a sense, is leaning too much toward the experiential or emotional side in dealing with sin in the believer. Murray states, "The representatives of Keswick have a passionate concern for deliverance from the oppressing consciousness of sin and the dissatisfaction arising from this consciousness."[21] In Keswick's term, the consciousness of sin is a symptom of sin. Keswick is involved more with a symptom of sin than sin itself. This concept is easily understood from Keswick's physical notion of sin. Keswick views sin as a physical disease such as a wound. Physically speaking, Keswick deals with the outward effect of the disease rather than the cause of the disease. Thus, Keswick, rather than understanding sin theologically, deals with the psychological effect of sin in an effort to be free from sin itself. But in all fairness though, Keswick is to be commended for bringing out the reality of the tension and struggle in the believer's life. Murray's statement above should not be understood in the sense that believers do not have a concern for deliverance from the oppressing consciousness of sin and the dissatisfaction arising from this consciousness. Nothing could be further from the truth. It is from statements such as these that Wesleyans and Keswick believe that Reformed Christians use Romans 7:14–25 as an excuse for not progressing in their Christian life and being comfortable with their lethargic condition or status quo of their spiritual life.

Murray also warns Keswick that a pit of perfectionism is not far away from its tendency to deal only with the psychological effect of sin. This

---

20. Murray, Review of *So Great Salvation*, 83.
21. Murray, Review of *So Great Salvation*, 83.

insufficient and inadequate understanding of sin naturally breeds complacency; complacency is the snare of perfectionism. Keswick advocates do not explicitly state that they teach perfectionism. But they should always remember that the harmful pit of perfectionism is just a step behind them.

Fifth, Murray does not agree with Keswick's distinction between the gradual process of sanctification and the definite decision for holiness, which is a point in time. He elaborates this point:

> Keswick insists upon the distinction between the gradual and continuous process by which we are conformed to the image and character of Christ and the definite decision for holiness, the whole-hearted dedication to God, which is a point or crisis. But must we not bear in mind that decision for holiness or dedication to God is itself something to which progressive sanctification must be applied?[22]

The problem with Keswick is that it differentiates between progressive and crisis sanctification and makes them distinct and separate entities of sanctification which the believer has to work at or experience in this life. Therefore, for Keswick, the Christian life is a combination of crisis and progressive sanctification throughout the duration of the Christian life.

However, it would be unfair to accuse Keswick of separating progressive and crisis sanctification without any relationship between them at all. In fact, Keswick does teach that they are vitally related and that the believer's crisis experience should be the undergirding impetus for the progressive sanctification. But it takes a man's decision to obtain instantaneous sanctification through crisis, and he can have that experience many times throughout his life. Murray rejects this teaching and says that the definitive or instantaneous aspect of sanctification is a God-given gift and happens only once in the believer's life. Thus, progressive sanctification must apply to it and they are inseparably connected to each other.

John Murray's Doctrine of Definitive Sanctification

Murray's doctrine of definitive sanctification was little known until the late twentieth century, but it is beginning to get a recognition as an important doctrine in the soteriology from Christian theologians. In the midst of so much emphasis on the holy life of a Christian at the present time, Murray's doctrine of definitive sanctification needs to be assessed in the proper historical and theological context for its significance in the Christian church.

---

22. Murray, Review of *So Great Salvation*, 83–84.

In this part of the chapter the presentation of Murray's doctrine of definitive sanctification is divided into three sections. The first section includes the development of the doctrine, the second the explication of the doctrine followed by the significance of it in the third section.

Development of the Doctrine of Definitive Sanctification

Before going into the study of the content of the doctrine, it is necessary for us to look at the process of the development of the doctrine. Although in his presentation of the doctrine Murray did not state in any place whether he was responding to any particular teaching or movement, it may be said now that he was setting forth the doctrine of definitive sanctification in response to Keswick and indirectly to the holiness movement's teaching in general. Christian doctrines have to be understood in the context of Christian history. No doctrine is completely detached from the historical context in which it is developed. Even Murray himself stated, "The theology of one generation can never be divorced from historical antecedent."[23] Judging from Murray's writings on sanctification, his development of the doctrine of definitive sanctification may be divided into three stages.

First Stage

Murray's book review of Barabas's *So Great Salvation* in the *Westminster Theological Journal* in 1953 may be regarded as the first stage of the development of the doctrine. It is difficult to pinpoint exactly when he decided to work on the doctrine of definitive sanctification as the Reformed alternative to Keswick's teaching. But it is easily seen in this review that Murray entertained a special interest and concern for this subject.

In the review, Murray comments on Keswick's emphasis upon Paul's teaching in Romans 6 for sanctification. Keswick bases its teaching on sanctification, especially instantaneous sanctification, heavily upon this chapter. It will be seen in this section that Murray also bases his doctrine of definitive sanctification on this chapter. Although it is difficult to conjecture whether Romans 6 played the important and decisive role for sanctification in Murray's theology prior to this event, it seems that Murray's use of Romans 6 for definitive sanctification did not come about without the influence of Keswick.

---

23. Murray, "Foreword," viii.

Murray's review contains some germinal ideas on definitive sanctification. In commenting on Romans 6:14, he asserts that it teaches the believer's definitive and decisive breach with sin, "specifically with the rule and power of sin." This point is resounded again and again in his later writings on sanctification. Murray also sets forth the idea of the actual victory of a believer in Christ rather than Keswick's positional victory.[24] This may be regarded as germinal and important in the formulation of this doctrine, although in what sense the victory is actual needs to be developed further. In this review are included some germinal ideas and a basic description of definitive sanctification, but the terms "definitive" or "definitive sanctification" are not used.

Second Stage

The second stage of the development covers from 1955 to 1959 during which Murray's three books, *Redemption Accomplished and Applied*, *Principles of Conduct*, and the commentary *The Epistle to the Romans*, were published. In *Redemption Accomplished and Applied*, published in 1955, Murray has a section on sanctification. Although he does not have a separate section on definitive sanctification, the first three pages of this section contain the basic ideas of definitive sanctification. Murray writes:

> And this victory is actual or it is nothing. It is a reflection upon and a deflection from the pervasive New Testament witness to speak of it as merely potential or positional. It is actual and practical as much as anything comprised in the application of redemption is actual and practical.[25]

It is clearly seen from statements such as those above whom Murray is responding to, even though he does not use the word "Keswick," nor does he use any one of Keswick's works as a reference. He is firmly rejecting Keswick's positional victory and setting forth the idea of actual victory in Christ.

It is much clearer whom Murray has in mind when he is penning the following statements, "Perfectionists are right when they insist that this victory is not achieved by us nor by working or striving or laboring; they are correct in maintaining that it is a momentary act realized by faith."[26] Such statements as these are not found in B. B. Warfield's *Perfectionism*. Here Murray acknowledges that some elements of the perfectionists'

24. Murray, Review of *So Great Salvation*, 81.
25. Murray, *Redemption*, 142.
26. Murray, *Redemption*, 143.

teaching are correct. So in a sense, Murray indirectly admits that Warfield's response from the wholly progressive aspect of sanctification was not a fully balanced response to the perfectionists' teaching on sanctification. One cannot ignore the once-for-all aspect of sanctification. Murray writes that this blessing cannot be separated from the state of justification. The term "definitive" is still not used in *Redemption Accomplished and Applied* in describing the once-for-allness of sanctification.

In *Principles of Conduct* published in 1957, Murray sets forth the principle of the dynamic of the biblical ethic on the idea of definitive sanctification. Although the term "definitive sanctification" is not used, the term "definitive transformation" is used to describe the definitive once-for-allness of the breach with sin and its power.[27] In this book, Murray cites Romans 6 extensively to describe the "definitive transformation" of the believer in Christ. At one place he expounds:

> Hence, if we died with him, we also died to sin once for all. And 'we who died to sin, how shall we any longer live therein?' (Romans 6:2). It is this concept of having died to sin that expresses, perhaps more eloquently than any other in Scripture, the definitive cleavage with sin which takes place when in the work of God's grace a person is united to Christ.[28]

Murray equates "our old man has been crucified" (Romans 6:6) to "we died to sin" (Romans 6:2) —the definitive and decisive breakage with sin. This definitive transformation of the believer is the foundation of a holy Christian life or progressive sanctification.

Murray speaks of the definitive and progressive aspect of sanctification in terms of the indicative and the imperative in Romans 6. He writes, "It is all summed up in the simple proposition that the indicative underlies the imperative, and the assurance of the indicative is the urge and incentive to the fulfillment of the imperative."[29] Thus, definitive sanctification is the driving force of progressive sanctification. Murray explains how these two are weaved together in the believer's life as mysterious as they are:

> The deliverance in view must therefore apply to all sin, and the inescapable inference is that the sin which still inheres in the believer and the sin he commits does not have dominion over him. Sin as indwelling and committed is a reality; it does not lose its character as sin. It is the contradiction of God and of that

---

27. Murray, *Principles of Conduct*, 211.
28. Murray, *Principles of Conduct*, 204.
29. Murray, *Principles of Conduct*, 220.

which a believer most characteristically is. It creates the gravest liabilities. But by the grace of God there is this radical change that it does not exercise the dominion.[30]

Thus, Murray shows that the idea of definitive sanctification is something to which progressive sanctification must be applied.

Murray's commentary, *The Epistle to the Romans*, includes exegetical material supporting the idea of definitive sanctification. In exegeting Romans 6:2, "we died to sin," Murray explains:

> If we view sin as a realm or sphere then the believer no longer lives in that realm or sphere. And just as it is true with reference to life in the sphere of this world that the person who has died "passed away, and, lo, he was not: yea, I sought him, but he could not be found" (Psalms 37:6; cf. 103:16), so is it with the sphere of sin; the believer is no longer there because he has died to sin. Failure to appreciate this premise upon which the subsequent argument rests and of which it is an expansion will distort our understanding of this chapter. The believer died to sin once and he has been translated to another realm.[31]

He shows that it is imperative to understand the idea of the definitive aspect of sanctification in order to correctly expound Romans 6.

In several places in this book, it seems that Murray is in dialogue with Keswick. At one place he writes, "That believers 'walk' in newness of life indicates that the life is not conceived of as otiose possession but as engaging the activity of the believer."[32] In this statement, Murray seems to refute Keswick's positional victory, which remains as otiose possession unless realized in the believer's experience. At another place he writes, "We are not commanded to become dead to sin and alive to God; these are presupposed. And it is not by reckoning these to be facts that they become facts."[33] Such statements seem to be a response most suitable for Keswick. The reader will recall that Keswick teaches that a positional victory becomes experiential by reckoning through the faith of the believer. Also on the exposition of Romans 6:12, Murray uses the illustration of the slave who has been set free. This illustration seems to be similar to that of Evan Hopkins in which he explains the difference between the legal and actual freedom of man.[34]

---

30. Murray, *Principles of Conduct*, 220.
31. Murray, *Romans*, 213.
32. Murray, *Romans*, 217.
33. Murray, *Romans*, 225–26.
34. Murray, *Romans*, 227. Hopkins, "Our Old Man," 175–76.

In his *The Epistle to the Romans*, Murray delineates and illustrates the idea of a definitive aspect of sanctification. But the term "definitive sanctification" as such is not used. The second stage of the development of the doctrine of definitive sanctification includes an explanation of the idea of definitive sanctification. But the term "definitive sanctification" is not used and the ideas are not organized into a doctrinal form.

Third Stage

The third stage of the development of the doctrine of definitive sanctification is from 1962 to 1967 during which the articles "Sanctification" in *Christianity Today* and "Definitive Sanctification" in the *Calvin Theological Journal* were published by Murray. In these two articles, he coined the term "definitive sanctification" and introduced an organized doctrinal presentation of definitive sanctification.

In his article "Sanctification" in *Christianity Today* is first seen the term "definitive sanctification." Not only is this term used in this article, but also Murray distinguishes between definitive and progressive sanctification and commences the discussion with definitive sanctification. He asks a rhetorical question, "What is this definitive sanctification?" Murray answers his own question:

> There are various ways in which it can be characterized. The specific and distinguishing action of each person of the Godhead at the inception of the state of salvation contributes to the decisive change which this sanctification denotes, and not only contributes but insures the decisive nature of the change itself. But perhaps the most significant aspect of New Testament teaching and the aspect requiring particular emphasis is that a believer is one called by the Father into the fellowship of his Son (1 Cor. 1:9). Union with Christ is the pivot on which the doctrine turns, specifically union with him in the meaning of his death and the power of his resurrection.[35]

Murray also in this article introduces definitive sanctification as a *sine qua non* of sanctification and treats it on par with progressive sanctification. He emphatically notes the importance of definitive sanctification. "The virtue of accruing from the death and resurrection of Christ affects no phase of salvation more directly than that of insuring definitive sanctification. If we do

---

35. Murray, "Sanctification," 30.

not reckon on and with this relationship, we miss one of the most cardinal features of redemptive provision."[36]

The culmination of Murray's presentation of definitive sanctification is the article "Definitive Sanctification" in the *Calvin Theological Journal* in 1967. In this article, he systematically and categorically sets forth this doctrine. Murray notes that this teaching has been neglected by Christians. He argues, "But it is a fact too frequently overlooked that in the New Testament the most characteristic terms used with reference to sanctification are used not of a process but of a once-for-all definitive act."[37] He continues, "It would be, therefore, a deflection from biblical patterns of language and conception to think of sanctification exclusively in terms of progressive work."[38]

Murray introduces Romans 6:1—7:6 as the primary text for definitive sanctification. Referring to "we died to sin" in Romans 6:2, he writes that "it is a cleavage, a breach, a translation as really and decisively true in the sphere of moral and religious relationship as in the ordinary experience of death."[39] In this article, Murray uses other Scripture passages such as 1 John 3:6–9, Ephesians 2:1–6, and others to explain the doctrine.

The third stage of the development of the doctrine of definitive sanctification by Murray is characterized by the introduction of the term "definitive sanctification" and the systematic presentation of the doctrine. What is more noticeable in these writings is that the tone of the writing does not seem to be responding to a certain group but rather simply setting forth what the doctrine of definitive sanctification is couched in biblical terms.

Explication of the Doctrine of Definitive Sanctification

Sanctification is generally spoken of as a process. Murray is the first Reformed theologian who spoke of definitive sanctification in a doctrinal form. He pointed out that more characteristic terms are used in the New Testament for a definitive act than for a process. Therefore, a study of sanctification exclusively from a progressive aspect gives an imbalanced and distorted view of sanctification. But to describe definitive sanctification requires a theologically sound framework in order not to fall into a fallacious teaching. Murray states, "To speak of sanctification as definitive might appear to deny its

---

36. Murray, "Sanctification," 30.
37. Murray, "Definitive Sanctification," 5.
38. Murray, "Definitive Sanctification," 6.
39. Murray, "Definitive Sanctification," 7.

progressive nature and open the door to the fallacy by which the doctrine has so frequently been distorted."[40]

Having this thought in mind, Murray's doctrine of definitive sanctification is explicated in this section. This section includes the definition, basis, and nature of definitive sanctification followed by its relationship with progressive sanctification.

The Definition of Definitive Sanctification

Murray defines definitive sanctification as a decisive sanctifying act, a once-for-all sanctification, which is completed in the believer's life as it brings about a radical change in his relationship to sin and righteousness. Pivotal to defining definitive sanctification is "we died to sin" (ἀπεθάνομεν τῇ ἁμαρτίᾳ) in Romans 6:2. It means that the believer is once-for-all severed from sin as the dominion over him. Murray explains this point:

> The breach with sin and the newness of life are as definitive as were the death and resurrection of Christ. Christ in his death and resurrection broke the power of sin, triumphed over the prince of darkness, executed judgment upon this world, and by this victory delivered all those are united to him. Believers are partakers with him in these triumphal achievements.[41]

The believer's connection with the realm of sin has been severed once for all. The use of the aorist (ἀπεθάνομεν) denotes a particular moment in the believer's life when this definitive, irrevocable act has occurred. The irrevocable step has been taken in his life in that he is not ruled by the power of sin anymore. He is absolutely and completely freed from the power of sin.

Not only is the believer severed from the realm of sin once for all, but he also enters a new realm of righteousness. In dethroning sin from his life, the believer serves the new master, LORD Jesus Christ. He is now under the control of the provisions of grace. He is transferred from the servitude of sin to the freedom under the lordship of Jesus Christ.

Murray's definition of definitive sanctification mainly stems from "we died to sin" in Romans 6:2. His interpretation of this passage is generally in the tradition of Calvin and Charles Hodge. However, Murray is alone in bringing the importance and bearing of this passage upon the exposition of the whole chapter. He states, "So is it with the sphere of sin; the believer is no longer there because he has died to sin. Failure to appreciate this premise

---

40. Murray, "Sanctification," 30.
41. Murray, "Sanctification," 30.

upon which the subsequent argument rests and of which it is an expansion will distort our understanding of this chapter. The believer died to sin once and he has been translated to another realm."[42]

The Basis of Definitive Sanctification

Murray makes the believer's effectual union with Christ for the basis of definitive sanctification. Romans 6:3-5 is crucial for understanding this point. Commenting on this passage, Murray says:

> It is baptism into Jesus' death that makes valid the pivotal proposition, "we died to sin." Then Paul proceeds to identify believers with Christ in his burial and resurrection (Rom. 6:3-5). This means, therefore, that not only did Christ die, not only was he buried, not only did he rise from the dead but also all who sustain the relation to him that baptism signifies likewise died, were buried, and rose again to a new life patterned after his resurrection life. No fact is of more basic importance in connection with the death to sin and commitment to holiness than that of identification with Christ in his death and resurrection.[43]

He also says that union with Christ is the pivot on which this doctrine of definitive sanctification turns. The believer's union with Christ especially means here the union with him in his death and the power of his resurrection.

Murray is not the first one who stressed the importance of union with Christ for the basis of sanctification, especially definitive sanctification. In fact, Keswick, before Murray, asserted emphatically the importance of the union with Christ for the basis of sanctification. Barabas writes, "Another aspect is that when Christ died on the cross to sin, we were identified with Him in that death to sin. That is we died with Him. By our union with Him in His death we were freed from the penalty of sin and emancipated from the power of sin."[44] Even Charles Hodge explicitly teaches the absolute necessity of union with Christ for the believer's sanctification. In his typical writing style of filling many lines to complete just one sentence, Hodge comments, "All that the Scriptures teach concerning the union between the believer and Christ, and of the indwelling of the Holy Spirit, proves the supernatural character of our sanctification. Men do not make themselves holy; their holiness, and their

---

42. Murray, *Romans*, 213.
43. Murray, "Definitive Sanctification," 13.
44. Barabas, *So Great Salvation*, 88–89.

growth . . . are not due to their own fidelity . . . but to the divine influence by which they are rendered thus faithful."[45]

But what we need to refer back to regarding this matter is Walter Marshall's book, *Gospel Mystery of Sanctification*, first published in 1692. In this work, Marshall presents the idea of a once-for-all aspect of sanctification on the basis of fellowship and union with Christ. He writes:

> Another great mystery in the way of sanctification is the glorious manner of our fellowship with Christ in receiving a holy frame of heart from Him. It is by our being in Christ, and having Christ Himself in us—and that not merely by His universal preference as He is God, but by such a close union as that we are one spirit and one flesh with Him; which is a privilege peculiar to those that are truly sanctified. I may well call this a mystical union.[46]

Basically, Keswick's idea of the ground of positional sanctification and Murray's idea of the basis of definitive sanctification are not much different.

In setting forth the idea of the ground of sanctification, Keswick seems to emphasize the believer's death to sin with Christ.[47] Keswick's teaching on this point closely follows Marshall's statements. Marshall emphasizes:

> By His death, He freed Himself from the guilt of our sins imputed to Him, and from all that innocent weakness of His human nature which He had borne for a time for our sakes. And by freeing Himself, He prepared a freedom for us, from our whole natural condition, which is both weak as He was, and also polluted without guilt and sinful corruption. Thus the corrupt natural estate, which is called in Scripture the old man, was crucified together with Christ, that the body of sin might be destroyed.[48]

Marshall also emphasizes the believer's resurrection with Christ for the basis of sanctification. The idea of the believer's resurrection with Christ is also very important for Murray in teaching the basis of definitive sanctification. Murray's teaching on this point is very similar to Marshall's statements below. Again, Marshall explains:

> By His resurrection, He took possession of spiritual life for us, as now fully procured for us, and made to be our right and

---

45. C. Hodge, *Systematic Theology*, 3:218.
46. Marshall, *Sanctification*, 35.
47. Barabas, *So Great Salvation*, 88.
48. Marshall, *Sanctification*, 41.

> property by the merit of His death. Therefore, we are said to be quickened together with Christ, even when we were dead in sins, and to be raised up together.... His resurrection was our resurrection to the life of holiness.... We are married to Him that is risen from the dead, that we might bring forth fruit to God. Baptism signifies the application of Christ's resurrection to us as well as His death; we are raised up with Him, in it, to newness of life.[49]

Thus, Marshall's emphasis on the believer's death and resurrection with Christ closely resembles Murray's idea of the basis of sanctification in union with Christ.

Both Murray and Barabas refer to Marshall's book in their works, though generally.[50] It may seem that both of them got the idea for the basis of a once-for-all aspect of sanctification from Marshall's work. It nevertheless appears that Murray indirectly affirms Keswick's teaching at least on this matter.

Murray, having stated the union with Christ as the basis of definitive sanctification, probes into the question of how in this union of Christ the death and resurrection of Christ are related to sanctification. According to him, the death and resurrection of Christ are indirectly related to sanctification through the medium of justification from the progressive aspect of sanctification, but they are also directly related to sanctification from the definitive aspect of sanctification. For the purpose of definitive sanctification, Murray emphasizes the direct relationship between them:

> Or it might be said that by his death and resurrection Christ has procured every saving gift—the death and resurrection are therefore the meritorious and procuring cause of sanctification as well as of justification and in this respect are as directly related to sanctification as to justification.[51]

Statements such as those above are exactly what Keswick advocates would say (and have said many times) to those Christians who, following the tradition, only view sanctification progressively and, thus, see only the indirect relationship of the death and resurrection of Christ to sanctification through the medium of justification.

The difference between Keswick's and Murray's teachings at this juncture is that, whereas Keswick separates justification and immediate

---

49. Marshall, *Sanctification*, 42.
50. Murray, "Sanctification," 31; Barabas, *So Great Salvation*, 16.
51. Murray, "Definitive Sanctification," 14.

sanctification, though procured by Christ, by placing the "reckoning" process between them, Murray puts justification and definitive sanctification in a vital relationship in that both of them are given to the believer as the grace of God at the inception of the Christian life. But what the exact nature of the relationship between justification and definitive sanctification is, Murray does not say. Is justification also the foundation of definitive sanctification as well as progressive sanctification? Does justification come before definitive sanctification in the *ordo salutis*? These points would still have to be developed further in Murray's doctrine of definitive sanctification.[52]

The Nature of Definitive Sanctification

The nature of definitive sanctification entails two important questions: what really happens to the believer in definitive sanctification and when does it happen to him. It has been shown that Murray refutes Keswick's teaching of positional sanctification. He emphatically states that definitive sanctification is actual. The radical and definitive breach with sin is actual. The believer is once-for-all transferred from the realm of sin to the realm of grace. But in what sense is this change actual? Is there actual change inherent in the person as a believer?

Crucial for answering these questions is Murray's exposition of Romans 6:6. He interprets the "old man" (ὁ παλαιὸς ἡμῶν ἄνθρωπος) in this passage as "old self or ego, the unregenerate man in his entirety in contrast with the new man as the regenerate man in his entirety."[53] For Murray the old man and new man cannot coexist in the life of the believer. Commenting on the clause "our old man was crucified" (ὁ παλαιὸς ἡμῶν ἄνθρωπος συνεσταυρώθη), he writes:

> The old man has been crucified and that this is one of the ways in which Paul announces the definitive cleavage with the world of sin, which union with Christ insures. The old man is the unregenerate man; the new man is the regenerate man created in Christ Jesus unto good works. It is no more feasible to call the believer a new man and old man, than it is to call him a regenerate man and unregenerate. And neither is it warranted to speak of the believer as having in him the old man and the new man.[54]

---

52. These points will be developed in chapter 8 where my own position on these points is presented.

53. Murray, *Romans*, 219.

54. Murray, *Principles of Conduct*, 218.

Concerning "put off the old man" and "put on the new man" in Ephesians 4:22–24, Murray sees here that Paul speaks of putting off the old man and putting on the new man "in terms of result rather than in terms of exhortation."[55]

Murray's interpretation of "old man" in this way shows a radical departure from the traditional Reformed view of John Calvin and Charles Hodge who viewed the "old man" as the old nature which is gradually reduced in correlation to the growth of new man.[56] Murray's interpretation of the "old man" as the unregenerate man that cannot coexist with the new man makes a new chapter in the American Reformed view of sanctification.

Murray says that the radical change in definitive sanctification is actual and therefore it is experiential. What is that which is tangible in the realm of experience for the believer? Keswick teaches that the person who has gone through immediate sanctification is free from known sin. To repudiate this teaching, Murray cites 1 John 3:6–9, 5:16–18 to show that John here does not teach sinless perfection but some specific sin by "sin unto death" (ἁμαρτία πρὸς θάνατον). He goes to great lengths to show that this "sin unto death" is the denial of Jesus Christ as come in the flesh. Thus, the person who has gone through definitive sanctification is free from the sin unto death, or he does not and cannot deny Jesus as come in the flesh. Murray continues:

> The upshot of these propositions is simply that the believer confesses Jesus as come in the flesh, believes that this Jesus is the Christ and that he is the Son of God, and cannot apostatize from this faith. The believer is the one who has secured the victory over the world, is immune to the dominion of the evil one, and is no longer characterized by that which is the world, "the lust of the flesh, and the lust of the eyes, and the pride of life" (1 Jn. 2:16). It is, therefore, in these terms that we are to interpret the sin that the person begotten of God does not commit and cannot commit.[57]

Murray's attempt to forge a link between Paul's concept of definitive sanctification and John's concept of sin unto death is certainly worth of consideration. But he seems to particularize the actuality of definitive sanctification into an immunity from a specific sin. In other words, he still has to

---

55. Murray, *Principles of Conduct*, 215.

56. John Calvin writes, "The old man, as the Old Testament is so called with reference to the New; for he begins to be old, when he is by degrees destroyed by a commencing regeneration. But what he means is the whole nature which we bring from the womb, and which is so incapable of the kingdom of God, that it must so far die as we are renewed to real life." *Romans*, 224.

57. Murray, "Definitive Sanctification," 11.

explain why the believer who has gone through definitive sanctification experiences freedom only from the sin unto death when he has *actually* been freed from the dominion of *all sins*. Murray is not clear why there is a discrepancy in moving from actuality to experience in definitive sanctification.

The second important question in the nature of definitive sanctification is "When did a believer die with Christ and rise again?" Murray presents a two-pronged answer to this question. Past historical explanation demands that the believer died and rose again with Jesus Christ when he died and rose again. On the other hand, the ethico-religious explanation demands that the believer died and rose again with Christ in his actual life history. Murray argues that it is important to "stress both aspects, the past historical and the experiential in their distinctness, on the one hand, and in their inter-dependence, on the other."[58] These two are vitally related in that "the past historical conditions the continuous existential" in such a way that something occurred in the past historical makes necessary "what is realized and exemplified in the actual life history of the believer."[59] It is absolutely necessary to maintain these two perspectives in understanding the believer's identification with Christ. Murray explains:

> The experiential must not be allowed to obscure the once-for-all historical, nor the once-for-all historical so to overshadow our thinking that we fail to give proper emphasis to the way in which its meaning and efficacy come to realization in the practical life of the believer. In other words, due emphasis must fall upon the objective and subjective in our dying and rising again with Christ in his death to sin and living again to God.[60]

Thus, he nicely interweaves the past historical with the experiential aspects of the believer's identification with Christ in definitive sanctification.

The Relationship with Progressive Sanctification

Whereas definitive sanctification is a single, once-for-all sanctifying act occurring at the inception of the Christian life, progressive sanctification is a process which continues throughout the Christian life until the death of the believer. Murray shows a vital relationship between these two aspects of sanctification in the believer's life. He teaches that progressive sanctification is grounded in definitive sanctification:

58. Murray, "Definitive Sanctification," 19.
59. Murray, "Definitive Sanctification," 19.
60. Murray, "Definitive Sanctification," 19.

> To a large extent the progress of sanctification is dependent upon the increasing understanding and appropriation of the implication of that identification with Christ in his death and resurrection. Nothing is more relevant to progressive sanctification than the reckoning of ourselves to be dead to sin and alive to God through Jesus Christ (cf. Rom. 6:11).[61]

In the believer's life definitive sanctification is the foundation of progressive sanctification. It is because the believer has died to sin that he is able to fight the power of sin in his life. It is because the "old man" has died that the believer now can walk in the newness of the Spirit. Thus, the believer's death and resurrection with Christ have a direct effect on the progressive sanctification of the believer.

Though Murray's teachings on definitive sanctification and progressive sanctification may be expressed in terms of "indicative" and "imperative," Murray himself does not elaborate them very much in his writings. There certainly is in Murray's concept the relation of the indicative and imperative as is also expressed by Ridderbos in his great work, *Paul*. Ridderbos, in this work, repeatedly asserts that the "imperative rests on the indicative and that this order is not reversible." He states:

> By way of conclusion we may say that the imperative is grounded on the indicative to be accepted in faith once and for all and time and again anew. Because believers may know themselves as dead to sin and alive to God, they must present their body and their members to the service of righteousness. The imperative preaches rebellion against an enemy (sin), concerning which faith may know and must know again and again that it has been defeated.[62]

The above statements are along the same line with Murray's comments on Romans 6:12. Commenting on the imperative "let not sin reign" in this verse, Murray writes:

> The force of the imperative can be understood only in the light of the relation of the indicative to the imperative. Sin does not have the dominion—this is the indicative. This indicative is not only expressly asserted in verse 14, it is implicit in all that the apostle has argued in the verses that precede verse 12. Let not sin reign—this is the imperative. And it flows from the indicative. It

---

61. Murray, "Pattern," 2:311.
62. Ridderbos, *Paul*, 257.

is only because sin does not reign that it can be said, "Therefore let not sin reign."[63]

Thus, in both Ridderbos and Murray the indicative is foundational for the imperative in sanctification.

However, there is a difference between Murray's foundation and that of Ridderbos in sanctification. Ridderbos's foundation is the redemptive indicative dying and rising with Christ whereas Murray's is the believer's dying and rising with Christ in both past historical and experiential aspects. Thus, in a sense Murray's foundation for the imperative is a double foundation: the past historical and experiential indicative. He explains:

> Due emphasis must fall upon the objective and subjective in our dying and rising again with Christ in his death to sin and living again to God. It is only in this way that we can avoid the tendency to deny the vicarious significance of that which Christ wrought once for all in the realm of history as concrete and real as any other historical event.[64]

He preserves both an objective and subjective sense of the believer's dying and rising again with Christ, which is the basis for definitive sanctification of the believer.

Ridderbos views Paul's theology of salvation from the perspective of the *historia salutis* primarily. He emphasizes the importance of the *historia salutis* over *ordo salutis* in studying Paul's teaching on salvation. Ridderbos writes, "The great change of which Paul's preaching bears testimony is not in the first place the reversal in his mind with regard to the *ordo salutis*, but first and foremost with regard to the *historia salutis* in the objective sense of the word."[65] Christ's death and resurrection are thus interpreted from the redemptive-historical viewpoint. It may be said, therefore, that in Christ's death and resurrection the "eschatological gift" of sanctification is "breaking through as a reality already present."

Carrying this overarching theme in the theology of salvation, Ridderbos asks some critical questions which concern us most in relation to Murray's teaching here. Ridderbos precisely formulates this matter:

> Does he mean that what took place once in Christ is repeated and continued spiritually in those who are His? But how does he come to speak like this? Is this to be explained from an overpowering spiritual experience, a mystical union with Christ, a

---

63. Murray, *Romans*, 227.
64. Murray, "Definitive Sanctification," 19.
65. Ridderbos, *Time*, 48.

union enabling him to re-experience, so to speak, this process of death and resurrection spiritually?[66]

In answering these questions Ridderbos rejects the spiritual interpretation of this event and interprets it from the redemptive-historical viewpoint. He answers these questions unequivocally:

> No, when He died on Golgotha, they also died with Him, and when He arose in the garden of Joseph of Arimathea, they were raised together with Him.... the apostle does not appeal to the conversion of the faithful, but to their being included in Christ's death. And the same holds true for the resurrection, the exaltation in heaven, the coming back of the Church with Christ.[67]

Ridderbos thus makes clear that the believer died and rose with Christ, not in a metaphorical and spiritual sense, but in a historical sense. For him, the believer was included in Christ and has been present in him "through all the phases of the great history of salvation."

Murray, differing from Ridderbos's *historia salutis* approach to sanctification, here introduces the unique relationship in which progressive sanctification is grounded in definitive sanctification which is in turn based on the believer's dying and rising again with Christ in both past historical and experiential aspects. Progressive sanctification is thus grounded both in redemptive indicative and experiential indicative, if we may use these terms. By making progressive sanctification grounded in definitive sanctification in this way, Murray brings out a subjective sense as well as an objective one from the foundation of progressive sanctification. This may be one of the contributions Murray made to the doctrine of sanctification.

Significance of the Doctrine of Definitive Sanctification

Murray's doctrine of definitive sanctification is not well-known in the Christian church, though his work is beginning to get a recognition by some scholars recently.[68] While Murray's teaching may be viewed as one of the most important doctrines relating to the holy life of Christians, it seems that his teaching is not much appreciated for its significance among some Reformed theologians.[69] As Murray's teaching is being known and

---

66. Ridderbos, *Time*, 54.

67. Ridderbos, *Time*, 55.

68. Payne, *Already Sanctified*, 129; Park, *Driven by God*, 31; Peterson, *Possessed by God*, 63.

69. Fesko, "Sanctification," 197; M. Horton, *Covenant and Salvation*, 248. Fesko

studied by wider circle of theologians, the proper assessment of the significance of this doctrine is apropos today.

Recently some studies related to this subject have been propounded.[70] I feel, however, that the full aspect and significance of Murray's doctrine of definitive sanctification have not been delineated in these studies. Some studies tend to be purely exegetical, ignoring the historical and theological context of the doctrine, whereas others, on the other hand, tend to be highly historically oriented without theological and exegetical study. It has been shown in this study that the interpretation of Murray's definitive sanctification should involve all these aspects, and thus the significance of this doctrine should be sought in a historical, theological, and exegetical context.

Historical Significance

As with any other Christian doctrines Murray's definitive sanctification needs to be interpreted in a proper historical context. First, the significance of this doctrine in a historical sense is that it is a direct doctrinal response from the Reformed viewpoint to Keswick's teaching on sanctification. Though Murray did not explicitly claim it as such, it is clear from this study that Murray's definitive sanctification was developed out of a direct response to Keswick's sanctification. Murray's doctrine therefore must be interpreted in this historical context. Anyone who ignores this perspective will miss the full import and significance of this doctrine. It is regrettable that almost all the studies on sanctification by Christian writers, even Reformed, have overlooked this important point.[71] Rather than treating this doctrine simply as an exegetical interpretation of Romans 6, the doctrine must be seen as a direct doctrinal response by a Reformed theologian in the twentieth century to the victorious life movement, namely, Keswick. Murray's definitive sanctification stands as the foremost doctrinal response to the victorious life movement in twentieth-century America.

Second, since Murray's definitive sanctification is seen as a response to the victorious life movement, it falls into the historical progress of the Reformed response to the holiness movement in general. In the nineteenth

---

asserts that Murray's doctrine was derived from exegetical fallacy. Horton questions the reality of definitive sanctification in *ordo salutis*.

70. Payne, *Already Sanctified*, 129; Park, *Driven by God*, 31; Peterson, *Possessed by God*, 63; Adrian, "Definitive Sanctification"; Patterson, "Keswick Theology"; Eby, "Reformed Response"; Estes, "Death to Sin"; Maclemnan, "Romans 6."

71. Payne, *Already Sanctified*, 129; Park, *Driven by God*, 31; Peterson, *Possessed by God*, 63; Loucks, "Theological Foundations," 378; Eby, "Reformed Response," 137.

century, Charles Hodge pointed out the fallacies in the holiness movement's teachings. However, the foremost Reformed theologian to respond to the holiness movement in the late nineteenth century was B. B. Warfield. Warfield, often called the ablest American theologian, devoted his entire book, *Perfectionism*, to the description and evaluation of the holiness movement's teachings. His work on this subject is still considered one of the most exhaustive treatments of the holiness movement's teachings from a Reformed perspective.

However, as good and exhaustive as it was, Warfield's treatment of the holiness movement's teaching, particularly sanctification, dealt with this doctrine primarily from a progressive point of view. Warfield criticized and responded to the holiness movement's sanctification mainly from a progressive, gradual aspect of sanctification. As such, Warfield's response to the holiness movement's teaching was not a fully balanced response. The definitive aspect of sanctification was absent in his response to the holiness movement. This gap is filled by Murray's doctrine of definitive sanctification. Murray's definitive sanctification coupled with Warfield's *Perfectionism* comprise a fully balanced response to the holiness movement's teaching on sanctification. Thus, rather than seeing Murray's definitive sanctification as a historically isolated doctrine, it must be seen as the continuation of the Reformed response to the holiness movement on the matter of sanctification.

Third, Murray may be regarded as the one of the first theologians to correctly interpret Walter Marshall's teaching on sanctification in *Gospel Mystery of Sanctification*. It has been said that Keswick's teaching is a rehash of Marshall's sanctification in *Gospel Mystery of Sanctification*. While it cannot be denied that Marshall's work is one of the references Keswick advocates used in teaching sanctification, it was only one of the many sources they used and it certainly was not *the* textbook for Keswick's sanctification. Furthermore, in consulting Marshall's work it seems that they only extracted from it the materials that seemed to fit in their teaching. Barabas mentions Marshall's work in passing as one of the references for Keswick.[72] Keswick advocates such as Evan Hopkins and A. S. Wilson rarely cite Marshall's work.[73] W. H. Griffith Thomas shows a departure of Keswick from Marshall's work. In commenting about the insufficient content in Marshall's work, Griffith Thomas writes, "The special teaching of what holiness means and how it is to be obtained, was reserved for these latter days in close association with the Movement which resulted in the Keswick Convention."[74]

---

72. Barabas, *So Great Salvation*, 16.
73. Hopkins, *Law of Liberty*; A. S. Wilson, *Definitive Experience*.
74. Thomas, "Literature of Keswick," 223.

Therefore, the relationship between Marshall's work and Keswick is not as close as what some people make it out to be. What is taught in Marshall's work is certainly not the crisis or n^{th} degree sanctification but definitive sanctification which is correctly captured and formulated in a doctrinal form by John Murray. It may be that Marshall's work had not been appreciated as much as it should have been by the Reformed group which saw sanctification primarily from the progressive aspect. So, in this sense Murray may be the first Reformed theologian who saw and interpreted Marshall's definitive sanctification in a correct way.

Theological Significance

First, Murray's definitive sanctification is the first theological formulation of the definitive aspect of sanctification taught in Scripture by a Reformed theologian. As such, it captures and delineates the once-for-all aspect of sanctification and incorporates it into Reformed theology. No such doctrinal formulation as Murray's definitive sanctification is found in Charles Hodge's or Louis Berkhof's *Systematic Theology*, which are considered as the standard works of Reformed systematic theology. Murray's definitive sanctification is beginning to receive its deserved recognition by some Reformed theologians as it is being cited in the literature pertaining to sanctification.[75]

A similar concept may be found in Ridderbos in the form of "indicative" and "imperative." However, Ridderbos interprets the "indicative" of the believer's holiness in a historical sense.[76] Murray goes one step further. He interprets the "indicative" of the believer's sanctification in both a past historical and experiential sense. Murray sees both the objective and subjective meaning in the "indicative" of the believer's sanctification. Thus, Murray's definitive sanctification is important theologically because it is the first doctrinal formulation by an American Reformed theologian of the definitive aspect of sanctification, and it does not duplicate the teachings of the non-American Reformed theologians.

Second, Murray's definitive sanctification is the presentation of the once-for-all aspect of the Puritans' holiness teaching in the form of the Reformed doctrine. It is said that Marshall's *Gospel Mystery of Sanctification* is the last of the monumental Puritan works on the holiness of the Christian life. Marshall's work falls into the great tradition of the Puritan literature by Perkins, Sibbs, Baxter, and Owen in the sixteenth century

---

75. Hoekema, "Reformed Perspective," 78; Ferguson, "Reformed View," 58; Park, *Driven by God*, 31; Reymond, *New Systematic Theology*, 757.

76. Ridderbos, *Paul*, 254.

and the following centuries in Great Britain. Puritans were by and large Calvinists in their theology. So it seems proper that Marshall's teaching on sanctification is to be interpreted in the framework of the Calvinistic Reformed theology rather than in the tradition of the Wesleyan-Perfectionist teaching. Some elements of Marshall's teaching on sanctification, particularly the once-for-all aspect, have been the easy targets of Keswick's teaching in order to bolster the presumed orthodoxy and credibility of the Keswick movement. However, many Keswick advocates would agree that Marshall's teaching on sanctification is not the same as Keswick's crisis sanctification. This fact is easily seen in that although some Keswick advocates cite Marshall's work as one of the original sources for their teachings in a general sense, they do not delve into Marshall's teaching in detail to support their arguments for crisis sanctification.

Marshall's concept of once-for-all sanctification found its brilliant doctrinal form in the canvas of Calvinistic theology in the able and theologically adroit hands of John Murray. It must be remembered as well that Marshall's concept has originally been cast in the doctrinal mode of Calvinistic teachings. Thus, Murray's definitive sanctification constitutes an interpretation of Marshall's teaching in the way it was intended to be taught. In doing this, Murray captures and interprets the essence of the once-for-all aspect of the Puritans' holiness teaching in Reformed theology.

Third, Murray's doctrine of definitive sanctification fills the gap between justification and progressive sanctification in Reformed theology. It is understood that justification is the judicial basis for sanctification. It is commonly seen that justification is the act of God on the believer whereas sanctification involves the work of the believer led by the Holy Spirit. So there seems to be an abrupt change going from justification to sanctification in the believer's life. The intimately close relationship between justification and sanctification demands the smoothest transition from the stage of all God's work to the stage of the believer's work primarily. In order to bring justification and sanctification together in the closest relationship, one should not, however, confound justification with sanctification as to eliminate the distinctions between them, as Barth has done.[77] The goal is to put justification and sanctification together in the most intimate relationship with the realistic smooth transition between them rather than the seemingly artificial, abrupt change between them.

Murray's definitive sanctification serves to meet this purpose. The doctrine of definitive sanctification brings justification and sanctification into a most intimate relationship with the realistic and smooth transition

---

77. Berkhof, *Systematic Theology*, 537.

between them. It is not a theoretical doctrine but a biblical doctrine because it is fully based on Scripture. Scripture speaks of the holiness of the believer in realistic or "indicative" terms. The passages that teach the "indicative" of the believer's holiness have been shown amply in the previous section. These passages teach neither judicial holiness nor progressive sanctification but the definite, once-for-all transformation of the believer that has actually occurred in him. Only the doctrine of definitive sanctification can explain the true meaning of these passages. Progressive sanctification of the believer is possible not only because of justification but also because the transformation to holiness has actually occurred in him. Thus, the doctrine of definitive sanctification makes progressive sanctification possible and real while it itself is intimately related to justification.

Murray's definitive sanctification also gives a balanced approach to the soteriology in Protestant theology which put the main emphasis on the forensic doctrine of justification by faith in order to counteract the Roman Catholic Church's mysticism and the doctrine of infused grace. The doctrine of justification has been interpreted in a forensic sense whereas the doctrine of sanctification has been understood in a spiritual or pneumatic sense. Protestant theology has ascribed any pneumatic changes of man in salvation to sanctification in order not to confuse it with justification which is understood in a forensic sense. The result of this attempt is the separation between these very important doctrines which are so intimately and inseparably related to each other on the basis of the work of Christ. Murray's definitive sanctification brings these two doctrines together in a right intimate relationship on the basis of the death and resurrection of Jesus Christ. The idea of justification, Christ-for-us, and the idea of sanctification, we-in-Christ, nicely come together without confounding them in definitive sanctification. Thus, Murray's definitive sanctification fills the "invisible" gap between justification and sanctification in Protestant theology.

Exegetical Significance

First, Murray's definitive sanctification aids the reader's comprehension of the deeper import of the passages in Romans 6. Historically, Romans 6 has often been treated unfairly by many commentators. The teaching in Romans 6 certainly is not justification, nor is it progressive sanctification. It is placed between justification in Romans 5 and progressive sanctification in Romans 7. What is taught in Romans 6 has not been clear to many commentators and therefore the true meaning of the passages was not fully exegeted. They either interpreted it in a purely historical sense or claimed a perfectionist teaching based on this chapter. Murray may be regarded as the first theologian to bring out the depth and significance of the teaching in Romans 6 working from the perspective of definitive sanctification. His commentary, *The Epistle to the Romans*, richly exemplifies this fact.

Second, Murray's interpretation of the "old man" in Romans 6:6 shows a significant departure from the traditional Reformed interpretation of this passage, especially by John Calvin and Charles Hodge. Calvin writes:

> The old man, as the Old Testament is so called with reference to the New; for he begins to be old, when he is by degrees destroyed by a commencing regeneration. But what he means is the whole nature which we bring from the womb, and which is so incapable of the kingdom of God, that it must so far die as we are renewed to real life.[78]

In a similar vein Hodge writes, "*Our old man . . . is our corrupt nature as opposed to the new man, holy nature, which is the product of regeneration.*"[79] Murray, however, interprets "old man" as the unregenerate man which dies at the inception of the Christian life, "'Our old man' is the old self or ego, the unregenerate man in his entirety in contrast with the new man as the regenerate man in his entirety."[80] For Murray, the unregenerate man dies experientially at the moment of definitive sanctification such that the believer is a "new man." This is quite different from Calvin's and Hodge's teaching that the "old man" is the old nature which coexists with the new nature in the believer. Murray thus depicts regeneration as the absolute and complete change of the believer in a real sense.

Murray's interpretation of the "old man" in this way naturally leads to a different perspective on progressive sanctification. Rather than seeing the conflict in the believer as the struggle between the old nature and the new nature, Murray sees the conflict between the righteousness and the "garrison" of sin which lost the dominion over the believer. Thus, Murray's doctrine of definitive sanctification is significant exegetically in that it not only departs from the traditional Reformed position in its interpretation of the "old man," but also it provides another approach to the interpretation of the passages that teach conflict in the believer's life of progressive sanctification.

One of the Scripture passages that depicts the conflict of the believer in the progress of sanctification is Romans 7:22–23 which says, "For in my inner being I delight in God's law; but I see another law at work in me, waging war against the law of my mind and making me a prisoner of the law of

---

78. Calvin, *Romans*, 224.
79. C. Hodge, *Romans*, 197.
80. Murray, *Romans*, 219.

sin at work within me." Reformed theologians have viewed this conflict in the believer as the conflict between the spirit and the flesh. Calvin expresses this view in exegeting this passage:

> But we ought to notice carefully the meaning of the *inner man* and of the *members*; which many have not rightly understood, and have therefore stumbled at this stone. The inner man then is not simply the soul, but that spiritual part which has been regenerated by God; and the members signify the other remaining part; for as the soul is the superior, and the body the inferior part of man, so the spirit is superior to the flesh. Then as the spirit takes the place of the soul in man, and the flesh, which is the corrupted and polluted soul, that of the body, the former has the name of the inner man, and the latter has the name of the members.[81]

Hodge closely follows Calvin regarding the conflict of the believer in this passage. Hodge contends, "The one is I, i.e. my flesh; the other is I, i.e. my inner man. By the *inner man* is to be understood the "new man;" ... the soul considered or viewed as renewed."[82]

Murray, however, departs from this traditional Reformed interpretation of the passage in Romans 7:22–23. He equates the "inner man" with the deepest and truest self which is the "determinate will to the good." The antithesis in Romans 7 is between the law of sin and the law of God, not between the spirit (or soul) and the flesh. Murray explains this point:

> The antithesis between the law of sin and the law of God is registered in our persons in the warfare that is carried on in the realm of our consciousness between the dictates of sin and the law of God as that which is consented to, approved, and delighted in by our minds.[83]

Murray thus does not see the different parts of man in conflict with each other but sees the conflict between the law of sin and the law of God both of which try to lead the will of man to their own way. Therefore, Murray's concept of progressive sanctification is one of obedience by the will of the believer to the law of God rather than one of the renewal of the spirit and eradication of the flesh in the believer.

---

81. Calvin, *Romans*, 271.
82. C. Hodge, *Romans*, 235.
83. Murray, *Romans*, 267.

Conclusion

In this chapter, John Murray's response to Keswick's teaching of sanctification has been presented. Murray's response to Keswick began with his book review on Barabas's book, *So Great Salvation*, which is a definitive presentation of Keswick's teaching. In this review, he made several commendations of Keswick's teaching on sanctification. First, Keswick's emphasis on the believer's union with Christ for sanctification was cited as one of the commendable elements in Keswick's teaching. Second, Keswick's affirmation of the active participation of the believer in the gradual process of sanctification was also commended by Murray. Third, Keswick's effort to stress the importance of the work and presence of the Holy Spirit was commended. In a practical sense, Keswick's work of endeavoring to revitalize the church by stressing the ministry of the Holy Spirit in the believer's life was commendable.

Murray, however, pointed out the problems of Keswick's teaching. First, he criticized Keswick's superficial and shallow view of sin. Such a light view of sin, Murray warned, would lead them to perfectionism. Second, although he agreed with Keswick's view of the importance of Romans 6 for sanctification, Murray disagreed with Keswick on its teaching of positional sanctification. Murray asserted that the once-for-all aspect of sanctification in Romans 6 is actual and experiential without going through the reckoning stage, as taught by Keswick. Third, Murray pointed out Keswick's departure from the orthodox view of the teaching in Romans 7:14–25. He strongly objected to Keswick's view of seeing the notion of a defeated Christian in this passage. Fourth, he pointed out that Keswick was too caught up with the psychology of sin rather than really understanding what sin is. Here Keswick concentrated their effort in dealing with the psychological effects of sin rather than in understanding sin theologically first. Fifth, Murray criticized Keswick's differentiation of crisis and progressive sanctification which makes them distinct and separate entities of sanctification which a believer has to work at in his life.

Murray's presentation of his doctrine of definitive sanctification has been displayed as a part of the response to Keswick's sanctification, and the holiness movement's teaching in general. The development of Murray's definitive sanctification took about fourteen years from 1953 to 1967 involving three stages. Murray's review of Barabas's book was regarded as the first stage of the development of this doctrine. In this stage some germinal ideas such as the "decisive breach with the rule and power of sin" were seen in his writing. The second stage covered the period from 1955 to 1959 during which Murray published *Redemption Accomplished and Applied*, *Principles of Conduct*, and his commentary *The Epistle to the Romans*. He included his explanation of the idea of definitive sanctification in these writings. Moreover, Murray indirectly admitted that Warfield's response from the wholly progressive aspect of sanctification was not a fully balanced response to the holiness movement's teaching on sanctification. Though much of the concept of definitive sanctification was found in this stage, the term "definitive sanctification" was not used. In the third stage covering the time frame from 1962 to 1967, Murray set forth the concept of definitive sanctification in an organized doctrinal form. The articles "Sanctification" in *Christianity Today* and "Definitive Sanctification" in the *Calvin Theological Journal* included the term "definitive sanctification" and expounded the doctrine in detail.

In the explication of Murray's doctrine of definitive sanctification, Murray's teaching on the definition, basis, and nature of definitive sanctification have been presented as well as its relationship with progressive sanctification. He defined definitive sanctification as a decisive sanctifying act, once-for-all sanctification, which brought about a radical change in the believer's relationship to sin and righteousness. Murray emphasized the definitive and decisive breach from sin as dominion over the believer. He based definitive sanctification on the believer's effectual union with Christ. In doing this, Murray put justification and definitive sanctification in a vital relationship.

On the nature of definitive sanctification Murray said that the "old man" in Romans 6:6, interpreted as the unregenerate man, had died such that the change in the believer was actual and experiential. In interpreting the passage in this way, he departed from the traditional Reformed view of the "old man." Murray also pointed out that the change in the believer is both past historical and experiential. The believer died and rose again with Christ in a past historical sense, and he also died and rose again with Christ experientially at the inception of the Christian life. With regard to the relationship to progressive sanctification, Murray asserted that definitive sanctification is foundational for progressive sanctification. He demonstrated that progressive sanctification is grounded in definitive sanctification which is in turn based on the believer's union with Christ.

It also has been shown that the significance of Murray's doctrine of definitive sanctification may be seen in a threefold sense: historical, theological, and exegetical perspective. In a historical sense, this doctrine is developed out of the direct response to Keswick's sanctification. It is also historically significant because it falls into the historical progress of the Reformed response to the holiness movement in general. As such, it complements Warfield's response to the holiness movement's teaching in the late nineteenth century. Another significance of this doctrine historically is that it correctly interprets Walter Marshall's sanctification in *Gospel Mystery of Sanctification* from a Calvinistic, Reformed point of view.

Theologically, Murray's doctrine of definitive sanctification is the first formulation of the once-for-all aspect of sanctification into a doctrinal form by a Reformed theologian. Also, it is the presentation of the once-for-all aspect of the Puritans' holiness teaching in the form of Reformed doctrine. In this doctrine Marshall's teaching is interpreted in a way it was intended to be interpreted. Another important point theologically is that the doctrine of definitive sanctification fills a gap between justification and progressive sanctification in Protestant theology.

In an exegetical sense, Murray's doctrine of definitive sanctification established a right framework in which to understand truly the teaching of Romans 6 in its depth. Also, Murray's interpretation of the "old man" in Romans 6:6 as the "unregenerate man" discloses a momentous departure from the traditional Reformed view on sanctification. According to Murray, the "old man" died at the inception of the Christian life, and he does not exist any more in the believer. As such, there is no struggle between the "old man" and the "new man" in the believer. The struggle is between the righteousness and the "remnant" of sin in the believer.

Murray's doctrine of definitive sanctification is truly significant in many ways and as such it should be appreciated and utilized by the Christian church. More studies and efforts will be required to develop this doctrine into a more complete and elaborate form. This will be realized only when many Christian scholars and theologians delve into this doctrine and make it practical for believers of today. In an age when many believers swerve hither and thither seeking the holiness of life, the need for a biblically and theologically sound doctrine such as Murray's definitive sanctification is urgent. For this purpose, Murray performed a great service to the Christian church by setting the foundational stone on which to build a doctrine of Christian holiness which will be practical as well as theologically sound for all believers in Christ.

Chapter 7

Comparison of Keswick's Sanctification and John Murray's Definitive Sanctification

KESWICK'S TEACHING ON SANCTIFICATION and John Murray's response in the form of definitive sanctification played an important role in the development of the doctrine of sanctification in American Christianity. After studying these teachings separately in the previous chapters, we will in this chapter bring them together and examine them for the similarities and differences between them. The major elements of these teachings are compared side by side to assess strong and weak points of each side from the biblical perspective.

Similarities and Differences between Keswick's Sanctification and Murray's Definitive Sanctification

There are a number of similarities and differences between Keswick's sanctification and Murray's definitive sanctification. The similarities between these two will be examined first. The similarities between these two teachings are found in their historical and theological aspects.

Similarities between Keswick's Sanctification and Murray's Definitive Sanctification

The similarities between Keswick's sanctification and Murray's definitive sanctification may be discerned in the six aspects of these two teachings. Both of these teachings are involved in a progression of action-reaction phenomenon in the holiness movement in general. Also, these teachings are vitally connected to describing and promoting holiness of the Christian life.

Both teachings employ Romans 6 as the primary text on which to base their principal teachings. Thus, both Keswick and Murray teach that the believer's sanctification is based on the death and resurrection of Christ, or union with Christ. Furthermore, both of them specifically assert that the nature of sanctification they teach is instantaneous. They also distinguish the brand sanctification they teach from justification and progressive sanctification.

Action-Reaction Phenomenon in the Holiness Movement

In the course of time, the holiness movement assumed different forms and shapes and produced several branches in its progression in history. It cannot be denied that Keswick is one of these branches of the holiness movement and owed its existence deeply to it. This fact is affirmed by both protagonists and antagonists in their appraisal of Keswick. B. B. Warfield, who repudiates Keswick's teaching, puts Keswick in the holiness movement in his book, *Perfectionism*, and labels it "the victorious life movement" or "Quietistic Perfectionism," which suggests Keswick's indebtedness to the perfectionist teaching.[1] On the other hand, W. R. Thompson, who advocates Keswick, also argues that Keswick is closely linked to the ideal of Christian perfectionism in the holiness movement.[2] It may be maintained that American Keswick is a modified form of nineteenth-century perfectionism which drew heavy acrimonious criticisms for its Pelagian theology from Reformed theologians, especially Warfield. Thus, in this sense, Keswick, equipped and camouflaged with mild Calvinism, may be seen as a reaction of perfectionism to the heavy criticism of the Reformed theologians in the late nineteenth century.[3]

Likewise, Murray's definitive sanctification is also a reaction of the Reformed group to the modified form of the holiness movement, Keswick. Unlike other branches of the holiness movement such as the Pentecostal and Charismatic movements, Keswick, because of the appearance of its mild Calvinism, attracted many Reformed and Presbyterian Christians. Thus, Murray's definitive sanctification is a Reformed theological reaction to Keswick in which Murray attempted to expose the true nature of

---

1. Warfield, *Perfectionism*, 370.
2. Thompson, "Appraisal of the Keswick," 11.
3. Everett L. Cattel defines "mild Calvinism" as that which holds only three of Calvin's five points. However, in my opinion the five points of Calvinism come together or do not come at all. They are so interlinked with each other that one cannot be separated from another in Calvin's theology. "Appraisal of the Keswick and Wesleyan Contemporary Positions," 265.

Keswick's teaching and to set forth a Reformed alternative to Keswick's sanctification. Therefore, Keswick's sanctification and Murray's definitive sanctification are similar in the involvement of the action-reaction progression of the holiness movement in general.

Focus on the Holiness of the Christian Life

Keswick's sanctification and Murray's definitive sanctification are similar in that they both focus on the holiness of the Christian life. Keswick was especially organized for this purpose. Barabas writes, "Early Keswick meetings were called Convention 'for the promotion of practical holiness.' Keswick teaches that the Bible is first of all a practical book, and that when it is taken seriously life is revolutionized."[4] Thus, from the beginning Keswick was organized to focus on the holiness of the Christian life in a practical sense rather than disseminating a doctrinal truth on a certain subject of Christianity. As such, the believers are encouraged to take specific and practical actions to improve their spirituality. A. T. Pierson teaches the followers to remove any obstacles to the holiness of the Christian life. He writes, "The prompt renunciation of whatever is known or even suspected to be contrary to the will of God. Conscience must first of all be clean and clear of conscious disobedience or neglect of duty. Hindrances to holy living must be abandoned."[5]

Murray's definitive sanctification also focuses on the holiness of the Christian life. In his book review of Barabas's book, *So Great Salvation*, Murray commends Keswick for its endeavor to emphasize the ministry of the Holy Spirit for sanctification. Thus, in this commendation, Murray acknowledges that both he and Keswick, though with different teachings, are working toward the same goal, i.e., the accurate presentation of the biblical teaching on the holiness of the Christian life. Although Murray does not teach believers to take a certain action in a practical sense, his teaching surely focuses on holiness. He explains, "Every believer is a new man, that the old man has been crucified, that the body of sin has been destroyed, and that as a new man in Christ Jesus he serves God in the newness which is none other than that of the Holy Spirit of whom he has become the habitation and his body the temple."[6] Thus, both Keswick and Murray focus on the holiness of the believer's life by emphasizing the ministry of the Holy Spirit in him.

---

4. Barabas, *So Great Salvation*, 30.
5. Pierson, "Message," 90.
6. Murray, "Definitive Sanctification," 21.

Romans 6 as the Primary Text for the Teaching

Both Keswick and Murray use Romans 6 as the primary text for their teachings. Romans 6 has been called by Keswick "the Magna Charta of the soul and the Emancipation Proclamation of the Christian." Much of Keswick's crisis sanctification is based on this text. Likewise, Murray primarily bases the formulation of the doctrine of definitive sanctification on Romans 6. He calls the doctrine of definitive sanctification the hinge on which Romans 6 turns. In the article "Sanctification" in *Christianity Today*, Murray makes more references to Romans 6 than any other parts of Scripture for the presentation of definitive sanctification. Also in "Definitive Sanctification" in the *Calvin Theological Journal*, Murray states that no passage in the New Testament is more instructive than Romans 6 in teaching definitive sanctification.

Romans 6 had not been a primary text for the holiness movement's teaching until Keswick claimed it as such. In the same sense, Romans 6 had not played a major role such as Romans 7 for the Reformed study of sanctification until Murray introduced the distinctiveness of definitive sanctification taught in this text. Thus, Keswick's sanctification and Murray's definitive sanctification are similar in that they both utilize Romans 6 for their fundamental teachings and in the process, brought out the importance of this chapter for the study of sanctification.

The Basis of the Immediate Aspect of Sanctification

Another similarity between Keswick's sanctification and Murray's definitive sanctification is that they both base the immediate aspect of sanctification on the death and resurrection of Christ. In other words, both Keswick and Murray base sanctification on the believer's union with Christ. For Keswick, Barabas writes, "By our union with Him in His death we were freed from the penalty of sin and emancipation from the power of sin. All our sanctification therefore must be traced to, and rests upon, the atoning sacrifice of our LORD Jesus Christ."[7] For the doctrine of definitive sanctification Murray writes, "No datum is of more basic importance than the definitive breach with sin and commitment to holiness secured by identification with Christ in his death and resurrection."[8] In the above statements for Keswick's and Murray's teachings, the believer's union with Christ is emphasized for the ground of the immediate aspect of sanctification.

7. Barabas, *So Great Salvation*, 88–89.
8. Murray, "Sanctification," 790.

Both Keswick and Murray teach that the believer has been freed from the dominion of sin by virtue of union with Christ. As Murray emphasizes the resurrection of Christ in the believer's union with Christ, Keswick also underscores the importance of this truth. Barabas states, "It is a fact of great importance for the believer's sanctification that not only was he crucified with Christ, but that he was identified with Christ in His resurrection and ascension."[9] Thus, Keswick's sanctification and Murray's definitive sanctification are similar in that they are both grounded on the believer's union with Christ in his death and resurrection.

It is commendable both Keswick and Murray base their immediate aspect of sanctification on the union with Christ. It is no surprise to see Murray, as a Reformed theologian, bases his teaching on the union with Christ. Also the Keswick's approach, in spite of its Wesleyan perfectionism background, shows an earnest effort to emphasize the centrality of Christ in the experiential aspect of holy life.

The Instantaneous Nature of Sanctification

Keswick's sanctification and Murray's definitive sanctification are similar in their instantaneous nature of sanctification. Keswick's sanctification can be called more exactly a crisis sanctification based on positional sanctification. Barabas maintains, "Sanctification, in the sense of a definite decision for holiness, a thorough and whole-hearted dedication to God, the committal of the whole being to Him is a crisis, and the crisis must take place before we really know the process. Before you can draw a line you must begin with a point. The line is a process the point is the crisis."[10] By a crisis being the point, Barabas means that crisis sanctification is instantaneous as compared to the gradual process of progressive sanctification.

Murray also teaches that definitive sanctification is instantaneous in the Christian life. He states that the definitive and irrevocable breach with sin is an instantaneous and once-for-all act. Although Keswick's crisis sanctification is repeated in the Christian life as opposed to the once-for-allness of Murray's definitive sanctification, both of them occur instantaneously in the believer's life.

Aside from Wesleyan perfectionism since the eighteenth century, sanctification has been understood as a process throughout the Christian history. The concept of the instantaneous nature of sanctification was foreign to many Christian churches, especially in the Reformed circle. But

9. Barabas, *So Great Salvation*, 93.
10. Barabas, *So Great Salvation*, 93.

Keswick and Murray in their own way, Keswick by following the Wesleyan perfectionism tradition and Murray by reacting to Keswick theologically, brought out this particular biblical teaching to the fore and put it in the main stream of the Christian life in the evangelical church.

Distinction from Justification and Progressive Sanctification

Keswick's positional sanctification and Murray's definitive sanctification are distinguished from justification and progressive sanctification. Justification is the judicial proclamation of God's pardon of the sinner. Progressive sanctification is the gradual transformation of the believer through the work of the Holy Spirit into the image of Jesus Christ. Keswick's positional sanctification and Murray's definitive sanctification are neither forensic nor progressive in endowment of God's grace. Keswick's positional sanctification and Murray's definitive sanctification are similar in their function as the bridge between justification and progressive sanctification.

Differences between Keswick's Sanctification and Murray's Definitive Sanctification

Although there are some similarities between Keswick's sanctification and Murray's definitive sanctification, the similarities between these two teachings are outward in nature. As we move into specific elements of these teachings, we find that there are many differences between them. In this section the differences between Keswick's sanctification and Murray's definitive sanctification are presented in eight different categories.

Approach to the Study of Holiness

Although both Keswick's sanctification and Murray's definitive sanctification concentrate on holiness of the Christian life, the approach of these teachings to the study of holiness are quite different from one another. Keswick's sanctification takes the approach that is basically rooted in the perfectionists' teaching in the nineteenth century. Since perfectionists' teaching goes back to Wesleyan perfectionism in the eighteenth century in England, it may be said that Keswick's approach to the study of sanctification falls into the tradition of the Wesleyan-Arminian and perfectionist-Pelagian approach to the study of holiness of the Christian life. Murray's definitive sanctification, on the other hand, takes the Calvinistic, Reformed approach to the study of holiness of the Christian life.

N^{th} Degree Versus Once-For-All Sanctification

There is a difference between Keswick's sanctification and Murray's definitive sanctification in the repeatability of this experience. Keswick teaches that crisis sanctification is to be repeated many times throughout the Christian life. Evan Hopkins writes, "Is the crisis to be repeated? If I have once consecrated myself to God, am I not to consecrate myself to Him again? . . . I say, Yes, it is to be done again in the sense of restoration. You have slipped back, your attitude of consecration has not been maintained; you have to come back again, you have to repeat the act undoubtedly."[11] For Keswick, sanctification is comprised of crisis and process. Crisis is the driving force of process sanctification. Crisis enables the believer to make a quantum leap of spirituality and thereby enables him to begin process sanctification at the higher level of spirituality.

According to Keswick's sanctification, the believer may have many crisis sanctifications which may be termed as the first, second, third, . . . and n^{th} crisis sanctification. In fact, in Keswick's sanctification the more crises the believer has, the higher spirituality he will have in a shorter time. Keswick teaches that sanctification can be lost.[12] Therefore, a believer needs to have a crisis again in order to achieve sanctification. However, it does not teach that salvation is lost in the believer such that he needs to have the initial salvation crisis again.

Murray, on the other hand, teaches the once-for-allness of definitive sanctification. It happens at the inception of the Christian life only once and is never to be repeated in the life. Definitive sanctification cannot be lost by the believer. The person who has been truly born again by the Spirit has this blessing at the inception of his Christian life.

Therefore, there is a great difference between Keswick's crisis sanctification and Murray's definitive sanctification as far as the repeatability is concerned. Pictorially, Keswick's sanctification may be depicted as a combination of dots and short lines on a one-dimensional time axis if the dots represent crises and the short lines the process in sanctification. Then it is easy to understand Hopkin's statement that Keswick's sanctification is "a crisis with a view to a process."[13] Murray's sanctification curve on the

---

11. Hopkins, "Crisis and Process," 336.
12. Thompson, "Appraisal of the Keswick," 14.
13. Hopkins, "Crisis and Process," 332.

one-dimensional time axis would be just a straight line with a point at the beginning of the line. On this straight line the point represents definitive sanctification and the line represents progressive sanctification.

Positional Versus Actual Truth

Another difference between Keswick's sanctification and Murray's definitive sanctification is that the truth of the believer's death and resurrection with Christ is positional first for Keswick whereas it is actual for Murray. Keswick's positional sanctification is the condition in which the believer is set free from the dominion of sin. J. Robertson McQuilkin writes, "The first step is positional sanctification, in which the sinner is set apart from his or her sin for the purpose of becoming God's own possession."[14] Murray refutes this view and says that this truth involves more than just positional sanctification. It is actual and experiential in the believer. Murray argues, "This victory is actual or it is nothing. It is a reflection upon and deflection from the pervasive New Testament witness to speak of it as merely potential or positional."[15] For Murray, the victory that comes to the believer through definitive sanctification is actual and experiential. The victory over sin is experiential in the believer's life such that he does not and cannot commit the "sin unto death" in 1 John 5:16.

Keswick, on the other hand, teaches that this victory does not become experiential until the believer accepts the truth through a reckoning process by faith. This is the outworking of the believer's official position in his daily life. Thus, for Keswick this truth of the victory over sin may be lost forever from the believer unless he claims it by reckoning the truth. The victory over sin is a positional or potential blessing for the believer according to Keswick. However, for Murray this victory over sin is a blessing, actually given to the believer by God at the inception of the Christian life.

As was pointed out in chapter 6, Murray's concept of definitive sanctification is not much different from that of positional sanctification of Keswick, even though he tries hard to distinguish his concept from Keswick's. In fact, some scholars familiar with the instantaneous aspect of sanctification taught in Scripture use these terms interchangeably.[16]

---

14. J. R. McQuilkin, "Keswick Perspective," 158.
15. Murray, *Redemption*, 142.
16. Peterson, *Possessed by God*, 47; DeYoung, "Incentives," 49.

Relationship with Progressive Sanctification

Both Keswick and Murray teach that their crisis sanctification and definitive sanctification are closely related to progressive sanctification. According to Keswick, sanctification is comprised of crisis and process and crisis sanctification acts as the driving force for progressive sanctification. Crisis sanctification clears away the hindrances that may slow down the progress of sanctification. However, the nature of the relationship between Keswick's crisis sanctification and the progressive sanctification is different from the relationship of Murray's definitive sanctification with progressive sanctification.

While Keswick's crisis sanctification is the driving force for progressive sanctification, Murray's definitive sanctification is foundational for progressive sanctification. In Keswick, crisis helps the believer to achieve higher spirituality in progressive sanctification. For Murray, all believers are in progressive sanctification and they all have had definitive sanctification, and their progressive sanctification is based on it. In this sense, Murray's definitive sanctification is vitally and absolutely related to progressive sanctification in a much closer sense than Keswick's crisis and progressive sanctification.

Keswick makes crisis and progressive sanctification distinct by having the believer work at them separately. The believer needs to reckon, surrender or do other necessary activities in order to have crisis sanctification. He also has to work at the progress of sanctification everyday. In Keswick's sanctification crisis and progressive sanctification are considered as different stages. The believer has to work in order to achieve the corresponding sanctification.

Murray, on the other hand, teaches that definitive sanctification is a gift of God to the believer, therefore, it does not involve the believer's work. In progressive sanctification the believer needs to work at the growth of the spiritual life with the guidance of the Holy Spirit. Thus, they are not separate stages of sanctification which the believer has to work at. Definitive sanctification is the foundation for progressive sanctification.

Relationship with Justification

The relationship with justification is yet another difference found between Keswick's crisis sanctification and Murray's definitive sanctification. Both claim that their crisis and definitive sanctification are distinct from justification. Both Keswick and Murray see justification in the judicial sense of the declaration of the sinner to be righteous before God based on the work of Christ. Keswick teaches that the crisis sanctification may or may not happen at the time of the justification of the sinner. Murray, however, teaches that definitive sanctification occurs with justification at the inception of the Christian life.

Keswick's idea of the relationship between sanctification and justification is confounded in the way they define sanctification. Keswick divides sanctification into three stages: positional, experiential, and permanent. In positional sanctification are three elements: forgiveness, justification, and regeneration.[17] Thus, in their definition of positional sanctification they include the meaning of justification. Keswick's definition of positional sanctification is not distinctly set forth from justification.

It is seen that Murray clearly distinguishes definitive sanctification from justification. He also asserts that they are vitally and intimately related. However, he is not clear how justification and definitive sanctification are related logically in the *ordo salutis*.[18] Does justification come before definitive sanctification? Or do they come together logically in the *ordo salutis*?[19] Murray is not clear on this point although he clearly distinguishes justification and definitive sanctification.

Deliverance from Sin

There is a difference between Keswick and Murray in their conception of how the victory in Christ is translated into the actual experience in the believer's life. Keswick teaches that the believer who goes through Keswick's sanctification, especially experiential sanctification, is freed from known sin. The believer is freed from known sinful thoughts and actions. Canon W. Hay H. M. Aitken elaborates:

> Now dear brethren, from all such known sin—whether sins of heedlessness, as we call them, or sins of will—we are redeemed by the blood of the Lamb slain from before the foundation of the world for this very purpose; and because we are redeemed, therefore we have the right to be free. He that hath died is justified from sin, because the old man hath died, and only because he has died.[20]

17. J. R. McQuilkin, "Keswick Perspective," 158–60.

18. The *ordo salutis* is defined as the way of salvation. Berkouwer, *Justification*, 25.

19. This is one of the elements of definitive sanctification that needs to be developed further in this doctrine. My view on this matter will be presented in chapter 8.

20. Aitken, "Full Deliverance," 166–67.

Keswick advocates distinguish known sin from sins of ignorance and say that believers with Keswick's sanctification are delivered from known sin.

Murray, however, repudiates this view of Keswick. He teaches that the believer with definitive sanctification does not and cannot commit the "sin unto death" in 1 John 5:16. Murray writes that according to 1 John 3:6–9 and 5:16–18, "the regenerate does not commit sin, it is surely justifiable to conclude that the sin he does not commit is the sin unto death."[21] As such, the believer is protected from apostatizing the gospel of Jesus Christ. Murray explains, "We must infer that the sin a regenerate person does not commit is the denial of Jesus as come in the flesh or indeed the failure to confess Jesus Christ as come in the flesh."[22] Thus, in Murray's definitive sanctification the believer is freed from the sin unto death.

On this subject of the actual experience of the believer, there is yet work to be done on both Keswick's sanctification and Murray's definitive sanctification. Keswick's teaching of the believer's deliverance from known sin is a troubling one. Treating and defining sin in this way is very subjective because what may be a known sin to one may not be a known sin to another. Also, when they begin to treat "unknown sin" as flaws or short-comings, they are on the expressway to Pelagian perfectionism. Murray, on the other hand, seems to particularize the victory over all sins by naming one specific sin, the sin unto death in 1 John 5:16. Also Murray, by having the believer protected from apostatizing the gospel, seems to describe the condition of the believer rather than the deliverance from a specific sin for the believer. J. I. Packer calls the definitive experience of sanctification the transfer from the unnaturalness to naturalness of motivational holiness.[23] Motivational holiness makes the believer naturally to do godly actions and unnaturally to commit sin by yielding to the desires of the flesh. The discussion of this matter will be developed further with the inclusion of my view in the next chapter. In concluding the discussion here, I point out again that there is a difference between Keswick's sanctification and Murray's definitive sanctification in how the victory in Christ is translated into the experience of the believer.

Counteraction Versus Eradication

Another difference between Keswick and Murray is the way the Holy Spirit works in the believer. Keswick teaches that the Holy Spirit works

---

21. Murray, "Definitive Sanctification," 11.
22. Murray, "Definitive Sanctification," 11.
23. Packer, *Keep In Step*, 107.

against the law of sin by counteraction whereas Murray teaches that the work of the Holy Spirit is the eradication of the corrupt nature. Barabas writes, "Keswick leaders often say that God's method of sanctification is not suppression or eradication, but counteraction."[24] The power of the Holy Spirit, which counteracts the power of the law of sin in the believer, is a mightier force than the power of the law of sin. Thus, the believer is delivered from the power of sin and is free to walk the path of sanctification. Barabas offers an illustration:

> One not yet given, but frequently used, is the story of Peter walking on the water. We are told that he was able to walk on the water not in virtue of anything that Christ had wrought in him, or because his tendency to sink had been eradicated by the power of Christ, but because through faith-contact with Christ he was perpetually receiving a supply of divine power which completely counteracted his weight. He was kept from sinking, moment by moment, as long as he was in contact by faith with the source of all power.[25]

Although Keswick advocates may find the above illustration to be supportive of their teaching of counteraction of the Holy Spirit in the believer, I find this illustration to be totally inappropriate for the subject at hand. First, Peter's weight is not some evil force or agent such as the law of sin which should be eradicated eventually from the kingdom of God. Second, the people who teach eradication may just as well argue for their position from many incidents where Christ healed or "cleansed" the diseases of the people, such as leprosy. This is clearly "cleansing" or eradication of the disease or germs of disease by the power of Christ.

As opposed to Keswick's teaching of counteraction, Murray teaches eradication by the Holy Spirit. He writes, "If we are to use any of the terms . . . with reference to the grace of God as it is brought to bear upon the corrupt nature, . . . eradication . . . is the only proper one."[26] By this progressive eradication of "inward corruption" the believer is progressively conformed to the image of Christ. Murray, however, is not clear how this inward corruption is different from the "old man" which according to him died once-for-all in the believer's death with Christ.[27] In asserting eradication by the

24. Barabas, *So Great Salvation*, 94.
25. Barabas, *So Great Salvation*, 95.
26. Murray, Review of *So Great Salvation*, 80–81.
27. It seems that eradication by the Holy Spirit is also against sin itself in order for Murray to be consistent with his view of "old man." My view and suggestion on this matter will be presented in chapter 8.

Holy Spirit, Murray closely follows the Reformed tradition as opposed to Keswick's teaching of counteraction.

The Time of the Believer's Union with Christ

There is yet another difference between Keswick's sanctification and Murray's definitive sanctification as to when the believer's union with Christ occurs. Murray sees both the past historical and the experiential aspects in the union with Christ. Keswick, on the other hand, does not have an elaborate discussion on this subject. Keswick's teaching seems to be concentrated on the past historical aspect of the union with Christ. Barabas notes, "When Christ died on the cross to sin, we were identified with Him in that death to sin. That is, we died with Him. By our union with Him in His death we were freed from the penalty of sin and emancipated from the power of sin."[28] Barabas here emphasizes the past historical fact of the death of Christ. The fact of the believer's death to sin with Christ at the time of Christ's death is objective truth, or positional sanctification in Keswick's terminology. This positional sanctification becomes subjective experiential sanctification after the believer goes through the reckoning process by exercising the faith. Murray's view on this subject is that the believer's union is both past historical and experiential. In the past historical sense, the believer died to sin with Christ at the time of his death and resurrection. This past historical truth conditions the experiential truth. The believer actually died to sin and resurrected with Christ in his life history. Murray gives the reason for asserting the both aspects of the union with Christ, "It is only in this way that we can avoid the tendency to deny the vicarious significance of that which Christ wrought once for all in the realm of history as concrete and real as any other historical event."[29] Thus, Murray preserves the past historical and the experiential fact of the believer's death and resurrection with Christ in the vital relationship in the union with Christ, whereas Keswick emphasizes the believer's past historical death to sin with Christ which becomes the experiential truth for the believer after the reckoning process.

---

28. Barabas, *So Great Salvation*, 88–89.
29. Murray, "Definitive Sanctification," 19.

Conclusion

The comparison of Keswick's sanctification and Murray's definitive sanctification has been presented in this chapter. The similarities between these two doctrines are found in six elements of their teachings.

First, Keswick's sanctification and Murray's definitive sanctification are similar as they are involved in the action-reaction phenomenon in the holiness movement. B. B. Warfield responded from the Reformed position to perfectionism in the late nineteenth century. Warfield's criticism on perfectionism was responded by American Keswick with a modified form of perfectionism camouflaged with mild Calvinism. Murray's definitive sanctification was the response from the Reformed position to Keswick's sanctification, an offspring of perfectionism of the nineteenth century.

Second, they are similar in that they both focused on the sanctification of a believer. Keswick was especially organized to promote the holiness of the Christian life. Murray's definitive sanctification also focuses on the holiness of the believer in a definitive sense. By focusing on the holiness of a believer both Keswick's and Murray's teachings are vitally related to the daily life of a believer.

Third, Romans 6 is the primary text for both Keswick's and Murray's doctrines. Keswick called this chapter the "Magna Charta of the soul and the Emancipation Proclamation of the Christian." Murray also said that the doctrine of definitive sanctification is the hinge in which Romans 6 turns.

Fourth, the basis of the immediate aspect of sanctification is similar in Keswick's and Murray's doctrines. Both Keswick and Murray based sanctification on the believer's union with Christ. The believer's death to sin and resurrection with Christ are emphasized for the basis of sanctification. Both Keswick and Murray taught that the believer is identified and united with Christ by virtue of his death and resurrection with Christ.

Fifth, Keswick's sanctification and Murray's definitive sanctification are similar in their instantaneous nature of sanctification. Keswick's crisis sanctification based on positional sanctification is instantaneous. Crisis sanctification is instantaneous compared to the gradual process of progressive sanctification. Murray also teaches that definitive sanctification is instantaneous in the Christian life. He states that the definitive and irrevocable breach with sin is an instantaneous and once-for-all act.

Sixth, both Keswick and Murray distinguished their teachings from justification and progressive sanctification. Justification is the judicial proclamation of God's pardon of the sinner whereas progressive sanctification is the gradual transformation of the believer into the image of Jesus Christ. Both Keswick and Murray assert that their distinctive teachings are on the immediate aspect of sanctification which is far different from the judicial proclamation of the God's pardon of the sinner and the gradual transformation of the believer.

The similarities between Keswick's sanctification and Murray's definitive sanctification are outward in nature. However, as we move into the specific details of these teachings, we find many differences between these two in eight different categories.

First, the approaches of these teachings to the study of sanctification are different from each other. Keswick advocates used the approach that was rooted in perfectionism in the nineteenth century. It fell into the tradition of the Wesleyan-Arminian and perfectionist-Pelagian approach to the study of holiness. Murray's definitive sanctification, on the other hand, took the Reformed approach to the study of holiness of the Christian life.

Second, there is the difference between Keswick's and Murray's teachings in the repeatability of the experience of instantaneous sanctification. Whereas Keswick taught that crisis sanctification is to be repeated many times throughout the Christian life, Murray taught the once-for-allness of definitive sanctification. It happens at the inception of the Christian life only once and is never to be repeated in the life.

Third, the truth of the believer's death and resurrection with Christ is positional first for Keswick whereas it is actual for Murray. Keswick's positional sanctification is the condition in which a believer is set free from the dominion of sin. Murray's definitive sanctification, on the other hand, is actual and experiential. In definitive sanctification the victory over sin is experiential in the belier's life such that he cannot commit the sin unto death in 1 John 5:16. Keswick, on the other hand, asserted that this victory does not become experiential until the believer accepts the truth through the reckoning process by faith.

Fourth, there is the difference between these two teachings in the nature of their relationship to progressive sanctification. Whereas Keswick's crisis sanctification is the driving force for progressive sanctification, Murray's definitive sanctification is foundational for progressive sanctification. According to Murray, all believers have gone through definitive sanctification which is absolutely foundational for their progressive sanctification. Thus, Murray's definitive sanctification is vitally related to the progressive sanctification in a much closer sense than Keswick's crisis and progressive sanctification.

Fifth, Keswick taught that crisis sanctification may or may not occur with justification at the inception of the Christian life. Murray, on the other hand, asserted that definite sanctification occurs at the inception of the Christian life, possibly with justification.

Sixth, there is also a difference between Keswick and Murray in how the victory in Christ is translated into the actual experience in the believer's life. Keswick taught that the believer who goes through crisis sanctification is delivered from known sin while Murray taught that he who goes through definitive sanctification is delivered from the sin unto death. However, on this point Keswick's view seems to be leaning toward Pelagian perfectionism whereas Murray seems to particularize the victory over all sins by naming one sin, the sin unto death in 1 John 5:16.

Seventh, Keswick's and Murray's teachings are also different in the way the Holy Spirit works in the believer. Keswick taught that the Holy Spirit works against the law of sin by counteraction. The power of the Holy Spirit, which counteracts the power of sin in the believer, is a mightier force than the law of sin. Thus, the believer is freed from the dominion of sin in the Christian life. Murray, however, taught that the work of the Holy Spirit in the believer is the eradication of corrupt nature.

Eighth, the believer's union with Christ is taken in a past historical sense by Keswick while it is viewed as both past historical and experiential by Murray. Keswick emphasized the past historical fact of the death and resurrection of Christ. The fact of the believer's death to sin with Christ at the time of his death is objective truth, or positional sanctification in Keswick's term. In Murray's definitive sanctification, the past historical truth conditions the experiential truth. The believer actually died to sin and resurrected with Christ in the believer's life history. Thus, Murray emphasized both the past historical and the experiential aspects in the believer's union with Christ.

Murray's doctrine of definitive sanctification is an invaluable concept for understanding the once-for-all aspect of sanctification, as taught in Scripture. However, this doctrine needs to be developed and refined more in order to function as a *bona fide* element in the *ordo salutis*, and to provide actual and practical benefits to believers in the pursuit of holiness in the Christian life.

Chapter 8

Definitive Sanctification in Salvation of Man

MURRAY'S DOCTRINE OF DEFINITIVE sanctification is an invaluable and seminal concept on which to build the once-for-all and immediate aspect of sanctification as taught in Scripture. Murray formulated and introduced this doctrine in 1960s, and it was not well-known until the late twentieth century in the Christian church, even in the Reformed circle.

However, in recent years many scholars have begun to emphasize the indicative expression pertaining to sanctification in Scripture and have asserted the "once-for-allness and immediate aspect" of sanctification, whether they call it "positional," "definitive," or "accomplished" sanctification in their writings.[1] Therefore, it is reasonable to assume that there is a theological consensus formed in the Christian church for explicating and propagating this doctrine for promoting the holy life of believers. Although a question was raised about the soundness of biblical foundation for this doctrine,[2] the ample evidence for the biblical basis of the doctrine is documented by many scholars.[3]

It is encouraging to see that the current scholarship with respect to sanctification begins to treat the idea of definitive sanctification on par with progressive aspect of sanctification. However, more development and refinement are needed in order for this doctrine to be a full-fledged doctrine in the *ordo salutis* such as regeneration, justification, or progressive sanctification, and to be treated as such.

---

1. Payne, *Already Sanctified*, 5; Peterson, *Possessed by God*, 47; Park, *Driven by God*, 29; Grudem, *Systematic Theology*, 747; Reymond, *New Systematic Theology*, 756.

2. Fesko, "Sanctification," 197.

3. Cunnington, "Definitive Sanctification," 234; Payne, *Already Sanctified*, 5; Peterson, *Possessed by God*, 47; Park, *Driven by God*, 29.

In this chapter some elements of the doctrine of definitive sanctification are further elaborated and refined in an effort to develop it to a more biblically and theologically sound doctrine in Christian theology. To this end six elements of the doctrine will be examined and elaborated in detail including soteriological ramifications each elaboration or refinement of the element might engender. First, in what sense is definitive sanctification actual in the believer? In other words, what "actually," not theoretically, happens to the believer in definitive sanctification? Second, what is the experiential effect of definitive sanctification in the believer? The experiential and irrevocable effect in the believer as the result of definitive sanctification is at issue here. For example, does definitive sanctification make a believer immune from certain sin? Third, Murray says that because victory in Christ is actual, it is experiential. Is this true in spiritual life? Or is there a logical fallacy in his argument? Fourth, what is the exact relationship between justification and definitive sanctification? How is each element related to the union with Christ? And their logical relationship in the *ordo salutis* needs to be clarified. Fifth, what is it that is being eradicated by the Holy Spirit in the believer who has been definitively sanctified? Also, how does this process of eradication occur in the believer? Sixth, what is the relationship between definitive sanctification and progressive sanctification? For this question, the relationship between definitive and progressive sanctification is examined with a monergistic perspective of soteriology. The answers to these questions above will strengthen and refine the doctrine of definitive sanctification in an effort to establish it as a full-pledged doctrine in soteriology.

Actuality of Definitive Sanctification

What actually happens to a believer in definitive sanctification? Murray says that there is a decisive breach with sin as the dominion, and a new relationship with righteousness. The believer is translated from the realm of sin to the realm of the grace of God. His ethical and spiritual orientations are changed. Murray uses the term "transformation" of the believer in definitive sanctification. But Murray's description of the change of the believer in definitive sanctification is more of a translation in the sense of the believer's transference from one realm to another rather than the actual change or transformation in the nature of man. The issue at hand is what actually happens to the nature of man, both body and soul, material and immaterial being, if it happens at all. Is there the inherent change or transformation of the nature of man in definitive sanctification?

Murray's description of the change of the believer in definitive sanctification is primarily relational. Man's relation to sin and to righteousness is changed in definitive sanctification. Man's living sphere is changed from the world of sin, in which sin is the master, to the world of righteousness, in which the LORD Jesus Christ is the master. These descriptions are all relational changes in the believer. Murray's description of the change of man in definitive sanctification in a predominantly relational sense might compel Keswick advocates to view Murray's definitive sanctification as their positional sanctification even though he uses a different term. What needs to be included in Murray's definitive sanctification is the explication of the actual change that happens to the being or nature of man if there is the inherent change in man.

Also, unless the critical concept of the breach with sin in definitive sanctification is explained in a transformational sense, a criticism like Fesko's that the breach with sin belongs in justification will not be obviated completely.[4] If the breach with sin belongs in sanctification, there must be actual transformation in man in the act of the breach. I believe that there are three changes that actually occur in the act of the breach with sin in definitive sanctification.

Transformation in the Nature of Man

The main concept of definitive sanctification is the radical breach with sin as the dominion, as taught in Scripture (Rom 6:11, 14, 18, 22; 1 Cor 6:11). But what does the "breach with sin" mean? Before tackling this question, we need to first think about what "sin" is. As Berkouwer writes about sin, "we cannot reflect on the essence or the character of sin unless we do so in relation to God," sin always concerns God.[5] So sin, though undefinable in a phenomenal world, is a spiritual entity since God is the ultimate spiritual Being.

Sin was first committed by angels, the spiritual beings (Gen 3:1; Isa 14:12–15; 2 Pet 2:4; Jude 6). Sin came into a being in a spiritual realm. In the garden of Eden Adam committed the sin by eating the forbidden fruit from the tree of the knowledge of good and evil. Since sin is a spiritual entity, Adam's sinning occurred in a spiritual realm although it involved him eating the forbidden fruit in the physical world. Committing a sin is essentially a spiritual act in a spiritual realm. Because of Adam's sin he along with all mankind became slaves to sin, or "fallen" men (John 8:43; Rom 6:18, 22). Being enslaved to sin is a spiritual phenomenon that happens in

---

4. Fesko, "Sanctification," 210.
5. Berkouwer, *Sin*, 283.

a spiritual realm. But the spiritual act of becoming enslaved to sin has the corresponding transformational effect in the phenomenal world. Adam and Eve, becoming enslaved to sin by disobeying God, had a transformation in their nature as their eyes were opened and could see their nakedness which they could not see before (Gen 3:7).

Adam's sinning, a spiritual act in a spiritual realm, caused his nature to be altered, which is an actual change in a phenomenal world. Adam, being enslaved to sin in a spiritual realm, became a man without a free will (John 8:32, 36; Rom 6:20; 8:2; 2 Cor 3:17; Gal 5:2). His will became bent toward evil and is trapped in that direction, resulting in no freedom in his life. Not only did Adam lose free will, but also his spiritual sense was extirpated such that he became a spiritually dead man (Eph 2:1). Adam along with the mankind became enemies of God (Rom 8:7). Also Adam's enslavement to sin in a spiritual realm transformed his nature such that his body actually became an instrument of wickedness in the phenomenal world (Rom 6:13). Thus, an act of sin in a spiritual realm has the corresponding transformational effect in the phenomenal world.

Freedom of Will

Just like the enslavement to sin, the breach with sin as the dominion in the believer's life is a spiritual act that occurs in a spiritual realm. Just as the enslavement to sin in a spiritual realm had the corresponding transformational effect in the nature of man in the phenomenal world, so does the breach with sin in the nature of man. The first of these transformations in the nature of man by the breach is that man actually becomes free, possessing a free will (John 8:32, 36; Rom 6:20; 8:2; 2 Cor 3:17; Gal 5:2). Paul writes, "Because through Christ Jesus the law of the Spirit who gives life has set you free from the law of sin and death" (Rom 8:2).

The salvation of man necessarily includes freedom. Man becomes a "new man" endowed with free will in the salvation. It is critical to understand that the will of an unbeliever, a fallen man, is not free. It is under the bondage of sin. Paul writes, "When you were slaves to sin, you were free from the control of righteousness" (Rom 6:20). So "will" becomes truly a free will through definitive sanctification. Liberation of will at the time of salvation is extremely important in the believer's life. Jesus says, "Then you will know the truth, and the truth will set you free . . . So if the Son sets you free, you will be free indeed" (John 8:32–36). Paul writes also, "It is for freedom that Christ has set us free. Stand firm, then, and do not let yourselves be burdened again by a yoke of slavery" (Gal 5:1). Scripture unequivocally teaches that the unbeliever's will is not free, but the believer's will is free. There is a radical difference between the unbeliever's will and believer's will.

Modern man thinks he has free will. That is because he has a power to choose either A or B. But defining the free will in this way is non-biblical and humanistic. Even Immanuel Kant, a secular philosopher, does not define a free will in this way. He says that man is free when he acts according to the categorical imperative, which is the built-in universal law. Of course, this is not a biblical definition. But it shows that even the secular philosopher does not view the free will as the power to choose either A or B in a physical world. Also the existential philosopher Jean Paul Sartre cries out that people's freedom is a curse. This is a cry of a modern man who asserts he is free and tries to live accordingly.

Man's freedom and existence have a sensible meaning only in the context of God, who is the source of them. Jonathan Edwards says that man's freedom and existence cannot be understood without first understanding the freedom and existence of God. This is in line with Scripture. "For in him we live and move and have our being" (Acts 16:28). A thought of the existence of man is possible only under the supposition of the existence of God. Pascal says that man does not know himself because he does not know God. Also, John Calvin writes in *Institutes* that man cannot see himself without thinking about God. Therefore, just as the discussion of man's existence is possible only in the existence of God, the freedom of man's will is understood only when we understand the freedom of God's will.[6]

God has a will. "Will" may be defined as that by which the whole person chooses anything. God's will is free. No believer will deny that God has a free will. But that does not mean that God has a power to choose evil. Scripture says, "God did this so that, by two unchangeable things in which it is impossible for God to lie, we who have fled to take hold of the hope set before us may be greatly encouraged" (Heb 6:18). God cannot lie. Scripture does not teach that God's will is not free because God cannot lie. It is absurd to say that God should not tell the truth always but should lie once in a while so that his will can be truly free. Thus, Scripture does not teach that God has to choose evil as well as good in order for his will to be free. God does not have a desire to choose evil and does not actually choose evil. But God's will is truly free. God's will is free because his will is exercised always in line with his attributes. Anything pertaining to evil is not God's attribute. God has a free will because his will acts freely, meaning that his will is always exercised in line with his attributes.

---

6. This part of discussion is extracted from my other writing, *Covenant Life*, 61–64.

Man has a will, too. But man as well as his will are creation of God. Man, as the image of God, is created to think after God's thoughts, love like him, and to will according to his will. So man's will is free when it is exercised according to God's will, which is always exercised in line with his attributes. Out of God's many attributes, one that depicts God best comprehensively is love. John writes, "Whoever does not love does not know God, because God is love" (1 John 4:8). Man is created as God's beloved, and the primary purpose of man's will given by God is to love God freely. God is man's object of true love. So man's will is free when it is exercised in line with true love, or choosing God. Included in this choosing are the nature and purpose of man. Thus, man's will is free when his will is exercised according to true love, which is in line with the nature and purpose of man. When his will is exercised in this way, man has a peace and a sense of freedom in his heart. Man is said to have a free will when he exercises his will according to the intent of the creator, the true love.

When Adam fell in the garden of Eden, he lost this free will. This tragedy caused the mankind to be born with a will that is under bondage. Martin Luther is very emphatic about this. Man, fallen, has no free will. The totality of man's being, including his will, is enslaved to sin (Rom 6:20). The fallen man's will is bent toward the lust of the flesh, the lust of the eyes, and the pride of life; which I call "counterfeit love." This "counterfeit love" has replaced the "true love" at the core of man's being. That is why the unbeliever could not help but sin in his life. He is gravely deceived by the dark force to choose the "counterfeit love," which never satisfies him but only elicits more desire of worldly things. He is in the depth of misery.

Only Jesus Christ can liberate a man from misery and slavery. He says, "If you hold to my teaching, you are really my disciples. Then you will know the truth, and the truth will set you free" (John 8:31–32). Jesus liberates whole person, including his will, from the bondage of sin. He does it by coming into him and abiding in him. Thus, man becomes a Christ-indwelling believer. What happens in definitive sanctification is that the true love is placed in the heart of man, displacing the "counterfeit love" and the will is bent toward the true love. In this way, the believer exercises his will in accordance with the true love, which makes the will to be free.

However, we know that the believer also falls into sin even though he has a will bent toward true love. Influenced by fleshly desires, he sometimes chooses that which is contrary to true love, thereby not exercising his will freely. If this happens, the inconsonance of his will with true love will cause anxiety and guilt, which will lead him to repentance. Thus the believer does not go to the endpoint of sin and stay there, but he comes back to true love through repentance.

204　THE GROUND OF HOLY LIFE

The transformation that occurs to the will of man due to the enslavement to sin and the breach with sin is illustrated in the Figure 1. The first man, Adam, had a free will, which was bent toward God, true love. But Adam chose evil, and thereby exercised his will not freely. His will became enslaved to sin, bent toward evil. A fallen man, an unbeliever, could not help but sin. His will is bent toward evil and he has no free will. In the salvation by God, man's enslaved will is transformed into free will in definitive sanctification. Even though the believer has a free will, his will is not the perfect free will like that of the glorified man. Here we see the "already" and "not yet" concept in the believer's free will. He already has free will, but it is not yet the perfect free will he will have in the eschaton. In this life the believer falls into sin, not exercising his free will freely. But he does not go to the endpoint of evil. He always eventually chooses God crossing from the road of evil to the road of God through repentance, and thereby manifesting the free will inside of him.

Figure 1: Change in the Will of Man Due to
Enslavement to Sin and Breach with Sin

Thus, we see there is an actual, radical change in the will of man through definitive sanctification. Paul says, "For we know that our old self was crucified with him so that the body ruled by sin might be done away with, that we should no longer be slaves to sin" (Rom 6:6). Believer must believe his old self is dead. Man whose will was a slave to sin and was incapable of choosing true love is dead. He is a new man now, who has free will to choose true love at every point of his life. The belief in this truth is crucial for progressive sanctification in the believer's life.

Spiritual Sense

Another actual transformation in the phenomenal world by the spiritual act of the breach with sin is the revivification of a spiritual sense in the heart of man, often called a sense of the heart or the spiritual sense.[7] The unbeliever or unregenerate man does not have this spiritual sense, and he is said to be spiritually dead according to Scripture. Jesus says to one of his followers, "Follow me, and let the dead bury their own dead" (Matt 8:22). Paul also says the unbeliever is spiritually dead, "As for you, you were dead in your transgressions and sins" (Eph 2:1). The unbeliever has a corrupt heart without a spiritual sense that creates evil thoughts constantly (Gen 6:5). Jeremiah laments about the man's miserable condition, "The heart is deceitful above all things and beyond cure. Who can understand it?" (Jer 17:9). A fallen man has no interest in holiness and he is an enemy of God (Rom 8:7).

Man's nature must be changed in order to be a man of holiness, without which he will not see the LORD (Heb 12:14). Jonathan Edwards writes about a change of man's nature in salvation, "The Scripture representations of conversion do strongly imply and signify a change of nature."[8] As he introduces the concept of "distinguishing signs of truly gracious and holy affections," he says that one of the distinguishing signs is the actual change of nature of man. In referring to 2 Corinthians 3:18 Edwards writes, "But all spiritual discoveries are transforming, and not only make an alteration of the present exercise, sensation, and frame of the soul; but such power and efficacy have they, that they make an alteration in the very nature of the soul."[9] There is an inherent change in the nature of man by the power of the Holy Spirit at the time of salvation.

The heart being the seat of man's being, a divine seed is implanted in the heart of man.[10] In the salvation of man, the Holy Spirit through definitive sanctification revivifies the spiritual sense and creates a new heart that yearns for holiness and has the capacity to feel it. This is a radical change in the nature of man that turns the man from wickedness to holiness. Edwards writes, "A man may be restrained from sin, before he is converted; but when

---

7. Edwards, *Religious Affections*, 267.
8. Edwards, *Religious Affections*, 267.
9. Edwards, *Religious Affections*, 267.
10. Edwards, *Religious Affections*, 267.

he is converted, he is not only restrained from sin, his very heart and nature is turned from it unto holiness; so that thenceforward he becomes a holy person, and enemy to sin."[11]

Walter Marshall has a similar concept for the new man and call it "holy frame of heart." J. I. Packer also concurs with the concept of a change at the core of man's being, the heart, in salvation:

> Also, they have been raised with him to walk in newness of life; this means that the power that wrought Jesus' resurrection is now at work in them, causing them to live differently because in truth they are different at the center of their being in what Paul in Romans 7:22 calls "my inmost self" and Peter in 1 Peter 3:4 calls "the hidden person of the heart." They have been changed by the dethroning in them of that allergic negative reaction to the law of God, which is called sin, and the creating in them what Luis Palau in the title of one of his books calls a "heart after God."[12]

This is the heart that "seeks God, love God, honor God, serve God, and please God."[13] This is the heart what the new man in Scripture signifies. This heart makes a believer truly and essentially a new man, not just religiously a new man. The believer's heart with a spiritual sense is truly different from that of an unbeliever.

In pursuing the holiness in the Christian life definitive sanctification is inextricably related to progressive sanctification. It is the foundation for progressive sanctification. Progressive sanctification involves the believer's effort in the pursuit of holiness in the Christian life. This Christian endeavor is possible only when he is able to distinguish holiness from other qualities or virtues of life and also has a desire for it throughout his life. Unless a fallen man is transformed in his nature to exercise this faculty before the process of sanctification begins, progressive sanctification is meaningless without a direction or impetus. The spiritual sense must be formed in the heart of man in an instantaneous and once-for-all act of the Holy Spirit in order for an earnest effort for progressive sanctification to begin.

Holy Spirit works on and through the heart with the spiritual sense for the sanctification of the believer. The immediate object of the spiritual sense is the beauty of holiness. Man in a fallen state has five senses in his being. But a regenerate man, a believer, also has a spiritual sense which should have the primary position and power over other senses in living a Christian life. The believer, still a physical being in this life, has to use these

---

11. Edwards, *Religious Affections*, 269.
12. Packer, *Keep In Step*, 107.
13. Packer, *Keep In Step*, 107.

five senses to live the earthly life, but should be reminded that these senses are tainted and corrupt and should yield to the primacy of the spiritual sense in the pursuit of holiness.

That is why Paul says to the believers to set their hearts on things above rather than on earthly things. He says, "Since, then, you have been raised with Christ, set your hearts on things above, where Christ is, seated at the right hand of God. Set your minds on things above, not on earthly things" (Col 3:1–2). The believer has a new heart with the spiritual sense revivified through definitive sanctification by the Holy Spirit. What Paul is essentially saying is that now relinquish the rein of your life to the spiritual sense because you have a new heart.

Body as an Instrument of Righteousness

The body is mysteriously and inextricably united with the soul in a man. The separation of the body and soul is death. As stated before, a spiritual act of sin has a corresponding transformational effect in the phenomenal world. As Adam committed the first sin in the garden of Eden, his body turned into something that was not before the sin. Before the sin, his body was an instrument to communicate with God and to have a fellowship with God, and possibly to worship God (Gen 3:8). But after the sin Adam uses his body to distance himself from God and hide him from God. He says to God, "I heard you in the garden, and I was afraid because I was naked; so I hid" (Gen 3:10).

Also, when Adam before the sin first saw Eve, he used his mouth and tongue to express his love for her, "This is now bone of my bones and flesh of my flesh; she shall be called 'woman,' for she was taken out of man" (Gen 2:23). But after the sin he uses the same mouth and tongue to accuse the woman and God for his sin, "The woman you put here with me—she gave me some fruit from the tree, and I ate it." And when Adam and Eve see themselves after the sin, they see a totally different thing with the same eyes, their nakedness. "Then the eyes of both of them were opened, and they realized they were naked, so they sewed fig leaves together and made coverings for themselves" (Gen 3:7). Their bodies are being used for the completely different purpose after they committed the sin.

Adam's enslavement to sin made his body an instrument that is totally useless for a spiritual purpose. In fact, his body became an instrument for selfishness, namely, an instrument of wickedness. Thus just as Adam's enslavement to sin made the body of man an instrument of wickedness, so does the breach with sin based on the work of Christ make the body of man an instrument of righteousness. This is what happens in definitive sanctification. The body of man is transformed into an instrument of righteousness from an instrument of wickedness by the Holy Spirit based on the work of Christ. Paul teaches this important truth, "Do not offer any part of yourself to sin as an instrument of wickedness, but rather offer yourselves to God as those who have been brought from death to life; and offer every part of yourself to him as an instrument of righteousness. For sin shall no longer be your master, because you are not under the law, but under grace" (Rom 6:13–14).

The union of the body with the soul in man is probably the greatest mystery pertaining to the nature of a human being. As Paul says the body is the house or the earthly tent the soul lives in, "For we know that if the earthly tent we live in is destroyed, we have a building from God, an eternal house in heaven, not built by human hands" (2 Cor 5:1). The body is so mysteriously, intimately, and inextricably united with the soul that the character or nature of the body is determined by the soul that lives in it. I do not mean a corpse by body, but a real living body that houses the soul in. So the nature of the body, a real living body, is determined by the kinds of the soul that lives in it. The body that houses a regenerate soul is completely different from the one that houses an unregenerate soul. It is not just that the purpose of the body is different. The body, which is mysteriously and inextricably united with the soul as one being, energized and guided by the regenerated soul, is completely different from the one that is energized and guided by the unregenerated soul. The body housing the regenerate soul can say "Jesus is the LORD" while the other body cannot (Rom 10:9; 1 Cor 12:3). Saul's body with the unregenerate soul was used to threaten and persecute believers, while Saul's transformed body, or Paul's body, was used to serve and love other people tirelessly.

When Adam committed the first sin, a spiritual act (though the body was used), it was not just the purpose of the body that was changed, but the body, becoming a part of the depraved human nature, was actually transformed into an instrument of selfishness, or wickedness. There was a real transformation in the nature of the body that it started to die (Rom 6:23). Adam's body, the living body, was actually and materially transformed into an instrument of wickedness whose end is death and decomposition, even though before the fall his body was undying and an object of God's blessing whose end was not death and decomposition. "God saw all that he had made, and it was very good" (Gen 1:31). Adam's body was a part of "all that he had made, and it was very good." But Adam's sin so radically transformed his body that it became an object of judgment that must die. Just as Adam's enslavement to sin changed his nature to a depraved one such that his body was transformed into an instrument of wickedness, so does the breach with sin based on the work of Christ transform the body of man into an instrument of righteousness.

Man's enslavement to sin caused by Adam's first sin brought about the radical and actual change in the nature of man in the phenomenal world. This change includes three different transformations in the nature of man. First, man lost the free will, and it became trapped in sinning for an evil purpose. Second, he also lost the spiritual sense in his heart and the heart became corrupted and the source of constant evil thoughts. Third, man's body was transformed into an instrument of wickedness. In totality man became a depraved man with the death waiting at the end of his life (Rom 6:23).

Man's breach with sin based on the work of Christ, the last Adam, also brought about the radical and actual change in the nature of man in the phenomenal world. This radical change for life includes three different transformations in the nature of a fallen man. First, man is restored and endowed with a true free will that always chooses God rather than evil. Second, he has a new heart with a revivified spiritual sense such that he desires and pursues the holiness in his life. Third, his body is transformed into an instrument of righteousness from an instrument of wickedness. These three transformations are inherent and irrevocable changes in the nature of man by the Holy Spirit through definitive sanctification. These transformations are summarized in Table 8:1. In totality a depraved man becomes a sanctified man in definitive sanctification with eternal life (Rom 6:23; 1 Cor 6:11).

	Before	After
Will	No Free Will	Free Will
	Will is enslaved to Sin always choosing Evil	Chooses God
Heart	Depraved Heart with Five Physical Senses	New Heart with Spiritual Sense along with Five Physical Senses
Body	Instrument of Wickedness	Instrument of Righteousness

Table 8-1 : Actual Transformation in the Nature of Man through Definitive Sanctification

Effect of the Breach with Sin

Just as the enslavement to sin by Adam's first sin is a history-altering event, so is the breach with sin by Christ, the last Adam, in a positive way. Berkouwer says that "sin is . . . a cataclysmic and disruptive power."[14] The cataclysmic power released by Adam's enslavement to sin derailed the human history and brought about the future filled with misery and death. On the contrary, the rectifying and healing power to the infinite degree brought by the breach with sin by Christ opened a new epoch that is moving toward eternal life and bliss for believers in Christ. It is important to understand and treat this definitive breach with sin by Christ as an epoch-making, cosmic, and gracious act of God in the plan of salvation of man. As such, it encompasses many of the blessings the new man is endowed with by the gracious hands of God. As we have seen above, the transformation of man's nature is an actual change in a phenomenal world, corresponding to the spiritual act in a spiritual realm. Aside from this transformation of man's nature, other definitive changes in man's life are effected by the breach with sin. These changes along with the transformation of man's nature characterize believers in Christ and differentiate them from unbelievers.

Change of Master: from Sin to God

The breach with sin effects the change of the master, from serving sin to God. Paul writes, "But now that you have been set free from sin and have become slaves of God" (Rom 6:22). Many, if not all, of fallen men think that they are the masters of their lives. This is probably one of the greatest and most effective lies *sin* instills in a head of fallen man. According to Berkouwer, sin manifests itself *sub specie boni* and hides its true nature.[15] Sin dulls man's mind to believe that he has the rein of his own life and controls his own destiny and that no one, including God, has a say on his life, when in fact his whole being is shackled to sin. Sin cunningly hides itself under the cover and projects the man as the grandmaster of his own life.

This is what happened to Eve in the garden of Eden. Refuting God's command not to eat the forbidden fruit, the serpent says, "You will not certainly die. . . . For God knows that when you eat from it your eyes will be opened, and you will be like God, knowing good and evil" (Gen 3:4–5). What the serpent essentially says to Eve is that "you will be the master of your life and control your own destiny." As soon as she buys into this idea,

---

14. Berkouwer, *Sin*, 261.
15. Berkouwer, *Sin*, 236.

she is engulfed with lust and pleasures of the world. For enticed Eve, "the fruit of the tree was good for food and pleasing to the eye, and also desirable for gaining wisdom" (Gen 3:6). This is the same, but very powerful and enticing, method the Satan has used since the beginning and of which the Apostle John warns us against, "For everything in the world—lust of the flesh, the lust of the eyes, and the pride of life—comes not from the Father but from the world" (1 John 2:16). Once man buys into the idea of being the master of his life, he is in no time thrown into the den of misery and anguish serving sin without the end.

Christ's saving work brought about the change of the master to a man, delivering him from the merciless despot. The new master, God, opened a new life and destiny for the man. He also finds his true identity and ultimate purpose of life in God, who is also his creator. Man finally comes back home to God, his creator and master, as Augustine says that "you made us for yourself and our hearts find no peace until they rest in you."[16] Pascal concurs:

> What else does this craving, and this helplessness, proclaim but that there was once in man a true happiness, of which all that now remains is the empty print and trace? This he tries in vain to fill with everything around him, seeking in things that are not there the help he cannot find in those that are, though none can help, since this infinite abyss can be filled only with an infinite and immutable object; in other words by God himself.[17]

The most important and ultimate matter for a created personal being is to know who or what the source or originator of him/her is and to be in a truthful or authentic relationship with that being. Without it everything he/she does is meaningless and aimless.

In God the true master, man finds his authentic self and peace with himself and everyone and everything around him. In God he recovers the past, sees the future and truly lives in the present. In this theocentric world view man discovers the order and beauty in the universe and sees virtues and vices in a human relationship as they really are. In having and serving God as the master, man discovers worship and finds his true spiritual identity in the backdrop of eternity of the spiritual world. The spiritual communion between two personal beings, man and God, is restored through this relationship, in which a loving and intimate communion transcends a mere slave-master relationship.

The loving and intimate communion between man and God reveals that God is not just a man's new master, but also his Father. Thus the

---

16. Augustine, *Conf.* 1.1.
17. Pascal, *Pensées*, 75

change of the master effected by the breach with sin is not just replacing one master with another. This change also brought about the change of the very nature of the master-slave relationship. This is more of a loving relationship between a father and son than an autocratic relationship between a master and slave. The best interest of the son or "slave" is at the fore in this relationship. The goal of this relationship is blessing and exaltation of the "slave" rather than exploitation and bondage. Mercy and goodness of God and gratitude and obedience of man characterize the relationship between the "master and slave" presented in Romans 6.

Change of Domain of Life: from Law to Grace

Another change effected by the breach with sin is the change of domain or realm of life of man. Man lived under the law before, but now lives under grace. Paul writes, "For sin shall no longer be your master, because you are not under the law, but under grace" (Rom 6:14). This is also a once-for-all, definitive change from one realm of life to another.

The law in Romans 6:14 should not be understood as the Mosaic law. Since the law is used as the antithesis to grace, the "law must be understood in much more general terms of law as commandments."[18] As grace is contrasted with law, not with sin, they are not expressions of rulers but domains of life or ruling principles. The law here is then a ruling principle that pronounces the condemnation of man. Grace, on the other hand, is God's sovereign and benevolent ruling principle that governs and empowers the redemptive life of man. Even though man lives in the same world physically before and after the breach with sin, he is instantaneously and definitively transferred from one spiritual "world" to another on the basis of the work of Christ.

In a world that has law as the ruling principle, everything man does is gauged and judged by the law. Everyone becomes a lawbreaker and a slave to sin in this world (Rom 3:23). Bondage and slavery to sin is a way of life in this domain of spiritual life. Man creates legalism in an effort to escape from an invisible prison of law and falls into hypocrisy, and thereby plunging into another form of bondage. Living under the law makes a man to dwindle into a legalistic, hypocritical sinner.

Grace, on the other hand, opens up a totally different realm of life for a man. The invisible prison called law disappears once-for-all and he

---

18. Murray, *Romans*, 229. Cranfield interprets the term in a similar way; however, Käsemann sees it in a narrow sense as the Torah. Cranfield, *Romans*, 320; Käsemann, *Romans*, 178.

is free from the law. The law becomes powerless and man is no longer ruled by it. Nor is he gauged or judged by the law any more. Man is totally free once-for-all and eternally. Under grace he is truly free, meaning that he becomes truthful or authentic to himself and everyone else. Freedom is a *sine qua non* quality for a truthful or authentic relationship between personal beings. Thus only in the realm of grace an authentic relationship between man and God is possible. In freedom man becomes who he must be and decides and acts as the authentic self who only desires to exude the image of God through him.

In Scripture the law and grace are juxtaposed together as that which bring condemnation and righteousness, respectively. Scripture teaches, "If the ministry that brought condemnation was glorious, how much more glorious is the ministry that brings righteousness!" (2 Cor 3:9). Other passages in Scripture also pose condemnation and righteousness as the opposite adjudications (Job 9:20; Ps 94:21; Rom 8:3-4). The idea of condemnation and of justification depending on one's relation to sin is taught throughout Scripture. The enslavement to sin under the law brings condemnation whereas the breach with sin under grace brings justification. Therefore, man lives as a condemned man under the law, but he is a righteous man under grace. This is not just a change in a forensic sense. It is improbable to think that man is declared righteous when he is not actually righteous before God's eyes. So it is an actual change in that a condemned man actually becomes a righteous man with imputed righteousness in him and on virtue of the union with Christ. This change from a condemned man to a righteous man is a once-for-all and definitive phenomenon in the spiritual life of man.

The law brings anxiety and fear. Man in the depth of his heart knows he is a lawbreaker and suffers the inexorable anxiety which comes from the divided heart. The anxiety leads to fear as the law demands the penalty or judgment on the man, the lawbreaker. The anxiety and fear are the ineluctable reality of life for a man living under the law. On the other hand, man under grace enjoys joy and thankfulness in his life. Paul exhorts believers in Thessalonica, "Rejoice always, pray continually, give thanks in all circumstances; for this is God's will for you in Christ Jesus" (1 Thess 5:16-17). The law belongs to an earthly realm in which anxiety and fear dominate whereas grace belongs to a heavenly realm in which joy and thankfulness abound.

Change of a Way of Life : from Wickedness to Holiness

The breach with sin also brings a change of a way of life. Man's former way of life is characterized as impurity and wickedness, which have been definitively changed to righteousness and holiness on virtue of the work of Christ. Paul writes, "Just as you used to offer yourselves as slaves to impurity and to ever-increasing wickedness, so now offer yourselves as slaves to righteousness leading to holiness" (Rom 6:19). The tense of παρεστήσατε, "you used to offer," is a "complexive aorist indicating a linear action which, having been completed, is regarded as a whole."[19] Cranfield explains, "it is consonant with a desire to emphasize the fact that this phase of their lives is a thing of the past."[20] The former way of living in impurity to wickedness is done away with. Paul now exhorts believers to live in a new way of life, as the imperative passive παραστήσατε, "offer or yield," "indicates that the thought is of the beginning of the new way of life which contrasts with the old."[21] A radically different way of living a life, which is so foreign to a fallen man, has been endowed to a believer, which is characterized as holiness or sanctification.

The new way of life includes, as the term holiness implies, a new motivation arising from a pure heart, a new heart with the spiritual sense. Jesus says, "Blessed are the pure in heart, for they will see God" (Matt 5:8). The writer of the Hebrews teaches, "Without holiness no one will see the LORD" (Heb 12:14). Holiness arises from a pure heart. Those with the pure heart will see the LORD because they are holy. The purity of heart is to will one thing, that is, to seek God's will in this world. God's will for his people is to "seek his kingdom and his righteousness" (Matt 6:33). The pure heart seeks earnestly to establish the kingdom of God in the world. The holy person is the one who wills with one undivided heart to establish the kingdom of God in the world. The kingdom of God is governed by God's immutable principle of love and righteousness or justice.

Love and justice are essential virtues taught by God's law in Scripture. Jesus says, "Love the LORD your God with all your heart and with all your soul and with all your strength and with all your mind; and, Love your neighbor as yourself" (Luke 10:27). Paul reiterates this teaching, "For the entire law is fulfilled in keeping this one command: 'Love your neighbor as yourself'" (Gal 5:14). For a believer love is the foundational motivation for everything he does in his life. His love for God should be the foundational motivation for serving and worshipping him. Likewise, his love for the fellow human beings should be foundational motivation for treating them fairly and equally. Love for the believer is now the foundational principle and motivation for everything he does in the world.

---

19. Cranfield, *Romans*, 326.
20. Cranfield, *Romans*, 326.
21. Cranfield, *Romans*, 305.

Justice is another foundational principle in the kingdom of God. Jesus sums up the Law and the Prophets in justice, "So in everything, do to others what you would have them do to you, for this sums up the Law and the Prophets" (Matt 7:12). In other words, it is a fair treatment for everybody. Treat others as you want to be treated by others. Justice means no favoritism to anybody. James writes, "My brothers and sisters, believers in our glorious Jesus Christ must not show favoritism" (Jas 2:1). Again he writes, "But if you show favoritism, you sin and are convicted by the law as lawbreakers" (Jas 2:9). Favoritism is not out of love but is from selfishness.

Love and justice are the foundational virtues a man should have in the kingdom of God. They are often misunderstood as two opposite qualities. Although they are clearly two distinctive virtues, the root of them is the same. Our God is the God of justice as much as the God of love. One virtue does not diminish another. Each virtue brilliantly manifests who God is and harmoniously work together in the kingdom of God, each maintaining its own brilliant and powerful force in the heart of man. In the believer's life justice should be motivated by love, and love should show its truthfulness in justice.

For the believer living a new way of life, love and justice are the foundational principles in life, shedding once-for-all the former way of selfishness and injustice. Holiness, the new way of life, requires a pure heart, which wills one thing, that is to seek the kingdom of God in the world.

Change of Destiny: from Eternal Damnation to Eternal Bliss

The breach with sin changes the destiny of man from eternal damnation to eternal bliss. Paul writes, "But now that you have been set free from sin and have become slaves of God, the benefit you reap leads to holiness, and the result is eternal life. For the wages of sin is death, but the gift of God is eternal life in Christ Jesus our LORD" (Rom 6:22-23). Because of the work of Jesus Christ, the destiny of man was once-for-all changed from death to eternal life. Along with the destiny, the whole outlook of man's life is changed. The roadmap of life is changed also. This is a cataclysmic change in man's spiritual life which would have irrepressible ramifications in every facet of his life.

Death in Romans 6:23 is death in a comprehensive sense culminating in eternal damnation. Death is earned by man. Death is the wages which sin pays.[22] This death is what Paul speaks about in Romans 5. He writes, "Therefore, just as sin entered the world through one man, and death through sin,

---

22. Cranfield, *Romans*, 329.

and in this way death came to all people, because all sinned" (Rom 5:12). Because of Adam's sin the destiny of the mankind was sealed in death. The death includes spiritual and physical death culminating in eternal damnation. Without the grace of Jesus Christ no one can escape from this miserable destiny of eternal damnation.

Contrary to the death befallen to man, eternal life is the free gift from God. It is given through the grace of Jesus Christ. Paul writes, "The law was brought in so that the trespass might increase. But where sin increased, grace increased all the more, so that, just as sin reigned in death, so also grace might reign through righteousness to bring eternal life through Jesus Christ our LORD" (Rom 5:20–21). Eternal life is given at the time of regeneration in this life and culminates in eternal bliss in heaven. Because of the work of Jesus Christ, the destiny of man is once-for-all changed to eternal bliss.

One might suggest that the change of destiny is more related to regeneration than to definitive sanctification. It is true that the bestowal of new life, or eternal life, is the essence of regeneration. However, the breach with sin has to happen before man receives eternal life and enjoys it with the security of eternal bliss. Enslavement to sin and eternal life cannot coexist in man, the saved man. Therefore, the change of destiny from eternal damnation to eternal bliss is one of the effects of the breach with sin in definitive sanctification. We understand, of course, that regeneration, justification, and definitive sanctification occur at the same time and work mysteriously together to bring a glorious salvation of man. But the change of man's destiny, as other effects mentioned above, cannot be separated from the breach with sin in a logical sequence. The effects of the breach with sin described in this section can be summarized as in Table 8:2.

	Before	After
Master	Sin	God (Jesus Christ)
Domain or Realm of Life	Law	Grace
Way of Life	Wickedness (Lawlessness)	Holiness (Sanctification)
Destiny in Eternity	Eternal Damnation (Death)	Eternal Bliss (Eternal Life)

Table 8-2 : Effects of the Breach with Sin in Man's Life

Experiential Effect of Definitive Sanctification

Murray says that the experiential effect of definitive sanctification is that the believer is immune from the sin unto death described in 1 John 5:16–17. He writes, "Everyone begotten of God believes and confesses that Jesus as come in the flesh is the Christ (cf. 1 Jn. 5:1) . . . the believer confesses Jesus as come in the flesh . . . and cannot apostatize from this faith."[23] We see in these statements that Murray is trying to translate definitive sanctification into the experiential life of the believer in some specific sense. However, there is a problem in presenting the protection from the sin unto death as the experiential side of definitive sanctification.

First, there is a disagreement among scholars as to what this "sin unto death" in 1 John 5:16–17 really means. Murray's interpretation of the "death" as the "spiritual death" closely follows the view of John Calvin and of Louis Berkhof.[24] However, some scholars interpret it as "physical death" which is also described in 1 Corinthians 5:5 where Paul speaks of physical death in order to save the spirit of the person. Adam Clarke, in his commentary, presents this view. He writes, "The *sin unto death* means a case of transgression, particularly of grievous backsliding from the life and power of godliness, which God determines to punish with *temporal death*, while at the same time he extends mercy to the penitent soul."[25] John Wesley also sees physical death in 1 John 5:16–17 and says that any penitent may find mercy through Jesus Christ.[26] Therefore, Murray's idea of basing the experiential side of definitive sanctification on the passage that is interpreted differently by respected Christian scholars does not carry the convincing argument for this idea.

Second, if the sin unto death is in fact the spiritual death, then it should undoubtedly be connected to Matthew 12:31–32, as Berkhof has done, where Jesus speaks of the "unpardonable sin." Berkhof explains the unpardonable sin, "The sin consists in the conscious, malicious, and willful rejection and slandering, against evidence and conviction, of the testimony of the Holy Spirit respecting the grace of God in Christ, attributing it out of hatred and enmity to the prince of darkness."[27] This sin makes conversion and forgiveness impossible. Berkhof does not say that believers are immune from committing this sin. In other words, there seems to be the possibility of the believers committing this sin, but the fact that they fear they might

---

23. Murray, "Definitive Sanctification," 11.
24. Calvin, *First John*, 273; Berkhof, *Systematic Theology*, 253.
25. Clarke, *1 John*, 925.
26. Wesley, *Works*, 2:239.
27. Berkhof, *Systematic Theology*, 253.

have committed this sin shows that they have not committed it. He construes, "In view of the fact that this sin is not followed by repentance, we may be reasonably sure that they who fear that they have committed it and worry about this, and who desire the prayers of others for them, have not committed it."[28] Thus, even if the sin unto death is interpreted as spiritual death, Murray's concept of the believer being protected from the sin unto death because of definitive sanctification does not find much support from another Reformed theologian, Berkhof.

Third, Murray does not explain why the believer with definitive sanctification is immune from only this sin, sin unto death, when he says that the believer is decisively severed and freed from the dominion of *all sins*. It is not clear to us why Murray insists that the believer with definitive sanctification is totally, undoubtedly, and eternally delivered from one sin, i.e., sin unto death. Is it because of Keswick's influence? Murray's desire to express definitive sanctification in a specific experiential sense might have been influenced by Keswick's teaching of the believer's deliverance from known sin. But when Murray expounds the sin unto death in 1 John 5:16, the purpose of bringing out this passage for the specific sin seems to fade. When Murray explains the sin unto death, it seems that he describes more of the state or condition of the believer rather than the specific sin from which the believer is protected. Murray writes, "The believer . . . cannot apostatize from this faith."[29] Or the believer has been transferred to a different state because of definitive sanctification, so that he cannot apostatize from the faith. Thus, Murray's explanation of the experiential side of definitive sanctification seems to be a description of the new state of the believer who has gone through definitive sanctification.

Progressive Sanctification as the Experiential Side of Definitive Sanctification

Rather than trying to translate the experiential effect of definitive sanctification into a specific sin, it is biblical and reasonable to view progressive sanctification as the experiential side of definitive sanctification. In other words, definitive sanctification is foundational for progressive sanctification. In definitive sanctification a believer is severed and freed from the dominion of sin. The believer experiences progressive sanctification because of and on the ground of definitive sanctification. He can now progress in his sanctification because he has been truly transformed inwardly by God in definitive

---

28. Berkhof, *Systematic Theology*, 254.
29. Murray, "Definitive Sanctification," 11.

sanctification. In the progress of sanctification, the believer will never again fall under the dominion of sin even though he may be influenced by it.

Progressive sanctification is the outward manifestation of inward holiness, which was endowed by the Holy Spirit in definitive sanctification. Scripture teaches inside-out sanctification, never outside-in sanctification. The believer can never make himself holy by outward work. The foundation is always inside, the energy comes from inside. Paul says to Colossians believers, " Since, then, you have been raised with Christ, set your hearts on things above, where Christ is seated at the right hand of God. . . . Put to death, therefore, whatever belongs to your earthly nature: sexual immorality, impurity, lust, evil desires and greed, which is idolatry" (Col 1:1–5). Again he writes, "Therefore, as God's chosen people, holy and dearly loved, clothe yourselves with compassion, kindness, humility, gentleness and patience" (Col 3:12). Sanctification is always an inside-out endeavor driven by God's grace, manifested in the outward characters of a believer as the fruit of the Holy Spirit.

Impossibility of Unrepentant Sin

The believer's life, or progressive sanctification, is an ongoing repentant life as he falls into sins and never reaches the perfection in this life. Since the believer is under the grace of God, he will not regress in his spirituality in his Christian life. The degree of the progress of spirituality may be different from one believer to another, but the sum total of spirituality at the end of life will always be progression, not regression. And definitive sanctification warrants this progression of sanctification in the believer's life. In other words, there will be no unrepentant sins in his life if he is on a true progressive sanctification based on definitive sanctification. So in a sense we can say that a believer is completely free from the unrepentant sin through definitive sanctification in his life.

This concept naturally leads to the logical conclusion that the believer will not committee the unpardonable sin if the unpardonable sin in Matthew 12:31–32 is understood as a persistent regress into impenitence as Berkouwer describes.[30] The believer will not fall into this spiritual darkness because of definitive sanctification. Or simply put, the believer with definitive sanctification will not commit the unpardonable sin in which the salvation is lost. Then it seems that we come to the same conclusion as Murray's but through a different path. But there is a difference between this view and Murray's. This view is not that definitive sanctification makes the believer

30. Berkouwer, *Sin*, 341.

immune from one sin, sin unto death, but that the believer's life will be characterized by a progress in spirituality without unrepentant sins because of definitive sanctification, such that he will not be in spiritual regression which may lead to the "sin unto death."

Thus, the actual transformation of the believer in definitive sanctification is to be emphasized as opposed to the attempt to translate definitive sanctification into protection from a certain sin. Because the believer has been truly transformed in definitive sanctification, he can experience the effect of that transformation in his daily life in the form of progressive sanctification. Progressive sanctification is the inseparable experiential effect of definitive sanctification.

Transition from Actual to Experiential

Murray teaches that in definitive sanctification victory in Christ is actual.[31] And because it is actual it is experiential. For Murray, victory in Christ is actual for the believer and is translated immediately and automatically—without any efforts of the believer—into the experience of being immune from the sin unto death. In this way, he seems to eliminate the reckoning process of Keswick. In Murray's definitive sanctification, victory in Christ for the believer is actual and experiential almost simultaneously. What is actual in definitive sanctification is almost simultaneously experiential in the believer's life.

However, Murray's actual and experiential aspect of definitive sanctification does not seem to be much different from Keswick's positional and experiential sanctification, except that a believer has to go through the reckoning process from positional to experiential sanctification for Keswick. So Murray's actual aspect of definitive sanctification does not seem to be different from Keswick's positional sanctification in spite of his insistence of its difference from Keswick's. He writes that this victory in Christ is not merely potential or positional. His argument seems to be that the actual aspect of definitive sanctification is different from Keswick's positional sanctification because the actuality of definitive sanctification is automatically experiential. In other words, for Murray definitive sanctification is actual, not positional, because it is experiential. So although he writes the statement "Because it is actual it is experiential," what he really means is that because it is experiential it is actual, not positional.

Also, Murray's statement "Because it is actual it is experiential" might stir up disagreement by some people. What is actual may not always be

31. Murray, *Redemption*, 142.

experiential in the life of a man. Suppose two generals who have been at war against each other sign the peace treaty to end the war and declare peace in the world. After signing the treaty, peace in the world is actual. However, there may be two soldiers from the opposite sides at the remotest place to whom the news of the peace treaty has not reached yet. When they cross each other, one gets shot from the other and is killed. What the soldier who is killed after the peace treaty experiences is not peace and happiness but war, pain, and death. So for this soldier what is actual is *not* experiential in his life. This illustration is not to prove Keswick's separation of positional from experiential sanctification at all. This is simply to show Murray's statement does not always hold true. The actuality and experience often do not correspond to each other in real life. I believe that the actuality of definitive sanctification should be found in the true and actual transformation of the nature of man in definitive sanctification.

Rather than attempting to prove the actuality of definitive sanctification by the experiential side of sanctification, the actuality of definitive sanctification should be found in the true and actual transformation of the nature of man. The nature of man is actually transformed in definitive sanctification. The believer as the new man has free will, the heart with a spiritual sense, and the body as an instrument of righteousness. The "old man" has died and the believer now is the "new man" (Col 3:9–10).

How much the believer enjoys or experiences what has actually happened in definitive sanctification in his daily life depends on his faith and obedience to the word. This faith is not the same as Keswick's "reckoning" which leads to crisis sanctification in the believer's life. The believer has to exercise his faith in order to experience existentially what has actually happened in his nature. This is an ongoing process which is the essential element of progressive sanctification.

Relationship between Justification and Definitive Sanctification

The relationship between justification and sanctification is one of the most important soteric issues in the plan of salvation of man. Ever since the Reformation the primacy has been given to justification over sanctification, as sanctification was understood as a process. Then when the doctrine of definitive sanctification was introduced in the middle of the twentieth century, this relationship became even more complicated. However, the correct conception of definitive sanctification in relation to justification is crucial to understand aright the whole process of salvation of man.

Direct Relation of Definitive Sanctification with the Union with Christ

One of the important elements in Murray's definitive sanctification is the relationship between definitive sanctification and justification. To bring out Murray's concept on this important point I quote Murray's statements in length:

> It might be said that the relation is that which justification sustains to sanctification, that the death and resurrection of Christ are directly the ground of our justification, that justification is the foundation of sanctification in that it establishes the only proper relation on which a life of holiness can rest, and that the relation of the death and resurrection of Christ to *sanctification* is this indirect one through the medium of justification. Or it might be said that by his death and resurrection Christ has procured every saving gift—the death and resurrection are therefore the meritorious and procuring cause of sanctification as well as of justification and in this respect are as directly related to sanctification as to justification. . . . He[Paul] brings the death and resurrection of Christ into a much more direct relation to sanctification by way of efficiency and virtue than these foregoing proposals involved. The truth is that our death to sin and newness of life are effected in our identification with Christ in his death and resurrection, and no virtue accruing from the death and resurrection of Christ affects any phase of salvation more directly than the breach with sin and newness of life. And if we do not take account of this direct relationship we miss one of the cardinal features on New Testament teaching.[32]

Murray, acknowledging justification as the foundation for the progressive aspect of sanctification, emphatically underscores the direct relationship of definitive sanctification to the union with Christ bypassing justification. One of Murray's contributions to Reformed theology may be that he put sanctification in direct relation to the death and resurrection of Christ. It is observed that Warfield says in responding to perfectionism that sanctification is by grace through faith. However, this statement has been taken in the sense of progressive sanctification. This statement is also true for definitive sanctification. Also, Calvin says that the union with Christ is foundational for both justification and sanctification. Murray does not disagree with Calvin or Warfield on this point at all. Murray actually presents this traditional Calvinistic position on this point in the first half of the above quotation. He

---

32. Murray, "Definitive Sanctification," 13–14.

fully agrees with these statements. But what he emphatically presents in the second half of the quotation is the phase of salvation that is *more directly* related to the union with Christ. This phase of salvation, more directly related to the union with Christ, is definitive sanctification.

It is interesting to note that Murray does not cite Warfield even once in support of the doctrine of definitive sanctification in his writings. This may be interpreted as either that Murray overlooked Warfield's statements pertaining to the teaching of definitive sanctification or that Murray did not find in Warfield any statement that unequivocally and substantially teaches definitive sanctification. Judging from Murray's character and diligence as a theologian, I prefer to choose the latter.

Reformed theologians have been stressing the process character of sanctification as opposed to the once-for-allness of justification in order to enunciate clearly the break with Roman Catholic Church. Roman Catholic Church teaches that "justification must be understood as the infusion of supernatural grace."[33] Reformed theologians object to this view and assert that justification is the declaration by God of the righteousness of a sinner on the ground of the work of Christ. Definitive sanctification is not the Roman Catholic Church's idea of justification because it involves the actual change of man by the power of God. Nor is it Osiander's idea of justification in which he actually mixes forgiveness of sin with rebirth. He also teaches the ontological change of man in justification by saying that "Christ's essence is mixed with our own."[34] Calvin rejects this teaching. Definitive sanctification and justification are different from each other, but they are vitally and intimately related to each other as they are both grounded on the union with Christ.

Justification and Definitive Sanctification in the *Ordo Salutis*

When it comes to the relation between justification and definitive sanctification, the logical relationship between these two in the *ordo salutis* should be considered.[35] Murray says that there is a very close direct relationship between

33. Berkouwer, *Sanctification*, 27.

34. Calvin, *Institutes*, 3.11.5.

35. *Ordo salutis* is understood as the order of the application and appropriation of salvation. In regard to justification and sanctification, however, it should not be taken as that sanctification is delayed well after the beginning of the Christian life. In order to eliminate this misunderstanding in the *ordo salutis*, Herman Ridderbos introduced another concept called *historia salutis* in which the general character of Paul's teaching is expressed in a new and broader outlook. Ridderbos writes, "Paul preaches justfication by faith, as opposed to Judaism, and Romans 4 is the great proof of this. But the

definitive sanctification and the union with Christ. However, he does not explicitly state whether justification logically comes before definitive sanctification or vice versa or if they come together logically in the salvation of man. By asserting definitive sanctification's direct relationship with the union with Christ and not being dependent upon justification, Murray seems to suggest the possibility of shifting the order of sanctification, definitive sanctification in this case, with respect to justification in the *ordo salutis*.

Although Murray does not give the complete *ordo salutis* with definitive sanctification in it, from his emphasis on the direct relationship with the union with Christ, it is reasonable to assume that definitive sanctification logically comes with justification, not after, in the *ordo salutis*. So their relationship in the *ordo salutis* may be written as justification/definitive sanctification or definitive sanctification/justification. Justification/Definitive Sanctification is one complete act of God. They are two sides of one coin. One stresses the judicial aspect and the other the actual transformational aspect of God's grace in the believer in the beginning of the Christian life. So if we may use Berkouwer's description of God's blessings of *ordo salutis* in concentric circles, the concentric circles of justification and of sanctification have been depicted as separate circles, one inside of the other, always justification inside of sanctification, showing sanctification's dependency on justification. However, in our case the circles of justification and of definitive sanctification should be on top of each other showing one line of the concentric circle in the top view. In this way, the distinctiveness of justification and of definitive sanctification is preserved as well as their two-side blessing of one complete act of God. By placing definitive sanctification in this way in the *ordo salutis*, we do justice to many Scripture passages that teach the indicative of the holiness of the believer.

By placing justification and definitive sanctification together in the *ordo salutis*, what I am actually saying is that God justifies and actually changes the inner man in the same logical order. Evangelical churches have been teaching that justification of man logically precedes the actual change of man by placing justification before sanctification in the *ordo salutis*.[36] Does God justify, or declare the righteousness of the sinner before

---

starting-point of Paul's preaching of justification by faith is to be found in the great turning-point in the *historia salutis*." Ridderbos, *Time*, 49.

36. In the nineteenth century A. Hodge observed the inseparable relationship between a forensic act of God and a subjective change in the moral character in the salvation of man. He proposed the interdependence between justification and regeneration in man's salvation. He wrote, "Thus it follows that the satisfaction and merit of Christ are the antecedent cause of regeneration; and yet, nevertheless, the participation of the believer in the satisfaction and merit of Christ (i.e. his justification) is conditioned upon his faith, which in turn is conditioned upon his regeneration. He must have part in

imputing the righteousness on him? I believe that God justifies the sinner and changes him by imputing the righteousness of Christ on him in one complete act. This is, however, totally and absolutely different from the Roman Catholic Church's doctrine of infused grace or Osiander's ontological change of man. In definitive sanctification, man's nature is changed to the "new man," but there is still a human nature, by the grace of God, and not mingled with the grace of God.

Righteousness and Holiness in the Salvation of Man

Justification and sanctification deal with righteousness and holiness respectively in the salvation of man. Justification and sanctification are the *duplex gratia* man receives in the salvation from God. Man cannot make himself holy, just as he cannot make himself righteous. This *duplex gratia* comes from the savior, Jesus Christ, the holy and righteous one (Acts 3:14).

Righteousness is endowed to a man through justification. Justification is a forensic act of God, in which a man is declared "righteous" based on the work of Christ. The forensic meaning of justification was firmly rooted in the Protestant theology in the Reformation. In justification the righteousness of Christ is imputed on a man, the sinner, and he is declared righteous. Righteousness means being "straight" or "right" with God. The man, a sinner, who puts his faith in Jesus Christ, is declared to be righteous or "right with God" on virtue of imputed righteousness of Christ in the court of God's law. This righteousness is understood to be the perfect righteousness in Protestant theology. The believer does not grow in righteousness in his Christian life, as opposed to holiness.

As opposed to an immediate, once-for-all act of justification, sanctification has been understood as a process, a life-long process in the believer's life. Sanctification deals with holiness. Holiness means separation and purity that has a strong connotation in the moral or ethical realm. Sanctification deals with a believer becoming holy in his being and life and never reaching the perfect holiness in this life. In sanctification the believer transforms into a holy person by the Holy Spirit. Unlike justification the believer in sanctification has to work or cooperate with the Holy Spirit. In Reformed theology this is expressed as a Spirit-led work. Thus in Protestant theology once one

---

Christ so far forth as to be regenerated in order to have part in him so far forth as to be justified." It seems that Hodge detected some type of an actual change of man in the beginning of the Christian life. However, without the benefit of the concept of definitive sanctification Hodge put himself in the precarious position of mingling justification with regeneration in the salvation of man. A. Hodge, "Ordo Salutis," 313.

becomes a believer, the burden of becoming holy far outweighs the burden of becoming righteous if the latter exists at all in the Christian life.

This is how justification and sanctification are viewed in the traditional Christian theology. So at the time of salvation a man, being given a new life, is justified with perfect righteousness once for all, but is not holy yet. In other words, God accepts a man who is righteous but not holy. Thus this theology, which emphasizes the primacy of righteousness, inadvertently creates a bifurcation of the *duplex gratia* which cannot be separated in the salvation of man.

Definitive sanctification preserves the *duplex gratia* at the time of salvation. Union with Christ is foundational for every element in the *ordo salutis*, including regeneration, justification, and sanctification. Regeneration, justification, and definitive sanctification happen at the same time in the salvation of man even though there is a logical order among them. Regeneration is an endowment of the new life in a man, whereas justification is a declaration of righteousness on man. Definitive sanctification is the breach with sin, which has the transformational effect in the nature of man in such a way that the man becomes holy before God. The transformational effect includes man's free will, the heart with a spiritual sense, and body becoming an instrument of righteousness. Therefore, what happens at the time of salvation is that a man is given a new life, eternal life, and becomes a "new man," and the new man is righteous and holy on virtue of his union with Christ who is holy and righteous. If man is united with Christ, he cannot be righteous without being holy.

Holiness is just as important as righteousness in the salvation of man, and in the relationship with God. Holiness is the distinctiveness of God's people in Scripture. God commands the Israelites to be holy because he is holy (Lev 11:44–45). Peter exhorts believers in the New Testament to be holy (1 Pet 1:15–16). It is unthinkable to say that man is righteous but not holy when he is given a new life and is accepted as a child of God. The *duplex gratia* of God is always endowed together in the salvation based on the union with Christ. At the time of salvation man is declared righteous through justification and is transformed into a holy man, a saint, through definitive sanctification (1 Cor 1:2). Justification and definitive sanctification always work together and cannot be separated. They are distinct from each other, but they together mysteriously create the spiritual totality of a "new man" God desires.

Thus, the intimate and vital relationship of justification and definitive sanctification with their distinct characteristics are absolutely essential in Christian theology. This vital relationship fills the gap between justification and progressive sanctification inadvertently left by the Reformation which has stressed the once-for-allness of justification as opposed to the process character of sanctification in an effort to refute Roman Catholicism's doctrine of infused grace into a believer. Perfectionism crept into this gap and wreaked havoc in the evangelical churches. The relationship between justification and definitive sanctification describes the judicial and actual transformational sides of the wonderful blessing of God without falling into perfectionism or the heretical doctrine of the Roman Catholic Church and of Osiander.

Eradication by the Holy Spirit in the Believer

Murray says that the "old man" has died to sin in definitive sanctification. He also says that "it is by progressive eradication of inward corruption that a believer is conformed to the image of Christ."[37] There is still the inward corruption in the believer even after definitive sanctification. The believer is decisively delivered from the dominion of sin, but the "garrison" of sin still remains in him. It does not dominate but influences his life. Thus, the struggle is between sin and righteousness or between the law of sin and the law of the Spirit in the "new man." The inward corruption in the believer is eradicated each day by the power of the Holy Spirit which will also eventually eradicate sin itself from the believer.

Murray does not seem to clarify the nature of the inward corruption and its relationship with sin remaining in the believer. More clarifications and refinements on this teaching are needed in order to understand how the eradication by the Holy Spirit occurs in the believer. Here in this teaching, we are reminded that the "old man" is dead and we are dealing with the "new man," who still has the inward corruption and the defeated sin in him. The relationship between these two and how they are eradicated by the Holy Spirit is the crux of the problem in this teaching.

The inward corruption in the believer is the earthly nature of a human being. Although he is endowed with the grace of definitive sanctification, he will never be perfectly holy as long as he remains in this earthly life. In definitive sanctification he is transformed into the new man who has free will, the heart with a spiritual sense, and the body that has been transformed into an instrument of righteousness. When these three elements of man's being work together following the guidance of the Holy Spirit, there is a progress or growth of holiness in the believer. This is how the believer is inwardly renewed day by day (2 Cor 4:16).

---

37. Murray, Review of *So Great Salvation*, 81.

The Heart of a Believer in Sanctification

What is most important in the life of sanctification is the heart of the believer. Jesus teaches the importance of the heart, "But the things that come out of a person's mouth come from the heart, and these defile them" (Matt 15:18). Paul urges Colossian believers to set their hearts on heavenly things, "Since, then, you have been raised with Christ, set your hearts on things above, where Christ is, seated at the right hand of God" (Col 3:1). Holiness starts from the purity of heart. This heart is ruled by the spiritual sense, overriding all other physical senses pertaining to the mundane things of life. The pure heart wills one thing. There is no division in the pure heart. The "will" attached to the pure heart will always choose God of holiness. As the will moves this way, the body is used as an instrument of righteousness to honor and glorify God. As long as this "new man" is manifested outwardly, the believer progresses in sanctification in his Christian life.

On the contrary, if the believer's heart is not ruled by spiritual sense and is divided, following other senses pertaining to mundane things, his "will" will inevitably choose what is against God of holiness. The believer in this case is living following his earthly nature. Paul warns believers about this life, "Put to death, therefore, whatever belongs to your earthly nature: sexual immorality, impurity, lust, evil desires and greed, which is idolatry. Because of these, the wrath of God is coming" (Col 3: 5-6). The believer's body is used as an instrument of wickeness committing these sins, and they are the outward manifestations of the inward corruption. The defeated sin in the believer gains a strength until a repentance is made to God. This is what happens when a believer falls into sin.

The Will of a Believer in Sanctification

The spiritual battle is on the heart and will of a believer in sanctification. If the heart is perfectly pure, the will moves to where the heart is and chooses the God of holiness. However, the believer's heart is seldom perfectly pure, meaning that the heart is divided. When the heart is divided, the "will" makes a decision either for holiness or against holiness, or wickedness. When the will makes a moral or spiritual decision in a spiritual life, it is either totally holy or totally wicked, no mixture of these two qualities in the voluntary action. The will makes countless moral or spiritual decisions like this in inner thoughts and outward actions throughout the Christian life. Holiness is the spiritual sum total of the effect on the inner man of the believer from these decisions up to that point of the life.

Therefore, the way to have a robust, progressive sanctification is to maximize decisions made by the "new man" whose life is guided by his transformed nature, with free will, the heart with a spiritual sense, and the body as an instrument of righteousness; and to minimize decisions made by the "new man" who has the transformed nature but whose life is nevertheless guided by his earthly nature. Thus eradication of the inward corruption is to eliminate the new man, the "latter new man," who willfully chooses wickedness, from the theater of one's Christian life. I am not suggesting there are two new men in the believer. The focus is on the will of one new man. To illustrate this point, an example might be that just because I hated my brother in the morning and loved him in the evening does not mean two men lived in me today. In one personal being of the believer, the "latter new man" comes out into the life because of an impure heart and imperfect free will that sometimes chooses wickedness over God.

Pure Heart and Free Will to Eradicate the Inward Corruption

The key to eliminating the latter new man, or eradicating the inward corruption, is to guard the heart and to exercise the free will as freely as possible, that is to choose God. Scripture teaches the importance of guarding one's heart, "Above all else, guard your heart, for everything you do flows from it" (Prov 4:23). Also believing God, serving God, and following God always unavoidably involve choosing one over another. Joshua tells the Israelites to choose, "But if serving the LORD seems undesirable to you, then choose for yourselves this day whom you will serve, whether the gods your ancestors served beyond the Euphrates, or the gods of the Amorites, in whose land you are living. But as for me and my household, we will serve the LORD" (Josh 24:15). Keeping the heart pure and choosing God will eradicate the inward corruption by eliminating the latter new man from showing up in real life. This mysterious combination of man's godly exercise and the gradual eradication of the inward corruption is guided and accomplished by the Holy Spirit. Using the means of grace and a man as an instrument, Holy Spirit transforms the heart into a pure heart and the free will into perfect free will progressively.

Pure Heart and Free Will to Eradicate the Remaining Sin

The "garrison" of sin, or remaining sin, is the thorn in the life of a believer. Can he get rid of it? Sin is not created by God and is non-being. Sin is a negation of God in any form. Unbelief is the encompassing negation of

God. A believer, though the new man, has the inward corruption, and sin resides in the corruption. Sin as non-being can only exist in that which it can corrupt. When the believer's free will moves toward wickedness, sin starts to take a form of a spiritual entity and manifests itself in the life of the believer. When the believer's free will moves toward God, the inner holiness is manifested outwardly, as sin as non-being does not exist. Or simply put, a movement of the will toward wickedness is like fanning the ember of corruption with filthy air, whereas a movement of the will toward God is like dousing the ember of corruption with the living water. As a believer, the new man, grows in holiness, the inward corruption is eradicated progressively by the Holy Spirit. As the inward corruption is eradicated through the sanctifying process, the remaining sin is also extirpated gradually by the Holy Spirit in the believer.

Relationship between Definitive and Progressive Sanctification

Definitive sanctification is inextricably related to progressive sanctification in the holy life of a believer. It is the foundation for progressive sanctification. Union with Christ is foundational for progressive sanctification through definitive sanctification. Progressive sanctification involves the believer's efforts in the pursuit of holiness in the Christian life. This Christian endeavor is possible only when he is able to distinguish holiness from other qualities or virtues of life and has a desire for it throughout his life. Unless a fallen man is transformed in his nature to exercise this faculty before the process of sanctification begins, progressive sanctification is meaningless without a direction or impetus. A spiritual sense must be formed, and desire for holiness must be created in man in an instantaneous and once-for-all act of the Holy Spirit, in order for an earnest effort for progressive sanctification to begin.

Inherent Impetus for Holiness

What makes a saved man, a believer, to desire and advance toward holiness, though he as an unbeliever had neither desire nor power to pursue it? In fact, he was "happy" with wickedness as long as it satisfied his selfish lifestyle. Why is there a sudden change? Why is there a sudden reversal of spiritual appetite? One of the reasons, as we explained in detail above, is the transformation of the nature of man through definitive sanctification. The transformations that occur in the nature of man are man's free will, the heart with a spiritual sense and the body as an instrument of righteousness. Especially, the new heart, the heart with a spiritual sense, powered by the Holy Spirit creates the insatiable desire and drive for holiness in the Christian life.

Jonathan Edwards calls this insatiable desire and drive for holiness a "divine taste."[38] The new man has a divine taste to distinguish the "spiritual and holy beauty of actions." He writes:

> Now as there is such a kind of taste of the mind as this, which philosophers speak of, whereby persons are guided in their judgement of the natural beauty, gracefulness, propriety, nobleness, and sublimity of speeches and action, whereby they judge as it were by the glance of the eye, or by inward sensation, and the first impression of the object; so there is likewise such a thing as a divine taste given and maintained by the Spirit of God, in the hearts of the saints, whereby they are in like manner led and guided in discerning and distinguishing the true spiritual and holy beauty of actions.[39]

The believer's new heart with the spiritual sense will motivate, drive, and guide him in discerning and pursuing the holiness in his Christian life. The "divine taste" is created and activated in the heart with the spiritual sense by the Holy Spirit, which will have an insatiable desire and drive for the beauty of holiness until it tastes the perfection set by the God of holiness. This is the inherent impetus for holiness created in man through definitive sanctification by the Holy Spirit.

This is the driving engine for progressive sanctification on the human side, while on the divine side the Holy Spirit, of course, is the agent of sanctification. In other words, in progressive sanctification the Holy Spirit will only work on those who are holiness-sensitive, not holiness-apathetic, believers. Holy Spirit will not force holiness on those who are apathetic toward or ignorant of the importance of holiness in their Christian life.

Holy Spirit works on and through the spiritual sense of the heart for sanctification as the believer desires and pursues holiness in life. The immediate object of the spiritual sense is the beauty of holiness. Man in a fallen

---

38. Edwards, *Religious Affections*, 209. J. I. Packer has a similar concept called motivational holiness. But motivational holiness is not created in the new heart. Rather, it was already in the spiritually dead man. "In the spiritually dead man motivational holiness is so unnatural as to be impossible, because at motivational level sin has the dominion all the time. But in the believer, who is united to Christ, motivational holiness is spontaneous and natural, and the unnatural thing is for him to do violence to his renewed nature by yielding to the desire of the flesh." *Keep In Step*, 107–8.

39. Edwards, *Religious Affections*, 208–9.

state has five senses in his being. But the believer, a regenerate man, also has a spiritual sense which should have the primary position and power over other senses in living a Christian life. The believer, still a physical being in this life, has to use these five senses to live the earthly life, but should be reminded that these senses are tainted and corrupt and should yield to the primacy of the spiritual sense in the pursuit of holiness. Thus, a goal of progressive sanctification is to let the spiritual sense have the primacy over other senses in living a Christian life.

That is why Paul exhorts Colossian believers to set their hearts on things above rather than on earthly things (Col 3:1–2). The believer has the new heart with a spiritual sense revivified through definitive sanctification by the Holy Spirit. What Paul is essentially saying is "now relinquish the rein of your life to the spiritual sense because you have a new heart." The Spirit-led life naturally leads to the on-going robust and healthy "divine taste" for holiness in the Christian life.

Indicative and Imperative in Sanctification

Scripture uses the indicative and imperative for sanctification indicating the definitive and progressive aspect of sanctification, respectively. The imperative is founded on the indicative just as progressive sanctification is founded on definitive sanctification. For the grace of holiness these two cannot be separated and work together in the Christian life. Ridderbos writes, "The imperative is grounded on the reality that has been given with the indicative, appeals to it, and is intended to bring it to full development."[40] They are not to be understood as two divisions of property that the indicative expresses the divine side and the imperative the human side in sanctification. Ridderbos explains:

> For the imperative not only has the function of bringing the new life denoted by the indicative to manifestation, but is also a constant touchstone for latter. And that not only because it is the criterion for the right functioning and self-realization of the new life, but also because it repeatedly places the new life itself under the condition of the manifestation of life demanded by the imperative.[41]

Both indicative and imperative of sanctification are God-driven work, even though man's obedience is required in the imperative of sanctification.

40. Ridderbos, *Paul*, 255.
41. Ridderbos, *Paul*, 255.

One cannot exist without the other in the salvation of man. If a man is truly a "new man," his obedience to God's word must be manifested in his life. Both aspects of sanctification comprise one complete act of God to transform a sinful man to a holy man in a sovereign redemptive plan of God. Ridderbos delineates this point:

> The explanation of this relationship lies in the fact that the reality described by the indicative, however much to be appreciated as the gift of God and the new creation, yet exists in the way of faith; while, conversely, the execution of the imperative is not in the power of man himself, but is no less a matter of faith. Indicative and imperative are both the object of faith, on the one hand in its receptivity, on the other in its activity. For this reason the connection between the two is so close and indissoluble. They represent two "sides" of the same matter, which cannot exist separated from each other.[42]

The importance of faith in sanctification, just as in justification, should not be overlooked just because man's work is involved in progressive sanctification. The inseparability and indissolubility of the indicative and the imperative accentuates the orthodox teaching that sanctification is by faith.

Inside-Out Holiness

Man does not, and cannot, make himself holy. God makes him holy. Sanctification like other elements in the *ordo salutis* is monergistic. Sanctification is the outward manifestation of inward holiness, which is endowed in man by God. Packer explains:

> We need then, to realize and remember that the believer's holiness is a matter of learning to be in action what he already is in heart. In other words, it is a matter of living out the life and expressing the disposition and instincts (that is, new nature) that God wrought in him by creating him anew in Christ.[43]

It is important to understand the "inside-out" character of holiness in sanctification, especially in progressive sanctification. Man's godly deeds do not make him holy, whether he is a believer or not. No human motivation or effort is contributed to make himself holy, or more sanctified. Scripture does not teach "outside-in" sanctification, where man makes himself holy by his own efforts. This kind of sanctification, which is

---

42. Ridderbos, *Paul*, 256.
43. Packer, *Keep In Step*, 107.

prevalent in man-made religions, breeds pride in man and is contrary to the very idea of holiness taught in Scripture.

Holiness in a biblical sense necessarily includes the idea of humility. Jesus Christ, who is called holy and righteous one, is the prime example of portraying this virtue in life. Inside-out sanctification is a monergistic and God's-grace-driven spiritual activity that makes a man to realize his spiritual impotence and to cling to the union with Christ more as he goes deeper into sanctification. For a believer, perfect holiness, which he is striving toward but can never achieve in this life, is the absolute and perfect union with Christ. Process of sanctification is nothing more than a gradual and upward manifestation of the inward reality of the believer, the union with Christ, outwardly through his words and deeds. The believer through this process transforms into an image of Jesus Christ, a humble, righteous, and holy man. This is done by the Holy Spirit, who bonds the believer and Christ into one. The monergistic operation of sanctification engenders the inside-out holiness in the believer.

Ridderbos points out the intimate relationship between the indicative and the imperative in Pauline teachings regarding the salvation of man. He writes:

> The indicative represents the "already" as well as the "not yet." The imperative is likewise focused on the one as well as the other. On the ground of the "already" it can in a certain sense ask all things, is total in character, speaks not only of a small beginning, but of perfection in Christ. At the same time it has its basis in the provisional character of the "not yet."[44]

In the redemptive history depicted by Paul the indicative and the imperative are so intimately close together that the imperative in a sense contains the inward meaning of "already" in the background. The imperative does not stand alone in Paul's protreptic writings on the redemption of man. Ridderbos further explains about the imperative, "there is in the 'not yet' the necessity for increasing, pushing ahead on the way that has been unlocked by the 'already.'" There is no autonomous drive in the imperative. In progressive sanctification there is no human motivation or external energy that initiates and keeps the process going. It is monergistic and internally originated and is by grace of Jesus Christ. The "already" holiness in the believer, on virtue of the union with Christ, comes out in the "not yet" realm through words and deeds of the believer energized and guided by the Holy Spirit.

---

44. Ridderbos, *Paul*, 257–58.

Conclusion

Murray's doctrine of definitive sanctification is an invaluable concept for understanding the once-for-all and definitive aspect of sanctification. However, it needs further development and refinement to be accepted as a *bona fide* soteric doctrine by the Christian church at large. To this end some elements of the doctrine are examined and refined for a clarification and improvement, such that the doctrine stands as an essential and independent element on par with other elements in the *ordo salutis* and that it proves to be a necessary and complementary doctrine to progressive sanctification as it engenders a monergistic characteristic of sanctification. In particular, six elements of the doctrine are critically examined and developed further in order to better understand the importance and necessity of this doctrine in the soteriology.

First, the actuality of definitive sanctification is to be found in the actual transformation in the nature of man. Murray's description of the change of a man in definitive sanctification is primarily relational. Rather, there is the actual, inherent change of the nature of man in definitive sanctification because the Holy Spirit comes into a man and transforms the very nature of man. In definitive sanctification man is endowed with free will, though it is not perfect. Also man's heart is transformed into a new heart with a spiritual sense. And man's body is transformed from an instrument of wickedness to an instrument of righteousness.

Second, Murray's argument that the experiential effect of definitive sanctification is the believer's being immune from committing the sin unto death is not persuasive. The sin unto death in 1 John 5:16 is interpreted as a physical death by some scholars. Also, in connection with the unpardonable sin in Matthew 12:31–32 Murray's assertion of the believer's protection from the sin unto death or the unpardonable sin is not shared by many scholars. Rather than trying to relate the experiential effect of definitive sanctification in this way, it is better to view progressive sanctification as the experiential side of definitive sanctification. Definitive sanctification is foundational for progressive sanctification. Definitive sanctification transforms a man into a new man such that he has desire and drive to pursue holiness in the Christian life. The believer, as a new man, experiences progressive sanctification because of, and on the ground of definitive sanctification.

Third, Murray says that victory in Christ is actual. He also says that because it is actual it is experiential. But that statement is not always true. What is actual may not always be experiential in the life of a believer. The victory in Christ is actual because it actually transformed the nature of man, and thereby man becomes a new man. The victory in Christ is actual because it actually and truly transformed man's will, heart, and body as an instrument of righteousness, whether the man consciously experiences it or not.

Fourth, Murray puts definitive sanctification in a direct relationship with the union with Christ, bypassing justification. He, however, does not elaborate how justification and definitive sanctification are related in the *ordo salutis*. Taking righteousness and holiness as inseparable graces in the salvation of man, it is logically appropriate to say that justification and definitive sanctification occur simultaneously at the inception of Christian life. They are two sides of one complete and gracious act of God in man. Justification is the judicial side of this blessing while definitive sanctification is the actual, or transformational, side of the blessing. However, they are distinct and totally different. By describing justification and definitive sanctification in this way one would not fall into Pelagian perfectionism or the Roman Catholic Church's or Osiander's heretical doctrine.

Fifth, the inward corruption in the believer is the earthly nature, and sin in the believer is the defeated sin. In definitive sanctification man is transformed into a new man with free will, the heart with a spiritual sense, and the body as an instrument of righteousness. These three transformed elements work together guided by the Holy Spirit to eradicate the corruption and sin. Keeping the heart pure and choosing God in daily life eradicates the inward corruption gradually in the believer. The mysterious combination of man's godly exercise and the Holy Spirit's guidance eradicates the corruption of man. As the inward corruption is eradicated through the sanctifying process, the remaining sin, which can exist only in the corruption, is also extirpated gradually by the Holy Spirit in the believer.

Sixth, the relationship between definitive and progressive sanctification is intimate and unbreakable as definitive sanctification is foundational for progressive sanctification. Definitive sanctification provides desire and drive for progressive sanctification. Formulating the concept of definitive sanctification in relation to progressive sanctification in this way effectuates the "inside-out" holiness and monergistic character of sanctification taught in Scripture.

The six elaborations and refinements on the concept of definitive sanctification show the importance of this doctrine in the theology based on a sovereign and gracious God. Without this doctrine justification becomes disjointed from sanctification and progressive sanctification tends to become legalistic. Since the Reformation the justification-centered theology emphasizing grace has triumphed in the Protestant church, with a good reason. However, it created an unintended consequence of bifurcation of righteousness and holiness. The message is that righteousness is by grace but holiness is by work. The Protestant church since then has tried to address the importance of holiness in the Christian life. The doctrine of definitive sanctification is one of the efforts to accomplish this purpose. There are others who likewise have emphasized the importance of holiness in the Christian life.

Chapter 9

The *Duplex Gratia* in the Protestant Church

WHAT IS GRACE? GRACE is undeserved blessing freely bestowed on man by God.[1] That is a simple enough answer. But do we humans really understand what this means? Can anything, even a tiniest thing, get done without us doing any kind of work in our life? Can we fathom the concept that man becomes right with God or righteous without himself doing any work at all? A description of the term "grace" seems simple, but understanding and application of it is never simple and easy; in fact, it is stupendously difficult for a finite human mind. It took about a millennium and a half for the simple teaching of "man's salvation is by grace of God," which is unequivocally taught in Scripture, to be declared and accepted as a *bona fide* doctrine of a Christian church, in this case the Protestant church.

Reaction to the Imbalance of *Duplex Gratia* in the Reformation

The Reformation in 1517, initiated by Martin Luther, put grace in the right place in the salvation of man by God. Or did it? Luther's proclamation of "justification by faith" certainly brought out the concept of grace to the fore and made it the centrality of Christian theology, or at least of soteriology. But to some people, just the profession of faith without an accompanying godly life was not good enough for the salvation, especially in the background of immoral lives of many people who claimed to be Christians. Thus was born the unending struggle between work and grace in the Christian life in the modern age. Did "salvation by grace of God"

---

1. Hughes, "Grace," 479.

make man's salvation too easy, thereby opening the floodgate for nominal Christians who are no different than pagans in their hearts?

Christian leaders and theologians in modern church age have tried to "rectify" this problem by injecting the necessity of works in the Christian life without making the salvation of man based on man's merit. Thus arose spiritual movements and theologies that put the emphasis on sanctification or on the importance of works in the Christian life. All these movements and theologies are considered to be reactions to the Reformation, which overemphasized justification at the expense of sanctification, thereby eclipsing the biblical balance of the *duplex gratia* in the salvation of man.

Pietism

In the Reformation, Luther's doctrine of justification paved a way for the salvation by grace of God and a direct and personal relationship between man and God without a human mediator. Although the Reformation liberated people in Europe from the Roman Catholic Church's shackles of law and tradition and opened a door for a genuine spiritual relationship with God, Luther was already disillusioned by the end of his life in many people who professed to be Christians but showed no sign of spiritual renewal in their lives.

After Luther's death the religious milieu of ecclesiastical formalism and spiritual laxity continued in Germany in much of the following century. In the late seventeenth century Philipp Spener (1635–1705), a Lutheran minister, appealed for a godly life of Christians and moral reform in the country. He took practical steps to revive church members and to reform the church in Germany. This is the beginning of the movement called pietism, and Spener is known as the father of pietism.

Spener's aim was to eliminate spiritual laxity and sterility from Lutheran church and to make Lutheran Christians "people of the heart for whom Christian living is the fundamental concern."[2] Pietists were primarily concerned with holy living, and they assiduously followed God's law to live a holy life. They required more than a memorization of confessional creed and intellectual assent to a doctrine, which they thought were not by themselves genuine signs of a true believer. For them, a transformation of life was the essential part of Christian life as they lived in the obedience to God's law.

Spener's teaching on holy living naturally leads to the emphasis on the experiential nature of Christian life rather than forensic character of salvation. Deviating from Luther's emphasis on justification, he stressed

2. Noll, "Pietism," 858.

more on the new birth, regeneration, that is directly related to the existential nature of salvation. Spener's emphasis on the new birth and new life led the theological pendulum to shift from a forensic element to an experiential element in salvtion; that is, from justification to sanctification. A doctrinal confession is not enough. A transformation of life to a godly life, holy living, is to be exhibited in the life of man who truly had the new birth. Moral changes which include setting aside worldly habits such as drinking and gambling must be shown in the man who goes through the life of sanctification.

In Dresden, Spener met August Hermann Francke (1663–1727) who became his successor in pietism. Francke became the leader of the newly founded University of Halle, which under his leadership became the center of pietism in Europe. Pietism at Halle stressed the practice of holy living such as caring for the poor and spreading the gospel. The university attracted many people who were committed to holy living and Christian service to others. Francke's best known student is Nikolas von Zinzendorf, who became the leader of the Moravian Church. Francke's emphasis on evangelism and missions was felt through Zinzendorf's Moravian Church, which sent out the missionaries to many parts of the world. Francke put his heart into evangelism and missions, and many missionaries were sent out from the university.

Pietism of Germany influenced the English speaking world with a far-reaching consequence. Most notable person influenced by pietism was John Wesley, founder of the Methodist church in England. Although the influence on Wesley was not directly from Spener or Francke, their teaching of pietism disseminated to him through Moravian Christians left an indelible mark on his teaching and ministry. Imbibing the Moravian teaching of pietism, Wesley devised his own brand of pietism, or holy living, called perfectionism, which in turn influenced American Christianity to a remarkable degree.

Assessment of pietism may be made from both sides of a theological aisle. The prominence of the experiential nature of Christian life tilted the movement toward subjectivism, even embracing the mysticism. Also, the emphasis on the individual interpretation of Christian teaching and experience made the movement without a representative doctrine by which it is theologically evaluated and upon which to build a theology in a systematic way. However, on the positive side pietism earnestly strived to stress the life of sanctification, which was eclipsed by the preponderant emphasis on the forensic nature of justification in the Reformation. In this sense pietism may be regarded as the first major reaction to the imbalance of the *duplex gratia* in the Reformation.

John Wesley's Perfectionism

As presented above and in chapter 2, the influence of pietism of Germany on John Wesley (1703–91) was substantial even though he never met Spener or Francke personally. Their teachings on holy living, sanctification, through Moravian Christians left a lasting impact on Wesley's teaching on salvation. Wesley, though not a systematic theologian *per se*, gave a theological framework to their ideas as he developed it to suit his own idea of sanctification in a broad context of salvation.

As with Spener, Wesley did not put much emphasis on justification at the inception of salvation although he taught it as an element in the order of salvation. What is more important for him is a steady and continual pursuit of holiness throughout the Christian life, which will eventually reach the climactic point of "mature" holiness, or perfection, in this life. This is absolutely essential before facing God as the judge at death, at which point the "final justification" occurs. Thus, although Wesley mentions justification in the beginning of salvation, it does not have the same import as for the Reformers two centuries earlier. In a practical sense the final justification of Wesley replaced *the* justification of the Reformers, who put a stupendous importance on the forensic declaration of justification at the *inception* of salvation.

Thus we see Wesley's attempt to "correct" the imbalance caused by the overemphasis on justification in the Reformation. What he is essentially saying is that if holiness is not seen in man's "Christian" life, then the veracity of justification must be questioned. This is a recurring theme in the Protestant theology in relation to grace versus work or law in the Christian life. In reacting to the imbalance of the *duplex gratia* of the Reformation, Wesley went further than German pietists by formulating his own doctrine of sanctification from practical teachings of the pietists. Rejecting Lutheran and Reformed theology, he employed his own brand of theology based on Arminianism to develop a doctrine of sanctification called perfectionism, which would put the primary emphasis on holiness in the Christian life.

Perfectionism, whether good or bad theologically, may be considered as an inevitable consequence of the Reformation, which overemphasized justification at the expense of sanctification and consequently produced many nominal Christians afterward. It so happened that it came in the person of John Wesley, a fierce evangelist with a theological mind, in a theological framework of Arminianism.

The Higher Life Movement in America

The higher life movement, often called victorious life movement, started in the 1850s with the publishment of William Boardman's book *The Higher Christian Life*.[3] However, the term "higher life movement" is used broadly here covering the holiness movement of Charles Finney, Oberlin perfectionism, and Keswick movement from the middle of the nineteenth century to the middle of the twentieth century for our discussion. Although all of these movements have their own distinctive characteristics, their primary focus is to promote holiness in the Christian life, and their teaching or theology was originated from Wesleyan perfectionism. What concerns us most is that how their teaching or theology was formulated in an effort to highlight holiness in the Christian life, which they saw was lacking in the believer's life.

Charles Finney's perfectionism and his theology in a broad sense speak loudly for man's work and man's ability to do it in salvation. His perfectionism generally follows Wesleyan perfectionism, except that his theology is more radical than Wesley's. Rejecting both Calvinism and Wesley's Arminianism, Finney employed Taylorism, which is essentially Pelagianism, to formulate his own brand of perfectionism and theology. He teaches that perfectionism is a Christian's duty, and he endows a man with the ability to achieve it. Thus man's work becomes important in Finney's soteriology such that his theology becomes semi-Pelagian similar to Roman Catholic Church's, except that in his theology a man, not the Church, endowed with the ability to achieve perfection is the ultimate decider of salvation. Then for all practical purposes his theology turns into Pelagianism.

Finney, sensing the overemphasis on the man's work in his theology, introduces a concept called "works of faith" to differentiate it from works of law. He subsumes all works pertaining to justification and sanctification under works of faith. However, a way to differentiate works of faith from works of law is arbitrary and subjective, which Finney uses to suit his theological purpose and to hide the Pelagian character of his theology. In doing so, he blurred the line between grace and work. Finney's overemphasis on sanctification, perfectionism in his case, without the monergistic foundation logically led him to semi-Pelagian theology with preponderant ideas of man's work and ability in the soteriology. An emphasis on the grace of holiness without the monergistic basis of theology is bound to produce a teaching that highlights man's work and minimize God's grace, thereby swinging the theological pendulum to the opposite side of the Reformation.

---

3. Naselli, *No Quick Fix*, 12.

Keswick in the middle of the twentieth century introduced a concept called "positional sanctification" that is supposed to come logically between justification and progressive or experiential sanctification in the *ordo salutis*. For positional sanctification Keswick teaches that the believer's victory in Christ is positional in a sense of potential, such that he has to go through the "reckoning" process to experience this blessing in his life. For Keswick, the positional sanctification includes the concept of justification and potentiality to become sanctified through the reckoning process. Thus, in Keswick sanctification became the centrality of the soteriology such that distinctiveness of justification was lost and the forensic character of salvation, which the Reformers had stressed so much, was minimized. Also man's surrender and faith, so-called "Let go and Let God" in Keswick's teaching, reveals Arminianism, or even Pelagianism, in their theology.

In Keswick the theological pendulum swung to the side of grace of sanctification just as in Finney's perfectionism but not as radically humanistic as Finney's perfectionism in their theology, but nevertheless achieved the same result. Keswick tried to incorporate God's sovereign grace into sanctification along with man's work, but in the process made God who is dependent on man's work to bring sanctifying work to the completion.

Dietrich Bonhoeffer's "Cheap Grace"

Dietrich Bonhoeffer (1906–45) was a Lutheran pastor and theologian who was killed by the Nazi government for his stand against Nazism during the World War II. His life and theology have influenced Christians worldwide after the war. Bonhoeffer's call for the life of discipleship is a piercing and thought-provoking message for Christians living in a secular and affluent world in the post-World War II era. Describing discipleship as following Jesus Christ under the yoke, he differentiates cheap grace from costly grace, the concept which is intimately pertinent to our discussion of sanctification.

Bonhoeffer begins with the state of the church today, "Cheap grace is the deadly enemy of our Church. We are fighting today for costly grace."[4] He describes cheap grace:

> Cheap grace is the preaching of forgiveness without requiring repentance, baptism without church discipline, Communion without confession, absolution without personal confession.

---

4. Bonhoeffer, *Cost of Discipleship*, 43.

> Cheap grace is grace without discipleship, grace without the cross, grace without Jesus Christ, living and incarnate.[5]

Cheap grace is an assent without a commitment, and it is an appearance without substance and power. Costly grace, on the other hand, is a commitment to the end, and it includes substance and power. Bonhoeffer construes about costly grace:

> Costly grace is the treasure hidden in the field; for the sake of it a man will gladly go and sell all that he has. It is the pearl of great price to buy which the merchant will sell all his goods. It is the kingly rule of Christ, for whose sake a man will pluck out the eye which causes him to stumble; it is the call of Jesus Christ at which the disciple leaves his nets and follow him. Costly grace is the gospel which must be *sought* again and again, the gift which must be *asked* for, the door at which a man must *knock*. Such grace is *costly* because it calls us to follow, and it is *grace* because it calls us to follow *Jesus Christ*.[6]

Costly grace includes a life of discipleship, which is the way of sanctification. Thus he says that justification by costly grace will lead to discipleship. However, justification by cheap grace will produce no discipleship; in fact, that justification is not the justification of a sinner at all. Bonhoeffer succinctly expresses the difference between costly grace and cheap grace. "The justification of the sinner in the world degenerated into the justification of sin and the world. Costly grace was turned into cheap grace without discipleship."[7]

Bonhoeffer points out that cheap grace was already in the Reformation church without accusing Martin Luther of causing this problem. He writes, "Cheap grace means the justification of sin without the justification of the sinner. Grace alone does everything . . . so everything can remain as it was before. . . . Well, then, let the Christian live like the rest of the world . . . That was the heresy of the enthusiasts, the Anabaptists and their kind."[8] The problem is that Luther recovered and taught costly grace but people did not understand the true meaning of grace, thereby taking it as a presupposition rather than the result. Bonhoeffer explains:

> Luther had said that all we can do is of no avail, however good a life we live. He had said that nothing can avail us in the sight of God but 'the grace and favor which confers the forgiveness

---

5. Bonhoeffer, *Cost of Discipleship*, 44–45.
6. Bonhoeffer, *Cost of Discipleship*, 45.
7. Bonhoeffer, *Cost of Discipleship*, 50.
8. Bonhoeffer, *Cost of Discipleship*, 43–44.

of sin.' But he spoke as one who knew that at the very moment of his crisis he was called to leave all that he had a second time and follow Jesus. The recognition of grace was his final, radical breach with his besetting sin, but it was never the justification of that sin. By laying hold of God's forgiveness, he made the final, radical renunciation of a self-willed life, and this breach was such that it led inevitably to a serious following of Christ. He always looked upon it as the answer to a sum, but an answer which had been arrived at by God, not by man. But then his followers changed the 'answer' into a data for a calculation of their own. That was the root of the trouble. If grace is God's answer, the gift of Christian life, then we cannot for a moment dispense with following Christ. But if grace is data for my Christian life, it means that I set out to live the Christian life in the world with all my sins justified beforehand. I can go and sin as much as I like, and rely on this grace to forgive me, for after all the world is justified in principle by grace.[9]

According to Bonhoeffer, Luther taught costly grace but his followers misconstrued it as cheap grace. Luther, with the background of an ascetic monkish life, unlikely taught the doctrine of justification by cheap grace, but justification by faith to many people without the background of an ascetic lifestyle seemed an easy salvation without any effort to live a godly life, thereby construing it as cheap grace. In the Reformation a religious euphoria of the freedom from shackles of Roman Catholic Church's laws may have fed the sentiment of cheap grace.

Regardless of the cause of cheap grace, scrutinizing the emphasis of justification by faith without discipleship or sanctification, Bonhoeffer poses a piercing question about the condition of the present church, "Was there ever a more terrible or disastrous instance of the Christianizing of the world than this?"[10] Christians without discipleship are not Christians at all. Discipleship is the true sign of a Christian. For Bonhoeffer, suffering is a sign of true discipleship. He writes, "Discipleship means allegiance to the suffering Christ, and it is therefore not at all surprising that Christians should be called upon to suffer. In fact, it is a joy and token of his grace."[11]

Bonhoeffer stresses discipleship, which is a life of sanctification that includes suffering, in order to "correct" the imbalance of the *duplex gratia* resulted from the Reformation. For him justification and sanctification must

---

9. Bonhoeffer, *Cost of Discipleship*, 50.
10. Bonhoeffer, *Cost of Discipleship*, 54.
11. Bonhoeffer, *Cost of Discipleship*, 91.

go together, and this is the true grace, costly grace. If there is no sanctification, then there was no justification.

New Perspective On Paul

The New Perspective on Paul (NPP) is a major shift on the interpretation of Pauline epistles that has risen in recent years. It started with E. P. Sanders in 1970s, and it quickly attracted many respected biblical scholars such as James D. G. Dunn and N. T. Wright. There are as many variants of this teaching as there are proponents of the NPP. However, two major propositions stand out from all of proponents of the NPP. First, contrary to the traditional Protestant church's teaching, the Judaism in the New Testament era, often called the Second Temple Judaism, did not teach salvation by works but rather taught that man entered into the covenant by God's grace and stayed in it through obedience to the covenant. Second, Paul's teaching on salvation should be understood in this Jewish context in that Christians are people in the covenant of God and their works of obedience to God's law are required for them to stay in the covenant and be saved ultimately. Thus, proponents of the NPP claim that the Reformers misunderstood the concept of justification as taught in Pauline epistles. Such a claim was viewed as an attempt to undermine the foundation of the Reformation and elicited hostile responses from some scholars in the Protestant church.

E. P. Sanders, the prime architect of the NPP, argues, "There does appear to be in Rabbinic Judaism a coherent and all-pervasive view of what constitutes the essence of Jewish religion and how that religion works."[12] He introduces the concept of "covenantal nomism" to summarize this coherent and all-pervasive view. Sanders explains this concept:

> The all-pervasive view can be summarized in the phrase 'covenantal nomism'. Briefly put, covenantal nomism is the view that one's place in God's plan is established on the basis of the covenant and that the covenant requires as the proper response of man his obedience to its commandments, while providing means of atonement for transgression.[13]

So the Jews get in the covenant by God's gracious election but need to obey the law to stay in the covenant. God rewards obedience but punishes transgression.

---

12. Sanders, *Paul and Palestinian Judaism*, 75.
13. Sanders, *Paul and Palestinian Judaism*, 75.

Dunn embraces Sander's reinterpretation of first-century Judaism and applies it to Paul's writings to churches in the New Testament. He writes:

> Sanders . . . has shown . . . that for the first-century Jews, Israel's covenant relation with God was basic, basic to the Jew's sense of national identity and his understanding of his religion. . . . for first-century Judaism everything was an elaboration of the fundamental axiom that the one God had chosen Israel to be his peculiar people, to enjoy special relationship under his rule. The law had been given as an expression of this covenant, to regulate and maintain the relationship established by the covenant. . . . That is to say, obedience to the law in Judaism was never thought of as a means of *entering* the covenant, of *attaining* that special relationship with God; it was more a matter of *maintaining* the covenant relationship with God. . . .
>
> Sanders has given us an unrivalled opportunity to look at Paul afresh, to shift our perspective back from the sixteenth century to the first century, to do what all true exegetes want to do—that is, to see Paul properly within his own context, to hear Paul in terms of his own time, to let Paul be himself.[14]

In this context works of the law understood by Dunn are identification markers of Jewish nation such as circumcision, Sabbath, and dietary laws, which served as barriers to exclude gentiles from salvation. Dunn explains:

> As I noted . . . this understanding of 'works of law' makes best sense of the phrase's use in the context in which Paul introduces it. . . . In Galatians 2. 16, . . . it . . . refers back to the issue at the center of the preceding controversies—circumcision and food laws. That is what was at issue—whether to be justified by faith in Jesus Christ requires also observance of these "works," whether, as the subsequent discussion makes clear, it is possible to conceive of a membership of the covenant people which is not characterized by precisely these works.[15]

So, good works, not works of the law, are the essential part of salvation, and thus needed for Christians to keep them in the covenant.

Another proponent of the NPP, N. T. Wright, who has been the major force in spreading this theology, redefines justification to accommodate covenantal nomism. He writes:

---

14. Dunn, *Jesus, Paul and the Law*, 185–86.
15. Dunn, *Jesus, Paul and the Law*, 220.

> The point is that the *word* "justification" does not itself *denote* the process whereby, or the event which, a person is brought by grace from unbelief, idolatry and sin into faith, true worship and renewal of life. Paul, clearly and unambiguously, uses a different word for that, the word "call." The word "justification," despite centuries of Christian misuse, is used by Paul to denote that which happens immediately after the "call": "those God called, he also justified" (Romans 8.30). In other words, those who hear the gospel and respond to it in faith are then declared by God to be his people, his elect. . . . They are given the status *dikaios*, "righteous," "within the covenant." . . . the fact that "justification" is not about "how I get saved" but "how I am declared to be a member of God's people," must always have an eye to the larger purposes of the covenant.[16]

Thus, jettisoning the Reformation's concept of justification, Wright introduces another justification, final justification, which is based on works until the end of life. He explains, "Paul has already spoken in Romans 2 about the final justification of God's people, on the basis of their whole life. This will take place at the end, when God judges the secrets of all hearts through the Messiah."[17] So Wright argues that initial justification, if we can call it as justification, is by faith whereas the final justification is by works.

The NPP proposed by its main proponents is neither new nor fresh in its explication of Pauline concept of justification or its reinterpretation of soteriology in general. Speaking from our present context of discussion on the *duplex gratia* after the Reformation, the NPP proponents emphasize the part of the Christian life pertaining to sanctification at the expense of justification. Their emphasis on man's works, though Spirit-led work in their thinking, inevitably led them to semi-Pelagian soteriology, which is not much different from Roman Catholic Church's teaching. And their concept of final justification is John Wesley's and Charles Finney's perfectionism of the eighteenth and nineteenth centuries all over again. The NPP was proposed not just to "correct" the imbalance of the *duplex of gratia* of the Reformation but to rebuild the foundation of the soteriology of the Reformation, but fell into Arminian and Pelagian camps.

---

16. Wright, *Paul*, 121–22.
17. Wright, *Paul*, 121.

Federal Vision

The Federal Vision (FV) is a recent theological movement that seeks to reinterpret a covenant in an ecclesiastical setting focusing on the objectivity of the covenant. Its seminal ideas started with Norman Shepherd in 1970s, and the main ideas were imbibed and developed further by other theologians and pastors of the Reformed and Presbyterian churches, most notably by scholars and pastors at the Auburn Avenue Pastor's Conference in 2002.[18] Although the current theological discussion is primarily confined to the Reformed circle, the eventual impact of the movement may be far-reaching, crossing the theological and ecclesiastical lines.

The foundational idea of the FV is that a covenant is conditional, thus minimizing sovereign grace and immutable will of God. Steve Wilkins, a proponent of the FV, explains:

> Covenant, therefore, is a gracious relationship, not a *potentially* gracious relationship. To be in covenant is to have the treasures of God's mercy and grace and the love which He has for His own Son given to you. But the covenant is not *unconditional*. It requires persevering faithfulness.[19]

So even if one is in the covenant, he can never be sure of his salvation until the end. He, in fact, may be proved to be a reprobate in the end. In order to get out of this theological quagmire, proponents of the FV invent two kinds of election: covenantal and decretal election. The decretal election is particularly related to the salvation. Rich Lusk explains the difference:

> Fourth, the warnings for us to come to grip with the strong covenantal language of the Scriptures. Calvinists are used to speaking in terms of God's decree. When we speak of the elect, the regenerate, the sanctified, and so forth, we usually have reference only to those who enter into final salvation. This *decretal* perspective is biblical and is important to maintain, but it is not the Bible's primary way of speaking. More often than not, the Bible speaks *covenantally* and does not draw immediate distinction between those in the covenant who are eternally saved and those who will someday apostatize. The Bible is a pastoral book and uses direct, personalized language to remind covenant members of their privileges and responsibilities.[20]

---

18. Shepherd, *Grace*, 83.
19. Wilkins, "Covenant, Baptism, and Salvation," 69.
20. Lusk, "New Life and Apostasy," 282–83. Italics are mine.

Those people who persevere to the end will prove to be in the decretal election. The others will be proved to be in the covenantal election and will be lost eternally.

This kind of thinking naturally leads to a concept of final justification and of final justification by works. Lusk explains the concept of final justification:

> All that to say: In the final installment of our justification, there is a very real sense in which works will be the decisive factor. If we take time to bother with the actual words of Scripture, this conclusion is unavoidable. It is so plain, one wonders how it could be missed or suppressed. God requires obedience just as surely as he requires faith. Obedience is not optional, but essential. At the same time, it is crucial for us to relate initial and final justification to one another in the proper way. We will develop the biblical picture as we go, but note at this point that initial justification by faith alone must, in some sense, serve as the foundation for final justification by works. At the very least, we can say initial justification puts us in a state of justification with God, which makes a final justification according to works possible.[21]

He further states, "Works of faith-filled obedience, in a secondary way, *cause* our final justification and salvation. Works are the *means* through which we come into possession of eternal life."[22] Reformers' concept of justification, which corresponds to initial justification in Lusk's thinking, is superfluous now because what matters for salvation is the final justification by works.

It is not difficult to see a close affinity between the FV and the NPP. The FV like the NPP attempts to eliminate "cheap grace" from the Christian life by accentuating works of obedience, or holy life, of a Christian. Even though their starting points are different, with the reinterpretation of the Second Temple Judaism for the NPP and the reinterpretation of covenant in the Reformed theology for the FV, they end up at the same point of highlighting the necessity and importance of man's works in salvation. The FV, just like the NPP, had to introduce the concept of final justification, which is really a justification by works. The FV in this regard is seen as another attempt to "correct" the imbalance of the *duplex gratia* in the Reformation

---

21. Lusk, "Future Justification," 10.

22. Lusk, "Tenses of Justification." Lusk tries hard to pull Calvin into the FV's camp by misinterpreting Calvin's writings. If Calvin taught final justification as Lusk claims, then John Wesley, who put final justification in the *ordo salutus*, ends up a Calvinist on this point.

by emphasizing the life after justification, the life of sanctification, primarily by Reformed theologians.

Definitive Sanctification in the *Duplex Gratia*

We have seen in the Christian history the six spiritual movements and/or theological teachings as "corrective" measures for the imbalance between justification and sanctification in the Reformation. Even though I agree with the argument that the Reformation's doctrine of justification by faith alone did not do justice to a life of sanctification and good works, I do not believe that any one of the corrective measures mentioned above renders a proper balance in the *duplex gratia* in the Reformation without falling into a Pelagian camp of theology.[23]

Paul asks believers a practical, yet theologically very profound, question, "Shall we go on sinning so that grace may increase?" (Rom 6:1). Is Christian's unholy life covered by God's grace, particularly the grace of justification? The answer is a resounding "no" as Paul says, "By no means!" (Romans 6:2). There is no "cheap grace"—a Christian must live a holy life if he is a true believer. Then how can he live a life of sanctification without making himself the achiever of this sanctification? Although this is a logical question arising from a seemingly rampant practice of cheap grace in the Christian life, Paul in Romans 6 neither asks this question nor gives an answer to this question. Rather, he teaches who the believer is; that is, who he is in Jesus Christ. We must first know that the believer is once-for-all and definitively made holy on virtue of the union with Christ. Granted, this does not seem like tackling the problem of unholy living of a Christian in a practical way, nor does it seem like providing practical steps to live a life of sanctification. However, we must take this step if we want to make any headway in solving the problem of the imbalance of the *duplex gratia* in the soteriology of Protestant theology. Although it seems to be a little step, it is a biblical way.

Grace as Power

Grace is a heavenly concept that can only be fully apprehended in a spiritual world. It usually means in this world an unmerited favor of God, or undeserved blessing of God. Although the meaning like this is generally correct,

---

23. Bonhoeffer's concept of costly grace for discipleship may be an exception to the critique mentioned here. However, it will be difficult to maintain the monergistic nature of salvation with sanctification devoid of a definitive aspect as the foundation.

it expresses only one aspect of this heavenly concept. In light of its biblical usage in the salvation of man, this meaning excludes other aspect of the term, which is intimately related with the transformation of man in a soteric life. Scripture teaches that in the outworking of God's plan of salvation grace is power, or more exactly it is God's benevolent power. Paul, who once was a persecutor of the church, writes, "But by the grace of God I am what I am, and his grace to me was not without effect. No, I worked harder than all of them—yet not I, but the grace of God that was with me" (1 Cor 15:10). For Paul, the grace of God is God's transforming power in him throughout his Christian life. In another place he also writes, "But he said to me, 'My grace is sufficient for you, for my power is made perfect in weakness.' Therefore I will boast all the more gladly about my weaknesses, so that Christ's power may rest on me" (2 Cor 12:9). Here grace and power are mentioned as working mysteriously together in Paul's life. God's grace always includes its inherent power to transform the man who receives it. Grace of righteousness is endowed to a man with power to make him righteous. Likewise, grace of holiness is endowed to a man with power to transform him into a holy person. God's grace without power is no grace at all.

The grace that is endowed to a man in sanctification, both definitive and progressive, is to be understood in this sense. Especially in progressive sanctification, man's work necessarily comes to the fore since it involves man's conscious efforts to live a life of sanctification. However, it is the grace that works in him throughout the process as Paul says in 1 Corinthians 15:10. Grace is not just a virtue, not even just power, but the personified power of Jesus Christ. So, in sanctification the subject is grace, and man is the object to be sanctified. Man, saved or not, does not and cannot sanctify himself. Grace uses a man's physical being as an instrument to make man's spiritual being holy, so that man's holistic being becomes sanctified. Therefore, whatever work man thinks he has done throughout this process is not his work, because he never was the subject of this spiritual endeavor. Grace was the primary subject. It is the grace that has done it. Then man can joyfully shout like Paul, "No, I worked harder than all of them—yet not I, but the grace of God that was with me" (1 Cor 15:10). Any good works done by a believer must be attributed to the grace that is in him.

Some theologians espousing the recent reinterpretation of Pauline epistles refer to Romans 2:6, where Paul says, "God will repay each person according to what they have done," to argue that the "final" justification will be by works. This obviously brought forth many negative reactions from theologians in the Protestant church. In response, they assert that they do not teach the salvation by works because the works done for the final justification are produced by the Spirit-led life of a Christian, hence salvation is by the grace of

God. The statement like this evidences that they underestimate, undervalue, and misidentify the grace of God. Grace is not a Christian's helper. Grace is the personified power of Jesus Christ in salvation.

Progressive sanctification is bound to be semi-Pelagian, whether we like it or not, unless we understand clearly the nature of definitive sanctification, especially the relationship between definitive sanctification and grace of God. In definitive sanctification the transformation occurs in the nature of man on virtue of the union with Christ.[24] It is by the sovereign grace of God. In definitive sanctification man's nature is transformed in such a way that man's physical being becomes a fit organ to be used as an instrument for sanctification by the grace of God, the personified power of Jesus Christ. So, the ensuing works for sanctification are done by the grace as the primary executor, even though man performs necessary activities using his physical organs.

Man contributes nothing to sanctification. Man becomes a fruit-bearing being only in the union with Christ. Jesus says, "I am the vine; you are the branches. If you remain in me and I in you, you will bear much fruit; apart from me you can do nothing" (John 15:5). It is not man, but man united with Christ, who does works for sanctification. In the union with Christ, grace, the personified power of Jesus Christ, uses a man to accomplish a godly purpose in and through him. Definitive sanctification is one aspect of man's union with Jesus Christ. Every aspect of man's union with Christ, or every element in the *ordo salutis*, should be seen through the lens of grace, the personified power of Jesus Christ.

Covenant as Driving Force

Why does a Christian have to live a holy life? The writer of Hebrews says, "without holiness no one will see the LORD" (Heb 12:14b). Referring to this verse, many Christian leaders teach that Christians must strive for holiness in this life. I agree with them that this is a reason for sanctification of Christians. But holiness should not be understood only as the goal in the Christian life. Otherwise, the goal becomes perfect holiness, that which Christians can never achieve but nevertheless have to strive for in this life. This would not give Christians a strong motivation to pursue holiness in their lives. All those spiritual movements and theologies presented in this chapter have risen to inject an impetus or motivation to Christians in their pursuit of holiness, which they as believers are supposed to do without

---

24. The transformation that occurs in definitive sanctification is described in detail in chapter 8.

any extrabiblical incentives. Some theologians even proposed a final test called "final justification" to keep Christians spiritually "sharp and alert" throughout their lives.

There is another reason taught in Scripture for a believer to be holy. In the Old Testament Israel is called a nation with distinct characteristics. They are people of covenant and a holy nation. A covenant is a sacred agreement between God and man regarding his life on earth. As the covenant is inextricably related to will of God, it includes the purpose of man's life in the world, or more specifically, the spiritual purpose of man's life in the world. So for Israel as a nation, their spiritual purpose as included in their national covenant is to live as a holy and righteous people from which the Messiah for the world will come. In order to accomplish this purpose, God made Israel holy, so they could live as holy people. "Do not profane my holy name, for I must be acknowledged as holy by the Israelites. I am the LORD, who made you holy" (Lev 22:32). Holiness is not the end for Israel. It is the means, spiritual means, to live a covenant life. It is the same for an individual. Samson was born and lived as a Nazirite. God tells Samson's mother about his life:

> Now see to it that you drink no wine or other fermented drink and that you do not eat anything unclean. You will become pregnant and have a son whose head is never to be touched by a razor because the boy is to be a Nazirite, dedicated to God from the womb. He will take the lead in delivering Israel from the hands of the Philistines. (Judg 13:4–5)

It includes Samson's spiritual purpose of his life and the way to live that life, a Nazirite life. So in Samson's life also, the life separated from other lives, a sanctifying life, is a means to achieve the covenant, the spiritual purpose, given by God.

The same principle applies to a believer in the New Testament. A believer is born with a God-given personal covenant, which includes his spiritual purpose of life in the world (Eph 1:4–5). He lives as a covenant man to accomplish the covenant, and the means to achieve that goal is holiness, the outward virtue of sanctification. The covenant gives the answer to "what" and sanctification to "how" of the Christian life. Without a firm belief and understanding of his personal covenant, a believer has no powerful motivation for sanctification.

The believer has been made holy as Israel was made holy by God (Lev 22:32). It is imperative to understand definitive sanctification as the *sine qua non* of a holy life of the believer. With definitive sanctification holiness becomes a means of the Christian life also, and without it holiness becomes the end only, that which man does not know where it ends. Who would embark on a journey without knowing the destination? Holiness is not the purpose of the Christian life, the purpose man can never fulfill. It is the means that comes with a purpose. A believer is holy now, not at the end of the life, on the basis of the union with Christ. For a believer the covenant gives the ongoing impetus for sanctification, and sanctification is the sign of covenant life.

Conclusion

It has been over five hundred years since the Reformation. More than anything else, what makes the Protestant church so distinctively different from Roman Catholic Church is the doctrine of salvation of man, the soteriology of Christianity. In the heart of the soteriology that separates these two churches is the doctrine of justification by faith. Justification by faith alone was the central doctrine of the Reformation, and other soteric grace such as sanctification was overlooked as the forensic nature of salvation was accentuated, thereby creating the imbalance of the *duplex gratia* in salvation. The upshot of the overemphasis of justification is a slew of Christians who profess to be in faith but do not manifest holy living in their lives. Many spiritual movements and theologies have risen in an effort to "correct" this problem by emphasizing sanctification in the Christian life. All of movements and theologies presented in this chapter are considered to be reactions to the Reformation, which overemphasized justification at the expense of sanctification, thereby eclipsing the biblical balance of the *duplex gratia* in salvation.

Pietism, originated in Germany about a century and a half after the Reformation, may be regarded as the first major reaction to the imbalance of the *duplex gratia* in the Reformation. Spener and Francke, the leaders of pietism, stressed the experiential nature of Christian life to cure the spiritual laxity and sterility of Lutheran Christians. They sensed that the problem was from the overemphasis of the forensic nature of salvation in the Reformation. Their teachings on sanctification, though not theologically formulated and leaning toward subjectivism, exerted a great influence on future leaders such as Zinzendorf and John Wesley.

John Wesley's perfectionism may be considered as an inevitable consequence of the Reformation, which produced many nominal Christians by overemphasizing justification at the expense of sanctification. Wesley employed Arminianism to develop his doctrine of sanctification and perfectionism. Wesley's perfectionism was an attempt to correct the imbalance of the *duplex gratia* with a theology in a systematic way. He in the process minimized justification and created overblown sanctification in his theology.

All of the higher life movements in America are descendants of Wesley's perfectionism in one way or another. Charles Finney employed Pelagian theology to formulate his own theology, and his perfectionism was the logical end of the doctrine of sanctification in this system. Another form of the higher life movement, Keswick also stressed sanctification but could not escape from emphasizing man's works in sanctification. All higher life movements are attempts to correct the imbalance of *duplex gratis* in the Reformation, but all these corrections are tainted with either Arminian or Pelagian theology.

Bonhoeffer's concept of cheap and costly grace epitomizes the problem caused by the overemphasis of justification in the Reformation and a solution to this problem. He clearly realized the imbalance of the *duplex gratia* in the modern church. He taught that discipleship of a Christian was the way to correct this problem of the imbalance. In viewing discipleship as the true sign of justification, Bonhoeffer put a great emphasis on the life of sanctification.

The NPP was proposed to correct the problem of the *duplex gratia* in the church by reinterpreting Pauline concept of justification in Scripture. Rejecting the Reformers' concept of justification, proponents of the NPP emphasized the necessity and importance of works and put a great emphasis on final justification in salvation. Their overemphasis on man's works in sanctification and the concept of final justification based on works logically led them to semi-Pelagian theology.

The FV like the NPP attempts to put a proper balance on the *duplex gratia* by accentuating works of obedience. Proponents of the FV reinterprets covenant in the Reformed theology in such a way that "final justification by works" becomes the deciding factor in the salvation of man. The FV is another attempt to correct the imbalance of the *duplex gratia* by emphasizing the life after "initial" justification, the life of sanctification, by Reformed theologians.

There is now, over five hundred years after the Reformation, a consensus in the Protestant church that there is the imbalance in the *duplex gratia* of soteriology in the Protestant theology. Many Christian leaders and theologians have attempted to render a proper balance to the *duplex of gratia* of the Reformation. They all stressed the necessity of man's works for salvation, and hence fell into the hand of humanistic theology, Arminianism or Pelagianism.

Man's works are needed in sanctification; however, progressive sanctification not founded on definitive sanctification is bound to lead the whole soteriology to an Arminian or Pelagian camp. It must be understood that the subject who does work in progressive sanctification is not the man, but grace of God, the personified power of Jesus Christ. This theological truth must be instilled in the mind of man through definitive sanctification. In progressive sanctification man is the object of sanctification, contributing nothing to his sanctification. So, with definitive sanctification it is possible to balance the *duplex gratia* without falling into Arminian or Pelagian theology.

Another problem with all these "corrective" measures to the imbalance in the *duplex gratia* is that holiness turns into perfect holiness, the goal, Christians must achieve in the end. Thus, holiness becomes the goal Christians must strive for but cannot achieve in this life. But holiness is the means, not the goal, of the Christian life, and personal covenant shows the purpose, or goal, of that life. A powerful impetus for holy life should come from the covenant, which is like a spiritual roadmap to Christians. A true believer must live a holy life as a covenant being in the redemptive plan of God. In definitive sanctification God initiates and energizes this process in his sovereign grace.

Bibliography

Adrian, Victor. "Definitive Sanctification." ThM thesis, Westminster Theological Seminary, 1961.
Ahlstrom, Sydney E. *A Religious History of the American People*. New Haven: Yale University Press, 1972.
Aitken, W. Hay H. M. "Full Deliverance." In *Keswick's Triumphant Voice*, edited by Herbert F. Stevenson, 160–71. London: Marshall, Morgan & Scott, 1963.
Aldis, W. H. "An Absolute Surrender." In *Keswick's Triumphant Voice*, edited by Herbert F. Stevenson, 289–95. London: Marshall, Morgan & Scott, 1963.
———. *The Message of Keswick and Its Meaning*. London: Marshall, Morgan & Scott, 1957.
Alexander, Donald L. "The Riddle of Sanctification." In *Christian Spirituality*, edited by Donald L. Alexander, 7–11. Downers Grove, IL: InterVarsity, 1988.
Atwater, Lyman H. "The Higher Life and Christian Perfection." *The Presbyterian Quarterly and Princeton Review* 22 (1977) 389–419.
Augustine. *Confessions*. Translated by R. S. Pine-Coffin. New York: Penguin, 1986.
Ayling, Stanley. *John Wesley*. Cleveland: Collins, 1979.
Barabas, Steven. *So Great Salvation: The History and Message of the Keswick Convention*. Westwood, NJ: Revell, 1952.
Berkhof, Louis. *Manual of Christian Doctrine*. Grand Rapids: Eerdmans, 1973.
———. *Systematic Theology*. Grand Rapids: Eerdmans, 1981.
Berkouwer, G. C. *Faith and Justification*. Translated by Lewis B. Smedes. Grand Rapids: Eerdmans, 1979.
———. *Faith and Sanctification*. Translated by John Vriend. Grand Rapids: Eerdmans, 1952.
———. *Sin*. Translated by Philip C. Holtrop. Grand Rapids: Eerdmans, 1980.
Boardman, W. E. *The Higher Christian Life*. Boston: Hoyt, 1858.
Bonhoeffer, Dietrich. *The Cost of Discipleship*. Translated by R. H. Fuller. New York: Touchstone, 2018.
Buswell, James Oliver. *The Christian Life*. Grand Rapids: Zondervan, 1972.
———. *A Systematic Theology of the Christian Religion*. Grand Rapids: Zondervan, 1972.
Calvin, John. *Commentaries on the Epistle of Paul the Apostle to the Romans*. Translated by Christopher Fetherstone. Grand Rapids: Baker, 1981.

———. *Commentaries on the First Epistle of John*. Translated by John Owen. Grand Rapids: Baker, 1981.

———. *Institutes of the Christian Religion*. Translated by Ford Lewis Battles. Edited by John T. McNeill. 2 vols. Philadelphia: The Westminster, 1960.

Carpenter, J. A. "Buswell, James Oliver." In *Dictionary of Christianity in America*, edited by Daniel G. Reid, 204. Downers Grove, IL: InterVarsity, 1990.

Cattel, Everett L. "An Appraisal of the Keswick and Wesleyan Contemporary Positions." In *Insights into Holiness*, edited by Kenneth Geiger, 264–79. Kansas City, MO: Beacon Hill, 1963.

Cho, David. *The Covenant Life*. Eugene, OR: Resource, 2020.

Clarke, Adam. *Commentary on the New Testament, 1 John*. Nashville: Abingdon, 1832.

Cox, George Leo. *John Wesley's Concept of Perfection*. Kansas City, MO: Beacon Hill, 1964.

Cranfield, C. E. B. *A Critical and Exegetical Commentary on the Epistle to the Romans*. Edited by J. A. Emerton and C. E. B. Cranfield. The International Critical Commentary. Edinburgh: T. & T. Clark, 1977.

Cumming, Elder J. *Through the Eternal Spirit*. Stirling: Stirling Tract, 1937.

Cunnington, Ralph. "Definitive Sanctification: A Response to John Fesko." *Evangelical Quarterly* 84.3 (2012) 234–252.

Dabney, Robert L. *Lectures in Systematic Theology*. Grand Rapids: Zondervan, 1972.

———. *Syllabus and Notes of the Course of Systematic and Polemic Theology*. Asbury Park, NJ: Presbyterian, 1885.

DeYoung, Kevin. "Incentives for Acting the Miracle." In *Acting the Miracle*, edited by John Piper and David Mathis, 43–64. Wheaton: Crossway, 2013.

Dieter, Melvin E. "The Development of Nineteenth Century Holiness Theology." *Wesleyan Theological Journal* 20 (1985) 61–77.

———. *The Holiness Revival of the Nineteenth Century*. Metuchen, NJ: The Scarecrow, 1980.

———. "The Wesleyan Perspective." In *Five Views on Sanctification*, 9–46. Grand Rapids: Zondervan, 1987.

Dunn, James D. G. *Jesus, Paul and the Law*. Louisville: Westminster/John Knox, 1990.

Eby, David L. "The Reformed Response to the Higher Life Movement." ThM thesis, Westminster Theological Seminary, 1982.

Edwards, Jonathan. *The Religious Affections*. Edinburgh: The Banner of Truth, 1986.

Elwell, Walter A., ed. *Evangelical Dictionary of Theology*. Grand Rapids: Baker, 1990.

Estes, Steven D. "Death to Sin in Romans 6." ThM thesis, Westminster Theological Seminary, 1987.

Ferguson, Sinclair B. *Devoted to God*. Edinburgh: The Banner of Truth, 2016.

———. "The Reformed View." In *Christian Spirituality*, edited by Donald L. Alexander, 47–76. Downers Grove, IL: InterVarsity, 1988.

Fesko, J. V. "Sanctification and Union with Christ: A Reformed Perspective." *Evangelical Quarterly* 82.3 (2010) 197–214.

Finney, Charles G. *Christ Our Sanctification*. Harrisburg, PA: Christian, 1942.

———. *Finney's Lectures on Systematic Theology*. Grand Rapids: Eerdmans, 1957.

———. *Lectures to Professing Christians*. Oberlin: Goodrich, 1879.

———. *The Memoirs of Charles G. Finney*. Edited by Garth M. Rosell and Richard A. G. Dupuis. Grand Rapids: Zondervan, 1989.

---. *Sanctification*. Edited by William Ernest Allen. London: Christian Literature Crusade, 1949.

---. *Sermons on Gospel Themes*. New York: Revell, 1876.

Flew, Newton R. *The Idea of Perfection in Christian Theology*. New York: Humanities, 1968.

Foster, Frank H. *A Genetic History of New England Theology*. Chicago: University of Chicago Press, 1907.

Freundt, A. H. "Dabney, Robert Lewis." In *Dictionary of Christianity in America*, edited by Daniel G. Reid, 336–37. Downers Grove, IL: InterVarsity, 1990.

---. "Thornwell, James Henley." In *Dictionary of Christianity in America*, edited by Daniel G. Reid, 1174. Downers Grove, IL: InterVarsity, 1990.

Grudem, Wayne. *Systematic Theology*. Grand Rapids: Zondervan, 1994.

Hamilton, James E. "Academic Orthodoxy and the Arminianizing of American Theology." *Wesleyan Theological Journal* 9 (1974) 52–59.

---. "Nineteenth Century Philosophy and Holiness Theology: A Study in the Thought of Asa Mahan." *Wesleyan Theological Journal* 13 (1978) 51–64.

Harford, Charles F., ed. *The Keswick Convention: Its Messages, Its Method and Its Men*. London: Marshall, 1907.

Harford-Battersby, Canon J. "The Cry of a Defeated Soldier." In *Keswick's Triumphant Voice*, edited by Herbert F. Stevenson, 111–17. London: Marshall, Morgan & Scott, 1963.

---. *Memoir of T. D. Harford-Battersby*. London: Seeley, 1890.

Hodge, Archibald Alexander. *The Confession of Faith*. Carlisle, PA: The Banner of Truth, 1978.

---. "The Ordo Salutis." *Princeton Review* (1878) 304–21.

---. *Outlines of Theology*. Grand Rapids: Eerdmans, 1928.

---. *Popular Lectures on Theological Themes*. Philadelphia: Presbyterian Board, 1887.

Hodge, Charles. *Commentary on the Epistle to the Romans*. Grand Rapids: Eerdmans, 1965.

---. "Finney's Sermon on Sanctification, and Mahan on Christian Perfection." *Princeton Review* 13 (1841) 231–50.

---. "Sanctification." *The Princeton Review* 39 (1867) 537–57.

---. *Systematic Theology*. 3 vols. Grand Rapids: Eerdmans, 1981.

Hoekema, Anthony A. "The Reformed Perspective." In *Five Views on Sanctification*, 59-90. Grand Rapids: Zondervan, 1987.

---. "Response to McQuilkin." In *Five Views on Sanctification*, 187-90. Grand Rapids: Zondervan, 1987.

Hoffecker, W. Andrew. "Hodge, Archibald Alexander." In *Dictionary of Christianity in America*, edited by Daniel G. Reid, 536–37. Downers Grove, IL: InterVarsity, 1990.

Hopkins, Evan H. "Christ Our LORD." In *Keswick's Triumphant Voice*, edited by Herbert F. Stevenson, 263–68. London: Marshall, Morgan & Scott, 1963.

---. "Crisis and Process." In *Keswick's Authentic Voice: Sixty-Five Dynamic Addresses Delivered at the Keswick Convention*, edited by Herbert F. Stevenson, 332–37. Grand Rapids: Zondervan, 1959.

---. "Deliverance From the Law of Sin." In *Keswick's Authentic Voice: Sixty-Five Dynamic Addresses Delivered at the Keswick Convention*, edited by Herbert F. Stevenson, 157–61. Grand Rapids: Zondervan, 1959.

———. "The Fulness of the Spirit." In *Keswick's Authentic Voice: Sixty-Five Dynamic Addresses Delivered at the Keswick Convention*, edited by Herbert F. Stevenson, 461–65. Grand Rapids: Zondervan, 1959.

———. *The Law of Liberty in the Spiritual Life*. Philadelphia: The Sunday School Times, 1957.

———. "Our Old Man Crucified." In *Keswick's Triumphant Voice*, edited by Herbert F. Stevenson, 172–78. London: Marshall, Morgan & Scott, 1963.

Horton, Michael S. *Covenant and Salvation: Union with Christ*. Louisville: Westminster/John Knox, 2007.

Horton, Stanley M. "The Pentecostal Perspective." In *Five Views on Sanctification*, 103–135. Grand Rapids: Zondervan, 1987.

Hughes, P. E. "Grace." In *Evangelical Dictionary of Theology*, edited by Walter A. Elwell, 479–82. Grand Rapids: Baker, 1990.

Hynson, Leon O. "Original Sin as Privation: An Inquiry into a Theology of Sin and Sanctification." *Wesleyan Theological Journal* 22 (1987) 65–79.

Käsemann, Ernst. *Commentary on Romans*. Translated by Geoffrey W. Bromiley. Grand Rapids: Eerdmans, 1986.

Keefer, Luke L., Jr. "Characteristics of Wesley's Arminianism." *Wesleyan Theological Journal* 22 (1987) 88–99.

Kim, Kwang Ryul. "A Tension Between the Desire to Follow the Example of Jesus' Life and the Desire to Trust in His Redemptive Work: The Theology of John Wesley Reflected in His *Christian Library*." PhD diss., Westminster Theological Seminary, 1992.

Klooster, F. H. "Berkhof, Louis." In *Evangelical Dictionary of Theology*, edited by Walter A. Elwell, 135. Grand Rapids: Baker, 1990.

Laidlaw, John. *The Bible Doctrine of Man*. Edinburgh: T. & T. Clark, 1895.

Lindstrom, Harald. *Wesley and Sanctification*. Wilmer, KY: Asbury, 1981.

Loucks, C. Mel. "The Theological Foundations of the Victorious Life." PhD diss., Fuller Theological Seminary, 1984.

Lovelace, Richard F. *Dynamics of Spiritual Life: An Evangelical Theology of Renewal*. Downers Grove, IL: InterVarsity, 1960.

Lusk, Rich. "Future Justification." http://trinity-pres.net/essays/_published_Future_Justification.pdf.

———. "New Life and Apostasy." In *The Federal Vision*, edited by Steve Wilkins and Duane Garner, 275–303. Monroe, LA: Athanasius, 2004.

———. "The Tenses of Justification." http://hornes.org/theologia/rich-lusk/the-tenses-of-justification.

Maclemnan, Calum. "Romans 6 As a Criterion for the 'Old Man/New Man' Conflict." ThM thesis, Westminster Theological Seminary, 1988.

Mahan, Asa. *The Baptism of the Holy Ghost*. New York: Palmer & Hughes, 1870.

———. "Doctrine of Sanctification." *Oberlin Evangelist*, August 22, 1848.

———. *Out of Darkness into Light*. New York: Garland, 1985.

———. *Science of Moral Philosophy*. Oberlin: Fitch, 1848.

Marshall, Walter. *Gospel Mystery of Sanctification*. Hertfordshire, UK: Evangelical, 1981.

Martin, W. W. "Insipid Christians." In *Keswick's Triumphant Voice*, edited by Herbert F. Stevenson, 133–38. London: Marshall, Morgan & Scott, 1963.

McQuilkin, J. Robertson. "The Keswick Perspective." In *Five Views on Sanctification*, 149–83. Grand Rapids: Zondervan, 1987.

McQuilkin, Robert C. "Victory in Christ." *The Sunday School Times*, September 9 and 16, 1939.

———. *Victory in Christ: or, Taking God at His Word: A Personal Testimony*. Columbia, SC: Columbia Bible College, 1939.

Mullin, R. B. "Hodge, Charles." In *Dictionary of Christianity in America*, edited by Daniel G. Reid, 537. Downers Grove, IL: InterVarsity, 1990.

Murray, Andrew. "The Carnal Christian." In *Keswick's Triumphant Voice*, edited by Herbert F. Stevenson, 84–93. London: Marshall, Morgan & Scott, 1963.

———. *The Holiest of All: An Exposition of the Epistle to the Hebrews*. New York: Revell, 1894.

Murray, John. "Definitive Sanctification." *Calvin Theological Journal* 2 (1967) 5–21.

———. *The Epistle to the Romans*. The New International Commentary on the New Testament. Edited by F. F. Bruce. Grand Rapids: Eerdmans, 1959.

———. "Foreword." In *The Problems of Original Sin in American Presbyterian Theology*, by George P. Hutchinson, vii–viii. Philadelphia: Presbyterian and Reformed, 1972.

———. "The Pattern of Sanctification." In *Collected Writings of John Murray*, 2:311. Edinburgh, England: The Banner of Truth Trust, 1977.

———. *Principles of Conduct*. Grand Rapids: Eerdmans, 1957.

———. *Redemption Accomplished and Applied*. Grand Rapids: Eerdmans, 1955.

———. Review of *So Great Salvation*, by Steven Barabas. *Westminster Theological Journal* (1953–54) 78–84.

———. "Sanctification." *Christianity Today*, May 11, 1962.

Naselli, Andrew David. *No Quick Fix*. Bellingham, WA: Lexham, 2017.

Noll, Mark A. "Glimpses of Finney." *The Reformed Journal* 36 (1986) 22–24.

———. "Pietism." In *Evangelical Dictionary of Theology*, edited by Walter A. Elwell, 855–58. Grand Rapids: Baker, 1990.

Packer, J. I. *Keep in Step with the Spirit*. Old Tappan, NJ: Revell, 1984.

———. "Keswick and the Reformed Doctrine of Sanctification." *The Evangelical Quarterly* 27 (1955) 153–67.

Palmer, Phoebe. *Faith and Its Effects*. New York: Garland, 1985.

Park, Jae-Eun. *Driven by God*. Göttingen: Vandenhoeck & Ruprecht, 2018.

Pascal, Blaise. *Pensées*. Translated by A. J. Krailsheimer. New York: Penguin, 1988.

Pask, Alfred H. "The Influence of Arminius on John Wesley." *London Quarterly and Holborn Review* 29 (1960) 258–63.

Patterson, Robert William. "Keswick Theology and American Evangelism." ThM thesis, Westminster Theological Seminary, 1982.

Payne, Don J. *Already Sanctified*. Grand Rapids: Baker Academic, 2020.

Peterson, David. *Possessed by God*. Downers Grove, IL: InterVarsity, 1995.

Pierson, Arthur Tappan. *The Keswick Movement*. New York: Funk & Wagnalls, 1903.

———. "The Message: Its Practical Application." In *The Keswick Convention*, edited by Charles F. Harford, 87–96. London: Marshall, 1907.

Piper, John. "Prelude to Acting the Miracle." In *Acting the Miracle*, edited by John Piper and David Mathis, 28–41. Wheaton: Crossway, 2013.

Pointer, S. R. "Shedd, William Greenough Thayer." In *Dictionary of Christianity in America*, edited by Daniel G. Reid, 1081. Downers Grove, IL: InterVarsity, 1990.

Pollock, J. C. *The Keswick Story*. Chicago: Moody, 1964.

Raser, Harold E. *Phoebe Palmer: Her Life and Thought*. Lewiston/Queenston: Mellen, 1987.

Reeves, James H. "Holiness and the Holy Spirit in the Thought of Charles G. Finney." Ph.D. diss., Fuller Theological Seminary, 1990.
Reymond, Robert L. *A New Systematic Theology of the Christian Faith*. Grand Rapids: Zondervan, 1998.
Ridderbos, Herman. *Paul: An Outline of His Theology*. Translated by John Richard DeWitt. Grand Rapids: Eerdmans, 1985.
———. *When the Time Had Fully Come*. Grand Rapids: Eerdmans, 1957.
Sandeen, Ernest. *The Roots of Fundamentalism*. Chicago: University of Chicago Press, 1970.
Sanders, E. P. *Paul and Palestinian Judaism*. Minneapolis: Fortress, 2017.
Sangster, W. E. *The Path to Perfection*. London: Hodder & Stoughton, 1943.
Scroggie, W. Graham. "Keswick's Distinctive Message." In *The Keswick Week: 1933*, 78–82. London: Pickering & Inglis, 1933.
Shedd, William G. T. *A Critical and Doctrinal Commentary upon the Epistle of St. Paul to the Romans*. New York: Scribner's, 1893.
———. *Dogmatic Theology*. Grand Rapids: Zondervan, 1953.
———. *Sermons to the Spiritual Man*. New York: Scribner's, 1910.
Shelley, Bruce. "Source of Pietistic Fundamentalism." *Fides et Historia* 5 (1972) 68–78.
Shepherd, Norman. *The Call of Grace*. Phillipsburg, NJ: P & R, 2000.
Smellie, Alexander. *Lift up Your Heart: Four Addresses on Sanctification*. London: Melrose, 1915.
Smith, G. S. "Atwater, Lyman Hotchkiss." In *Dictionary of Christianity in America*, edited by Daniel G. Reid, 392. Downers Grove, IL: InterVarsity, 1990.
Smith, Timothy L. *Called Unto Holiness: The Story of the Nazarenes: The Formative Years*. Kansas City, MO: Nazarene, 1962.
Snodgrass, W. D. "The Scriptural Doctrine of Sanctification Stated and Defended against the Error of Perfectionism." *Biblical Repertory* 14 (1842) 426–72.
Taylor, Howard, and Geraldine Taylor. *Hudson Taylor's Spiritual Secret*. Philadelphia: China Inland Mission, 1935.
Thomas, W. H. Griffith. "Christ as Our Priest." In *Victory in Christ*, 134–44. Philadelphia: The Board of Managers of Princeton Conference, 1916.
———. "The Literature of Keswick." In *The Keswick Convention*, edited by Charles F. Harford, 221–37. London: Marshall, 1907.
———. *The Victorious Life: Messages from the Summer Conference at Whittier, California, June Princeton, July Cedar Lake, Indiana, August*. Philadelphia: The Board of Managers of Victorious Life Conference, 1918.
Thompson, W. Ralph. "An Appraisal of the Keswick and Wesleyan Contemporary Positions." *Wesleyan Theological Journal* 1 (1966) 11–20.
Thornwell, James Henley. *The Collected Writings of James Henley Thornwell*. Edited by John B. Adger. Richmond: Presbyterian Committee, 1871.
Trumbull, Charles G. "The Faith for Victory." In *Victory in Christ: A Report of Princeton Conference*, 96–106. Philadelphia: The Board of Managers of Princeton Conference, 1916.
———. "The Let Go of Surrender." *The Sunday School Times*, September 16, 1911.
Tuttle, Robert G., Jr. "The Influence of the Roman Catholic Mystics on John Wesley." PhD diss., Bristol University, 1969.
———. *John Wesley: His Life and Theology*. Grand Rapids: Zondervan, 1979.

Tyson, John R. "Sin, Self and Society: John Wesley's Hamartiology Reconsidered." *The Asbury Theological Journal* 44 (1989) 77–89.
Van Til, Cornelius. *The Defense of the Faith*. Phillipsburg, NJ: Presbyterian and Reformed, 1967.
Vulgamore, Melvin L. "Charles G. Finney: Catalyst in the Dissolution of American Calvinism." *Reformed Review* 17 (1964) 33–42.
Wainwright, Geoffrey. "Perfect Salvation in the Teaching of Wesley and Calvin." *Reformed World* 40 (1988) 898–909.
Warfield, Benjamin Breckinridge. *Biblical and Theological Studies*. Edited by Samuel G. Craig. Philadelphia: Presbyterian and Reformed, 1968.
———. *Faith and Life*. New York: Longmans, Green, 1916.
———. *Perfectionism*. 2 vols. New York: Oxford University Press, 1931.
———. *The Plan of Salvation*. Grand Rapids: Eerdmans, 1942.
———. *The Power of God unto Salvation*. Philadelphia: Presbyterian Board of Publication and Sabbath-School Work, 1903.
———. "Sanctifying the Pelagians." *Princeton Theological Review* 1 (1903) 457–62.
———. *Selected Shorter Writings of Benjamin B. Warfield*. Edited by John E. Meeter. Nutley, NJ: Presbyterian and Reformed, 1970–73.
———. *Studies in Perfectionism*. Edited by Samuel G. Craig. Phillipsburg, NJ: Presbyterian and Reformed, 1968.
———. *Studies in Theology*. Edinburgh: The Banner of Truth, 1988.
Webb-Peploe, H. W. "Sin." In *Keswick's Authentic Voice: Sixty-Five Dynamic Addresses Delivered at the Keswick Convention*, edited by Herbert F. Stevenson, 31–40. Grand Rapids: Zondervan, 1959.
Wesley, John. *The Journal of the Rev. John Wesley*. Edited by Nehemiah Curnock. Vol. 1. London: Robert Culley, 1909.
———. *A Plain Account of Christian Perfection*. Louisville, Kentucky: Pentecostal, no date.
———. *The Works of John Wesley*. 14 vols. Grand Rapids: Zondervan, 1958.
Wheatley, Richard. *The Life and Letters of Mrs. Phoebe Palmer*. New York: Garland, 1984.
White, Charles Edward. "The Beauty of Holiness: The Career of Phoebe Palmer." *Fides Et Historia* 19 (1987) 22–34.
Wilkins, Steve. "Covenant, Baptism, and Salvation." In *The Federal Vision*, edited by Steve Wilkins and Duane Garner, 51–73. Monroe, LA: Athanasius, 2004.
Wilson, A. S. *Definite Experience: Convention Aid and Deterrents*. London: Marshall, Morgan & Scott, 1937.
Wilson, Robert H. "John Wesley's Doctrine of Sanctification." DMin diss., Fuller Theological Seminary, 1972.
Wood, Laurence W. "The Wesleyan View." In *Christian Spirituality*, edited by Donald L. Alexander, 95–118. Downers Grove, IL: InterVarsity, 1988.
Wright, N. T. *Paul: In Fresh Perspective*. Minneapolis: Fortress, 2009.

www.ingramcontent.com/pod-product-compliance
Lightning Source LLC
Chambersburg PA
CBHW070243230426
43664CB00014B/2397